Feminism, Economics and Utopia

What are the goals of feminist economics? This book examines the nature of utopia in feminist economics. Karin Schönpflug explores utopian concepts, particularly those related to work and reproduction, drawn from the writings of utopian thinkers and applied to feminist economics.

One part of this exploration relies on feminist, feminist economic and economic literature. The other part is based on empirical research: predominantly the analysis of the journal *Feminist Economics* and major anthologies of feminist economics. These two parts together give an overview of the situation of utopia in feminist economics and answer the following questions:

- Are there feminist, economic utopian visions amongst feminist economists? What are these visions?
- Is there a common vision for feminist economics or should there be?
- Can feminist economics be effective without a utopian vision?

The author also looks further into social arrangements, questioning the problems associated with the concepts of governance, nation-states, borders and institutionalized violence. Finally the rise of the utopian design of Neoliberalism, which has become mainstream thinking, is depicted as an example for the marketing and application of utopian ideas.

Inspired by utopian thinkers of the recent and not so recent past, this book does not offer straightforward solutions but rather encourages thought and questioning. It will appeal to feminist economists, historians and all those with an interest in utopian studies.

Karin Schönpflug is an Economist at the Austrian Ministry of Finance and also Lecturer at the University of Vienna, Austria.

Routledge Frontiers of Political Economy

1 **Equilibrium Versus Understanding**
Towards the rehumanization of economics within social theory
Mark Addleson

2 **Evolution, Order and Complexity**
Edited by Elias L. Khalil and Kenneth E. Boulding

3 **Interactions in Political Economy**
Malvern after ten years
Edited by Steven Pressman

4 **The End of Economics**
Michael Perelman

5 **Probability in Economics**
Omar F. Hamouda and Robin Rowley

6 **Capital Controversy, Post Keynesian Economics and the History of Economics**
Essays in honour of Geoff Harcourt, volume one
Edited by Philip Arestis, Gabriel Palma and Malcolm Sawyer

7 **Markets, Unemployment and Economic Policy**
Essays in honour of Geoff Harcourt, volume two
Edited by Philip Arestis, Gabriel Palma and Malcolm Sawyer

8 **Social Economy**
The logic of capitalist development
Clark Everling

9 **New Keynesian Economics/Post Keynesian Alternatives**
Edited by Roy J. Rotheim

10 **The Representative Agent in Macroeconomics**
James E. Hartley

11 **Borderlands of Economics**
Essays in honour of Daniel R. Fusfeld
Edited by Nahid Aslanbeigui and Young Back Choi

12 **Value, Distribution and Capital**
Essays in honour of Pierangelo Garegnani
Edited by Gary Mongiovi and Fabio Petri

13 **The Economics of Science**
Methodology and epistemology as if economics really mattered
James R. Wible

14 **Competitiveness, Localised Learning and Regional Development**
Specialisation and prosperity in small open economies
Peter Maskell, Heikki Eskelinen, Ingjaldur Hannibalsson, Anders Malmberg and Eirik Vatne

15 **Labour Market Theory**
A constructive reassessment
Ben J. Fine

16 **Women and European Employment**
Jill Rubery, Mark Smith, Colette Fagan and Damian Grimshaw

17 **Explorations in Economic Methodology**
From Lakatos to empirical philosophy of science
Roger Backhouse

18 **Subjectivity in Political Economy**
Essays on wanting and choosing
David P. Levine

19 **The Political Economy of Middle East Peace**
The impact of competing trade agendas
Edited by J.W. Wright, Jnr

20 **The Active Consumer**
Novelty and surprise in consumer choice
Edited by Marina Bianchi

21 **Subjectivism and Economic Analysis**
Essays in memory of Ludwig Lachmann
Edited by Roger Koppl and Gary Mongiovi

22 **Themes in Post-Keynesian Economics**
Essays in honour of Geoff Harcourt, volume three
Edited by Claudio Sardoni and Peter Kriesler

23 **The Dynamics of Technological Knowledge**
Cristiano Antonelli

24 **The Political Economy of Diet, Health and Food Policy**
Ben J. Fine

25 **The End of Finance**
Capital market inflation, financial derivatives and pension fund capitalism
Jan Toporowski

26 **Political Economy and the New Capitalism**
Edited by Jan Toporowski

27 **Growth Theory**
A philosophical perspective
Patricia Northover

28 **The Political Economy of the Small Firm**
Edited by Charlie Dannreuther

29 **Hahn and Economic Methodology**
Edited by Thomas Boylan and Paschal F. O'Gorman

30 **Gender, Growth and Trade**
The miracle economies of the postwar years
David Kucera

31 **Normative Political Economy**
Subjective freedom, the market and the state
David Levine

32 **Economist with a Public Purpose**
Essays in honour of John Kenneth Galbraith
Edited by Michael Keaney

33 **Involuntary Unemployment**
The elusive quest for a theory
Michel De Vroey

34 **The Fundamental Institutions of Capitalism**
Ernesto Screpanti

35 **Transcending Transaction**
The search for self-generating markets
Alan Shipman

36 **Power in Business and the State**
An historical analysis of its concentration
Frank Bealey

37 **Editing Economics**
Essays in honour of Mark Perlman
Hank Lim, Ungsuh K. Park and Geoff Harcourt

38 **Money, Macroeconomics and Keynes**
Essays in honour of Victoria Chick, volume one
Philip Arestis, Meghnad Desai and Sheila Dow

39 **Methodology, Microeconomics and Keynes**
Essays in honour of Victoria Chick, volume two
Philip Arestis, Meghnad Desai and Sheila Dow

40 **Market Drive & Governance**
Reexamining the rules for economic & commercial contest
Ralf Boscheck

41 **The Value of Marx**
Political economy for contemporary capitalism
Alfredo Saad-Filho

42 **Issues in Positive Political Economy**
S. Mansoob Murshed

43 **The Enigma of Globalisation**
A journey to a new stage of capitalism
Robert Went

44 **The Market**
Equilibrium, stability, mythology
S.N. Afriat

45 **The Political Economy of Rule Evasion and Policy Reform**
Jim Leitzel

46 **Unpaid Work and the Economy**
Edited by Antonella Picchio

47 **Distributional Justice**
Theory and measurement
Hilde Bojer

48 **Cognitive Developments in Economics**
Edited by Salvatore Rizzello

49 **Social Foundations of Markets, Money and Credit**
Costas Lapavitsas

50 **Rethinking Capitalist Development**
Essays on the economics of Josef Steindl
Edited by Tracy Mott and Nina Shapiro

51 **An Evolutionary Approach to Social Welfare**
Christian Sartorius

52 **Kalecki's Economics Today**
Edited by Zdzislaw L. Sadowski and Adam Szeworski

53 **Fiscal Policy from Reagan to Blair**
The left veers right
Ravi K. Roy and Arthur T. Denzau

54 **The Cognitive Mechanics of Economic Development and Institutional Change**
Bertin Martens

55 **Individualism and the Social Order**
The social element in liberal thought
Charles R. McCann, Jnr.

56 **Affirmative Action in the United States and India**
A comparative perspective
Thomas E. Weisskopf

57 **Global Political Economy and the Wealth of Nations**
Performance, institutions, problems and policies
Edited by Phillip Anthony O'Hara

58 **Structural Economics**
Thijs ten Raa

59 **Macroeconomic Theory and Economic Policy**
Essays in honour of Jean-Paul Fitoussi
Edited by K. Vela Velupillai

60 **The Struggle Over Work**
The "end of work" and employment alternatives in post-industrial societies
Shaun Wilson

61 **The Political Economy of Global Sporting Organisations**
John Forster and Nigel Pope

62 **The Flawed Foundations of General Equilibrium Theory**
Critical essays on economic theory
Frank Ackerman and Alejandro Nadal

63 **Uncertainty in Economic Theory**
Essays in honor of David Schmeidler's 65th birthday
Edited by Itzhak Gilboa

64 **The New Institutional Economics of Corruption**
Edited by Johann Graf Lambsdorff, Markus Taube and Matthias Schramm

65 **The Price Index and Its Extension**
A chapter in economic measurement
S.N. Afriat

66 **Reduction, Rationality & Game Theory in Marxian Economics**
Bruce Philp

67 **Culture and Politics in Economic Development**
Volker Bornschier

68 **Modern Applications of Austrian Thought**
Edited by Jürgen G. Backhaus

69 **Ordinary Choices**
Individuals, incommensurability, and democracy
Robert Urquhart

70 **Labour Theory of Value**
Peter C. Dooley

71 **Capitalism**
Victor D. Lippit

72 **Macroeconomic Foundations of Macroeconomics**
Alvaro Cencini

73 **Marx for the 21st Century**
Edited by Hiroshi Uchida

74 **Growth and Development in the Global Political Economy**
Social structures of accumulation and modes of regulation
Phillip Anthony O'Hara

75 The New Economy and Macroeconomic Stability
A neo-modern perspective drawing on the complexity approach and Keynesian economics
Teodoro Dario Togati

76 The Future of Social Security Policy
Women, work and a citizens basic income
Ailsa McKay

77 Clinton and Blair
The political economy of the third way
Flavio Romano

78 Marxian Reproduction Schema
Money and aggregate demand in a capitalist economy
A.B. Trigg

79 The Core Theory in Economics
Problems and solutions
Lester G. Telser

80 Economics, Ethics and the Market
Introduction and applications
Johan J. Graafland

81 Social Costs and Public Action in Modern Capitalism
Essays inspired by Karl William Kapp's Theory of Social Costs
Edited by Wolfram Elsner, Pietro Frigato and Paolo Ramazzotti

82 Globalization and the Myths of Free Trade
History, theory and empirical evidence
Edited by Anwar Shaikh

83 Equilibrium in Economics
Scope and limits
Edited by Valeria Mosini

84 Globalization
State of the art and perspectives
Edited by Stefan A. Schirm

85 Neoliberalism
National and regional experiments with global ideas
Edited by Ravi K. Roy, Arthur T. Denzau and Thomas D. Willett

86 Post-Keynesian Macroeconomics Economics
Essays in honour of Ingrid Rima
Edited by Mathew Forstater, Gary Mongiovi and Steven Pressman

87 Consumer Capitalism
Anastasios S. Korkotsides

88 Remapping Gender in the New Global Order
Edited by Marjorie Griffin Cohen and Janine Brodie

89 Hayek and Natural Law
Eric Angner

90 Race and Economic Opportunity in the Twenty-First Century
Edited by Marlene Kim

91 Renaissance in Behavioural Economics
Harvey Leibenstein's impact on contemporary economic analysis
Edited by Roger Frantz

92 Human Ecology Economics
A new framework for global sustainability
Edited by Roy E. Allen

93 Imagining Economics Otherwise
Encounters with identity/difference
Nitasha Kaul

Feminism, Economics and Utopia

Time travelling through paradigms

Karin Schönpflug

Routledge
Taylor & Francis Group
LONDON AND NEW YORK

First published 2008
by Routledge
2 Park Square, Milton Park, Abingdon, Oxon OX14 4RN

Simultaneously published in the USA and Canada
by Routledge
270 Madison Ave, New York, NY 10016

Routledge is an imprint of the Taylor & Francis Group, an informa business

Typeset in Times New Roman by
Taylor & Francis Books
Printed and bound in Great Britain by
Antony Rowe Ltd, Chippenham, Wiltshire

British Library Cataloguing in Publication Data
A catalogue record for this book is available from the British Library

Library of Congress Cataloging in Publication Data
Schönpflug, Karin.
Feminism, economics, and Utopia : time travelling through paradigms / Karin Schönpflug.
1. Feminist economics. 2. Free enterprise. 3. Utopias. I. Title.
2007034849

ISBN13: 978-0-415-41784-6 (hbk)
ISBN13: 978-0-203-93071-7 (ebk)

Contents

We alone can devalue gold
by not caring
if it falls or rises
in the marketplace.
Wherever there is gold
there is a chain, you know,
and if your chain
is gold
so much the worse
for you.

Feathers, shells
and sea-shaped stones
are all rare.

This could be our revolution:
To love what is plentiful
as much as
what is scarce

(Alice Walker, *We Alone*, 1993)

Preface

In the tradition of radical feminist thought, this book is meant to be an *appeal*: It is an appeal to dare, an appeal to dream, to leave one's designated sphere of thinking, to surpass the narrow borders of scientific thought, to free the forgotten specters from their archives, to look up marginal knowledge in all corners of the world, to travel and to learn with an open mind. This also entails the attempt at being reciprocal, unbiased, and willing to create a new paradigm far afield from dual hierarchies, casting off concerns of complying with the canon of the academe. Feminist economists could embrace the challenge to leave the tight control of the discipline of economics and could rise from the barren fields of bureaucratic storage and manipulation in the king methodology of econometrics by going beyond the existing system of political-economy and its prognostic timelines for the future with its function as railroad tracks leading to more of the same. Let's not worry about careers, tenure, and publication lists: feminist economists could be the "engineers of social change" (Folbre 2005) instead of the bystanders in a profit-driven economics of exploitation, destruction, and perpetual growth. Creative imagining of forgotten, banned thinkers may serve as an indicator towards a truly alternative economics far from the greedy behavior of "homo oeconomicus."

In one of the first anthologies of feminist economics Marianne Ferber and Julie Nelson introduce the working methods of feminism and feminist economics. They list four approaches: the affirmative; the empiricist (as Sandra Harding describes the neoclassical feminist economics); the approach via feminist difference; and the post-modern constructivist approach. One approach comes short in this list of possible options for feminist economics to operate: the creative, innovative, not realized, ergo utopian stance. Although it may not be classified as its own *modus operandi*, the quest for the utopian potential within the other four approaches seems complicated: Are there economic visions to be created with the (standard) tools of feminist economics? Is this a goal this discipline pursues? Or is the main purpose one of critique or deconstruction?

Throughout my research I have encountered utopian moments in all feminist economics approaches; however, a coherent utopian vision of feminist economics was nowhere to be found. Interestingly, digging deeper revealed quite a bit of revolutionary potential. Given the strength of utopian studies as a new discipline and the lack of alternative societies and models to desire (or fear) – enhanced through the fall of the Soviet Union and the cultural and economical spread of the hegemony of Neoliberalism – it seems there is a readiness to incorporate new ideas, to afford alternative concepts a place within policy recommendations. Many problems of late capitalism may be on the verge of becoming overpowering, such as: the ageing of the population in combination with a reduction of fair distribution in most "developed" countries; the increasingly strong push of the population of "developing" nations to join the rich "first world countries;" problems related to climate change, pollution, and a lack of sustainable economics; the change in working conditions, the polarization of wealth and distribution worldwide. I think that an alternative to today's very limited social and economic political aspirations could offer a comprehensive vision of feminist economics with unified recommendations for economic policy based on respect for people and nature, real choice, solidarity across the lines of sex, gender[1] and peoples, extending beyond profit and utility maximization.

The following posting by Andrew Hoerner on the Femecon mailing list triggered my thought process regarding feminist economics and utopia. Hoerner asks:

> When you live in a slave society and dream of the abolition of slavery, what do you dream? Of a world of masters, but without their power? Of a world of slaves, but without mistreatment? Of a world of balance in which the yin of slavery and the yang of mastery is brought into balance in every heart? Or do we dream of a new kind of person, a free citizen, neither master nor slave nor a mixture of the two, a being in no way defined by the roles of the old system?
>
> I think the goal of feminism is neither to make men like women nor to make women like men, but rather to abolish men and women as social categories, leaving behind only people with different genitalia, like the abolition of slavery leaves behind people with different skin colors. I do not think we know what these new beings will look like. But when i look at the privileges that patriarchy grants men, i often ask "Is this a privilege everyone should have? Or is this a privilege no one should have?" And when i see the injuries and the wisdom that many kind of hardship, oppression, and service to others can bring, i ask "Is this a lesson everyone should learn? Or is this a lesson no one should learn?"
>
> Occasionally i even think i know the answers to these questions. But often not.
>
> (J. Andrew Hoerner)[2]

In the following pages, I will consider and explore utopian concepts, particularly those relating to work and reproduction, governmentality and epistemology, drawing from the writings of utopian thinkers. I will also reflect on the role of feminist science as such and contemplate what has been done so far in feminist economics.

In this project I have tried to find answers to the questions Hoerner raises, but often found myself going down long alleys of related issues, traveling form one noteworthy site to another, re-reading my findings, where some seem very exciting and relevant, others more like necessary background tapestry, which may be skipped in practical reading if they turn out too dreary.

Apart from my appeal this book will not offer straightforward solutions. It invites you to dare to sit down and think, to envision and to create a passage into a better world, maybe with the help of some utopian thinkers who have passed on long ago …

Acknowledgments

This book would not have been possible without the help of an array of people: Drucilla Barker, who worked with me on the outline of this book, which was before just a version of my dissertation, and who was always there for questions and great advice; my dissertation advisors Peter Rosner, Franz Ofner, Susan Feiner, and Waltraud Ernst; my friends and colleagues who helped me read the first chapter drafts and gave me wonderful feedback on all my shortcomings and encouraged me to continue writing: Claudia Goutrié, Christine Klapeer, Roswitha Hofmann, Vina Yun, Marty Huber, Marjolein van der Veen, Doris Weichselbaumer, and Walter Oetsch. Thanks go to IAFFE as an organization for providing a strong support and collective encouragement, and individual members of IAFFE for inspiration, positive energy, and happy spirits to work on this project, particularly Ulla Grapard, Irene van Staveren, Nancy Folbre, Lee Badgett, Gillian Hewitson, and many others; and to Erika Doucette and Nicole Lundeens for helping me with the traps of the English language and proofreading everything. Others who have helped me with insightful comments or literature recommendations are plentiful, amongst them: Hanna Hacker, Else Hansen, Birthe Marker, Nicole Lieger, Martin Neubauer, and Susanne Nadenicek. Thanks are also due to my superiors at the Austrian Ministry of Finance who agreed to give me the time to write this book: Alfred Katterl, Erhard Moser, and Thomas Wieser; to the project International Development of the University of Vienna, in person especially Elke Christiansen and Walter Schicho, for providing me with material resources and a friendly, appreciative academic context; also to the Lesbian Center, Lila Tipp of Vienna, for lending me an office; and to the very competent and helpful librarians at the Economics Institute of the University of Vienna: Gabriela Freisehner, Guenther Mueller, Rainer Sauer, and Christine Scheich. I would also like to thank Angelika Eisterer for bearing the brunt of the emotional support necessary for completing a book; and finally my parents, Herta and Fredi Schönpflug who never doubted that I would be writing a dissertation in the first place.

1 Introduction

Contents guideline

With its argumentation this book follows a cyclical pattern of related fields: time, place, knowing, action.

In this case, *time* is associated with utopian moments throughout history; whenever the utopian impulse incessantly tries to break with the given status quo, to escape its given historical context in different periods of time. Still, for instance, feminist movements and theories of different time periods, such as those of the first- and the second-wave women's movements, are not easily comparable due to their given historical settings. The utopian *moment* in those aspirations for alternatives may, however, be comparable. Finally, an interesting notion related to the time issue is that rational science and its economic theory postulate an ahistoric character: a way of thinking that has always been here.

The category of *place* is also highly important in this endeavor. As with the time component, the case of utopian place is also removed from its given, located in a place of nowhere, inaccessible. Even more striking is the remoteness of feminist theory, since *knowing* becomes obtruded from generation to generation; feminist knowledge is buried in secluded archives. A working place for theory building has not yet become properly established and locations such as universities often demand great compromises in furthering scientific developments of feminist knowledge – provided that one agrees that feminist knowledge could be produced in contemporary university systems. The opposite of the place of the secluded archive is the marketplace of ideas: a system of discursive competition in which only a few ideas will become part of the canon and shape what we "know."

Knowing and knowledge production are slippery terrain: in aiming to establish a knowledge which is better than that provided by patriarchal, rational science, feminist theory runs the risk of losing its radical edge. Science needs to be objective and rational to create an acceptable truth. Feminist epistemology usually tries to comply with these rules, but feminist activism and practice-based theories of feminist movements have mostly declared themselves highly partisan for women as an oppressed group and their causes, rather than objective.

Action is what may follow a certain consciousness. The linkage between feminist theory and feminist action is described in feminist utopian visions and utopian novels. While still removed from actual occurrence, feminist theory is put into practice by the utopian authors of the feminist movement and incorporating the findings of feminist theories. In this regard, feminist utopian models are less thought experiments than serious indicators for political action.

Where is it all headed?

First of all, in Chapter 2, I demonstrate that feminist utopias explore and categorize gender relations roughly in three groups: those with gender equality; those with gender inequality; and those with fluid, non-binary conceptions of gender. In this section I introduce the feminist utopian texts I will be using throughout this volume. This chapter continues by looking at gender relations in economic theory, first in mainstream economic theory and then in feminist economics. Chapter 3 is concerned with the history of epistemology and science, and the associated gender roles and scientific paradigms and the consequences and opportunities this bears for feminist economics' epistemology today. Chapter 4, on methodology, completes this theoretical section and presents tools based on time, place, knowing and action, all applicable to the analytical section.

In Chapter 5 I present my first layer of analysis to examine the element of "work" as depicted in mainstream and feminist utopia, Marxism, and feminist economics. The second layer of analysis is concerned with feminist economic theory's approaches to utopia. In Chapter 6 I analyze the journal *Feminist Economics* for some answers, using quantitative and qualitative approaches. In Chapter 7 I look into social arrangements and utopian ideas for different constructions of society, focusing on two examples from feminist utopia that I find refreshing. I will try to question the problems associated with the concept of nation-states and their secluded territories and what this means for feminist theory and utopian thinking. I will look at the issue of borders and the violence that is employed to protect them, and then I will talk about the concepts of citizenship and subjectivity in both the status quo and utopian model societies. Chapter 8 demonstrates an example of the rise of the utopian idea: of Neoliberalism that has become mainstream thinking. This should serve as an example for the marketing of ideas, generally encouraging new thinking as becoming potentially influential. This chapter includes an example of the diversity of views in feminist economics, in this case associated with the ideal of the *free market*. The very last sections of this chapter are concerned with options for alternative strategies. This is the point where this book only indicates the range of possible opportunities by giving a few, sparse indicators of different options but fails to offer a solution itself.

Before getting started, this introduction aims to clarify some definitions and problems associated with the project.

"Nowhere" versus the "negative hermeneutic of exposure"

Discourses on social transformation such as feminism, feminist economics, and utopia not only are concerned with a field of probable developments, but also map out a timeline spanning (undesirable) social situations in the past to a present where odds can be reconsidered and change initiated towards a (more desirable) future. The situation in the present requires an analysis of "what went wrong" in the past, but there is an equal need for careful planning of future improvements. Jennifer Burwell points out two strategies useful for inducing social change:

> One seeks to envision a radical, qualitative break from existing conditions, the other is based on deconstructing society's claim to unity and legitimacy.
>
> (Burwell 1997: ix)

The radical break is associated with a clearly utopian planning momentum, where the deconstruction is associated with the critical analysis of the past. Both strategies are dependent on each other; standing alone, Burwell sees that they are restricted by their own weaknesses:

> The utopian constructions are hindered by creating an inaccessible "nowhere" where social contradictions have already been resolved, a critical connection to contemporary conditions and the setting into the "good place" is not being considered. The critical, more post-structuralist approach on the other hand confines itself to a "negative hermeneutic of exposure" but fails to present positive alternatives.
>
> (Burwell 1997: ix)

The limitation of one approach is the absence of the other impulse – the utopian vision needs to be tied to historical conditions; the critique needs to come with a utopian horizon in order to achieve distance from present conditions. How does that conflict present itself in feminist economics? Feminist economics, as a relatively young discipline, utilizes (at least) the four methodological approaches described by Ferber and Nelson (1993). In *Feminist Economics* (1999) Gillian Hewitson also lists a diversity of approaches for feminist economics (constructionist, empiricist, and poststructuralist). The utopian approach could be seen as another more unconventional approach within feminist economics, sometimes as its own approach, and at other times, to some degree, as an element of other methodological approaches.

Another thought connected to the different approaches is that the utopian stance can also reflect different levels of radicalism within feminist thinking. The difference is related to a historical development, and it is interesting to note that some developments in feminist radicalism followed a chronologically linear path whereas others did not. Reactionary backlashes in feminist economic theory and practice have occurred in all time periods.

Therefore a timeline of radicalism in feminist theory and economics would meander back and forth, thus depicting the backlashes in radicalism of thought. Another question may be whether on average feminist theory and feminist economics were actually more radical in the past than now. The answer certainly depends on one's perspective regarding radicalism, criticism, and utopianism in feminist thought and feminist economics but also as an appropriate analysis of historical contexts.

Another complication is that the timeline actually follows a dual path, as there are differences among types of radicalism. On the one hand, there is critical radicalism (such as in poststructuralism) and, on the other hand, there is utopian radicalism. And the question whether a certain model of feminist economics could be considered radically utopian rather than just "imaginary" remains to be asked. Whether one equates "utopian" with unfeasible and irrational wishful thinking or whether one assumes that utopia is a creative force essential to and inherent in all scientific thought seems to appear simply as an afterthought; however, this is actually at the core of the problems listed so far.

One good, yet more complicated, answer relating to the timeline, radicalism, and the parallel paths of exploration of feminist theory is provided by Jenny Wolmark in her discussion on *Science Fiction, Feminism and Postmodernism*. Wolmark unravels the issue of historical and contemporary feminism and its radicalism and stages of backlash using Julia Kristeva's three-tiered model of feminist struggle. The three stages of Kristeva are:

> [first] a feminism which is centered on the liberal struggle for equal rights for women; the second stage is a separatist feminism of difference which asserts that women are of value in themselves as women, rather than in terms of a patriarchal order which excludes them; the third stage is one in which all binary oppositions are deconstructed.
>
> (Wolmark 1994: 20)

Kristeva's three stages are reflected in the parallel worlds in Joanna Russ's utopian novel *The Female Man*, which I will discuss in Chapters 2 and 5.

It can be argued that it is impossible to separate the different stages, let alone opt for one at the expense of the others, as each stage is fully implicated in the others. Postmodern approaches attempt an additional view on the problem of these three stages, which not only sees them as chronological events with backlashes, as has been argued before, but at the same time sees the stages as parallels to each other, and also as linked to other issues, which fan out into a more complex subject space interlinking with different streams of thought:

> Unlike Kristeva, however, I assume that feminists today have to hold all three positions simultaneously. Simply to take up Kristeva's 'third position' of deconstructed identities, as she herself advocates, is clearly impossible. For, if we live in metaphysical space, our necessary utopian

> wish to deconstruct sexual identities always runs up against the fact that patriarchy itself persists in oppressing women as women. We must, then, at once live out the contradictions of all three feminisms and agonistically take sides: simply sitting on the fence will never demolish patriarchy.
>
> (Wolmark 1994: 20)

Feminist economics is still struggling to locate itself somewhere in the open field of feminist science: while philosophers, such as Kristeva, see the development of feminism as parallel streams, a more integrative view, such as described just above by Wolmark, will find that the streams of feminism in fact interlink, whereas the feminist biologist Donna Haraway describes feminism as expanding into the wider subject space of a matrix and, finally, feminist utopianists collapse the whole construction into a single point or even a void, an abyss, a "nowhere" (Utopia). Deconstructive thought does offer a pathway to the "no-place" in the utopian sense, but whether it offers a feasible passage to a "better place" too shall be further explored – this finding of a passage should indeed be one of the tasks of feminist economics. Nevertheless, the issues of identity and economics are intertwined. It seems as if feminist work needs to take place everywhere, always, and simultaneously. This is somewhat reminiscent of the idea of a "*true* modern woman": housewife, mother, successful business manager and volunteer; nothing is too much for her. In another light it sounds like a "nice" compromise and a comforting thought when one is tempted to evaluate one feminism as "better" than another, the idea that women have simply started to share their work and that there is no need for one woman to do everything everywhere on her own. However, whether it is politically a given that all feminist deeds are good deeds in regards to a common feminist economics goal is a core focus of my contemplations.

Socialism, liberalism, feminism, and utopia

> All alternative economic systems are about organizing labor. That is the big question: How do we organize ourselves? And the point I am making is that when we answer that question, whether we are coming out from a corporate capitalist point of view or from a socialist point of view, we have to recognize that there is this kind of labor that is different than other kinds, that is not as reducible to the logic of exchange or to the logic of central planning and bureaucratic administration. It is an intrinsically personal, intrinsically emotional kind of exchange that requires long-term relationships between people. And that is not something that the grand theoreticians of capitalism thought about, and it is not something that the grand theoreticians of socialism thought about either. So it is in the middle, it is kind of neglected by both sides.
>
> (Folbre 2005, online)

Similarly to feminist economists pointing out androcentric bias in the models of mainstream economics, feminist theorists have looked at historical models of utopian thought and pinpointed gender imbalances imbedded in those ideal worlds. The similarities between constructions considered economic models and those subsumed under "utopian modeling" are quite interesting. What makes one model scientific and intrinsically economic, when another is considered purely utopian? The categories are fluid, i.e. Marx and Engels were forced to actively defend their work, declare it strictly scientific, and stress the difference between their models and those designed by early utopian socialists such as Owens and Fourier. Be they scientific or not, the visions in Marx and Engels' work were clearly utopian at some point, as they only became reality when Socialist and Communist political leaders started to apply their economic theories to real life.

The feminist critique of utopian models is shown to be closely intertwined with the critique of economic models by feminist economists. Jennifer Burwell points to a conflict between mainstream utopia and feminist utopian critique:

> All of mainstream utopia's ideal societies – from the genre's inaugural moment with Thomas More's *Utopia* through the end of the nineteenth century – are of more or less socialist nature. But in spite of its predominance, socialism as the informing vision of utopias has been interrupted on two occasions: once in the late nineteenth century, around the time of the "first wave" of American Feminism, and again in the 1970s, in conjunction with the evolution of contemporary feminism. Along with this "second wave" of feminism came a substantial change in the utopian form, which began to incorporate conflict, imperfection, difference, and transgression into representations of an ideal social space that traditionally had been defined by its harmony and its stature as a sutured totality.
>
> (Burwell 1997: x)

Burwell's statement is of interest insofar as she sees feminist visions as interrupting socialist ones; she also claims that there is a socialist predominance in utopian visions. Nevertheless utopian designs of liberalism have come to dominate and exert influence on the political and economic spheres today, Adam Smith's utopia of harmony or Milton Friedman's *Capitalism and Freedom* are examples of utopias of classical and neoclassical economics.

Utopia

On the one hand, a discourse on utopia is very exiting, since it leads to entering various disciplines: The idea of utopia appears in an array of academic disciplines in social sciences, philosophy, economics, women's studies;

as well as in practical political concepts, literature, products of the entertainment industry, people's everyday conversations, and so on. At the same time, this is one of the largest difficulties in a discourse on utopia; the concept meanders in and out of all kinds of subjects and needs a lot of chasing after to fence it in comprehensively. Already the problem of definition, if not only tackled etymologically, needs various layers of approaches. Thus, trying to grasp the utopian essence with an all-inclusive definition entails considering the diversity of utopia's aspects, implications, and its ability to crop up in very different fields. A useful starting point in doing so, chosen by Lucy Sargisson, is to consult an encyclopedia. The *Oxford English Dictionary* yields the following results:

> UTOPIA: An imaginary island, depicted by Sir Thomas More as enjoying a perfect social, legal and political system. ... 2. Any imaginary, indefinitely remote region, country or locality. 3. A place, space, or condition ideally perfect in respect of politics, laws, customs and conditions. ... 4. An impossibly ideal scheme, esp. for social improvement.
>
> (*Oxford English Dictionary*, in Sargisson 1996: 10)

The idea of the utopia as such has been existent more or less since people have started to reflect on living together as a society. The longing to at least imagine a better world far away, and most likely unapproachable from the one currently lived in, seems to be a common (Western) human trait. The definition of utopia used throughout this work is most closely related to Lucy Sargisson's and Tineke Willemsen's work, from which the following definition of utopia has been developed:

> The idea of "*Utopia*" was named by Thomas More's *Utopia*, published in 1516. (Utopia is a pun on two Greek terms, "ou topos" meaning no place and "eu topos" meaning good place.) A utopian vision can be seen as a thought experiment for philosophers, social scientists, economists, and other theoreticians, no matter whether they are feminists or not. Utopias reflect beliefs of what an "ideal" society should be like and also imply a critique of the current state of affairs.
>
> (compiled from Willemsen 1997: 3ff.)

Considering the value judgment in the definition of utopia, it is essential to point out that a "good" place might be good only for certain people, regardless if it might actually be a rather "bad" place for some others. The goodness of utopia depends on one's perspective; therefore, it is essential to include dystopias and not only eutopias in this definition. A dystopia is a "bad" place to be for some, but probably a good place to be for others. Those unhappy with the utopia would call it a dystopia, the ones happy with it a eutopia, both of which represent two sides of the same coin.

Basically, utopia is a non-existent location, which is a good place to be – at least for some people. (Let's not forget to ask: for whom? In a feminist utopia the answer should be: for women. Next question: For all women? Also for women of color? Also for the poor? . . .) Apart from the judgment on goodness, there is the paradox of the no-place, where things get "un-scientific" as some might be tempted to claim. But aren't most, even deeply mathematical, economic models simply unreal places as well? Let's leave the question of realism aside for now, and consider utopian models at least as seriously as mainstream economic models.

The inaccessibility of that better place, which is an essential feature, seems to serve as a protecting device, allowing fantasizing on improvements more freely. The inaccessibility can be created by use of space or time components. The important characteristic is that the utopia is removed from the situation of here and now. The utopias created in our days usually reflect on modern optimism towards unrestricted technological progress (this is also the "magic word" in economic growth theory); they are often fashionably situated in future worlds, allowing indefinitely progressive technological and other inventions to solve presently unsolvable problems. In the historical context of Thomas More's novel, it was fashionable to remove the utopia from the current world by situating it in a faraway, not yet discovered place; preferably an island. This interestingly reflects the belief in simply "finding" one's happiness by coming upon wealth (gold, diamonds, treasures, and luxury goods) and improving the economic well-being of nations via sailing and conquering. Such frankness in motivation is not possible in our socio-economic historic context anymore. One of the last famous thinkers of the tradition to create utopias barred from today by regional distance was the French play writer Jules Verne, who lived in the last half of the 19th century. His popular science fiction novels are set in utopian worlds on *Mysterious Islands* but he also contemplated journeys possible only in future dimensions in his *From the Earth to the Moon*. This rings in the nowadays most popular method of distancing utopias by setting them in outer space or in the future in places thoroughly removed from time. Einstein's findings in physics have replaced the glamor of discovering mysterious Terran lands; the mysteries of the unknown have shifted to truly inaccessible dimensions of time travel. Sometimes, the removal from reality does not take place in time or space, but is made by changing just one variable within a model of the present situation, which is also a traditional approach for economists, i.e. a disease that kills all males, and then planning out the consequences – as is done in Charlotte Perkins Gilman's *Herland* (Willemsen 1997: 4).

The negative connotation of the utopian concept ("daydreaming," "science fiction" . . .) usually devalues creative impulses brought forward in utopian visions, even though these ideas may eventually become precisely developed through technological progress at some future stage. Whether the concepts are considered too "daring," too "romantic," too "naïve," or too "Cassandrian" usually does not matter.

Utopian types

When thinking about the historical background of the utopian idea, Lucy Sargisson offers a classification of five historical types of ideal societies, of which utopia is only one. The first is named *Cockaygne* and is based on the medieval poem *The Land of Cokaygne.* This archetype is also known from medieval paintings. In Cockaygne, all wants and desires are fulfilled; it is a world of abundance in food and sex. There are self-roasting birds, rivers of wine, fountains of youth, wishing trees, and desirable sexual partners. "It is a hedonistic paradise; Cockaygne privileges material and sensual satisfaction and assumes natural abundance. Its inhabitants symbolize satiated desire" (Sargisson 1996: 15). A world where desires are satiated is certainly problematic from an economist's point of view. In traditional economic concepts utility (without budget constraints) will never reach a maximum; the graphical metaphor tries to represent most utility curves as mountains without a peak. The principle of never-ending growth to keep up with never-ending needs is one of the basic foundations of today's economy: it is in the formula for production-consumption-profit; it is the glue that keeps society alive in the way we know it. Criticism of the idea of never-ending growth is rare. Cockaygne is a revolutionary dream, certainly entirely impossible, but an interesting thought experiment for how the world could be. The idea of Cockaygne is at present still a very common, archetypal theme in fairytales and children's stories. Every child (in German-speaking contexts) is familiar with the myth of "*Schlaraffen-Land*," where no one needs to hold a job. Usually, the puritan moral at the end of the story stresses the concept of reward, ensuring the listening children that it is entirely non-pleasurable and boring to always get what you want without trying and working very hard for it.

The other types of ideal society in the five classifications include: *Arcadia*, the image of a pastoral setting of perfect natural beauty populated with morally or aesthetically motivated humans, where satisfaction is temperate; *The Perfect Commonwealth*, a society with a given moral code carried out by all of its members, as described in Ovid's *Golden Age*; and the *Millennium*, an ideal society in which people are bettered by an external force, a god-like figure creating or eliminating good or evil behavior. Only the fifth model of ideal worlds is what Sargisson describes as the true *Utopia.* Its difference to the other four versions of better worlds is that "in utopia there is no *deus ex machina*, nor any wishing away of the deficiencies of man or nature. . . . The utopia creates systems which will cope with these deficiencies" (Sargisson 1996: 16).

There are various other systems for classifying utopias; another example comes from Karl Mannheim:

> Mannheim categorizes utopian mentality in "modern times" into four stages which are historically, developmentally and dialectically interrelated: chiliastic, liberal-humanitarian, conservatism and socialist-communist.
>
> (Shafi 1990: 55)

Where Mannheim ranks utopias as evolving over time, other thinkers have certainly developed more and other means of categorization which shall be forgone at this point.

Functions of utopia

Trying to argue what makes one feminist economic concept utopian, rather than categorizing the issue simply as a feminist innovative expansion, is the most difficult evaluation which needs to be performed in this regard. A combination of Sargisson's approaches and Angelika Bammer's strategy is of great help. Bammer claims:

> one could argue that it is not the conceptual framework but the discursive strategies that makes a utopia "utopian." By making us read differently, they make us think differently. Or, simply put: they make us think.
> (Bammer 1991: 172)

The utopian content in works of feminist economics therefore shall be tested according to the following criteria, which I have derived from the concepts and definitions presented above:

- no place criterion/thought experiment;
- better place criterion/reflection on an ideal society;
- containment of a critique of the current status quo;
- a radical, qualitative break from the status quo.

The question arising at this point probably revolves around speculations on utopian models and utopian theories. What use are theories of better worlds, which are per definition far removed form reality and utterly inaccessible? Tineke Willemsen first brings up the importance of thought experiments. She argues that

> describing an ideal society in a realistic way allows scholars of all disciplines to present their views in a structured, yet imaginative way. Utopia presents an alliterative to the current situation. This form is therefore also useful for political theorists to abstract the idea that the current situation is not the only one thinkable, as people often seem to assume. A utopia is a vehicle for philosophers, social scientists, feminists,[1] and other theoreticians to present their ideas about what is just or correct in the form of a well-illustrated example. Creating a utopia on paper forces one to really think through the consequences of ethical principles. In terms of the natural sciences or psychology utopia can be described as a thought experiment in which a number of variables in the current situation are changed, and the consequences are predicted. In the social sciences, it can be called a simulation; a description of what

> will happen in society under certain conditions, when certain parameters achieve optimal values.
>
> (Willemsen 1997: 4)

This statement lists a whole array of functions of utopias: For one, utopias give structure to scientific thought and, second, they open up spaces for alternatives. Third, Willemsen states that utopia is a vehicle; a tool for scientists to experiment, simulate and model situations with changed parameters. For her, another purpose of utopias is to represent facets of the author's ideology. Utopias function as metaphors for carrying complex, beliefs, models, and doctrines. Explicit determination of issues of legitimization, fairness, happiness, etc. is a prerequisite for composing a utopian world. Codes for human behavior, as well as the organization of the utopian society, need to be specified. Especially regarding ideals, feminist utopias can vary tremendously, a notion worth exploring in this context.

Describing ideal communities also functions as a reflection of what the author thinks is wrong with the current situation:

> Utopias always imply a critique of the current state of affairs. Showing an alternatively possible or thinkable state of affairs implicitly – or sometimes explicitly – points to what is wrong in the present. The utopia functions as a mirror of our current society.
>
> (Willemsen 1997: 4)

Certainly, there are also negative functions of utopia for academic work. Some might include a danger of narrow-mindedness, obstructing the way to other arguments, or a general sense of being "unscientific."

Feminist theory and utopian visions

Definition problems arise not only in examining the question of what "true feminism" may be, as another problem lies within the complex of the "*feminist* utopia:"

> Feminism can take many forms, has many theories and ideologies and therefore probably no two feminists will agree as to what an ideal feminist society would look like. It is hardly even possible to give a definition of feminism that every feminist will agree with. The easiest way to describe a feminist utopia is to paraphrase a line coined by the first modern outspoken feminist in The Netherlands, Joke Smit. She wrote a song with a first line that has become almost proverbial in the Netherlands: There is a land where women would like to live. A feminist utopia would therefore be the description of a place where at least women would like to live.
>
> (Willemsen 1997: 5)

Tineke Willemsen, referring to this Dutch song, offers a suggestion for a basic common denominator for a feminist utopia: a land where women would like to live. This seems to be a very basic, lowest-level common denominator that unites all kinds of feminisms, and may even be in agreement with people who are not feminists. Of course, Willemsen's claim for a land where all women would like to live is fairly distorted. Consider the question of whether this land should be a place, like a Tupperware commercial, where the "domesticated housewife" would like to live. This spirals right back to the discussion on whether the judgments and evaluations of workers in Marxism or the judgments of the suppressed wives should be accepted from the theory building radical yet elitist thinkers. Bammer answers the question: "If women's utopias were different from men's, the question was: how? What was a feminist utopia?" (Bammer 1991: 25). Carol Pearson attempted to establish a set of criteria with which to describe and define the specifics of a feminist view: "Her first and foremost criterion was ideological: a feminist utopia, she posited, begins with the premise that patriarchy is an unnatural state. … Secondly, Pearson argued, a feminist utopia is defined by the nature of its vision, namely a vision of a world that is better – utopian – for women" (Bammer 1991: 25). Which women are the denominator still remains a problematic issue, and therefore when trying to envision more definite features of this utopia – the land where women would like to live – things become even more difficult: How should gender roles be recreated? How should working conditions be reshaped? What about reproduction and childcare? What about family structures and the construction and geography of nation-states and government? What about ontologies in science and scientific approaches altogether? What about feminist economics?

2 Gender relations

Gender relations in utopia

This section serves as an introductory chapter to the feminist utopias I will be relying on throughout this research. The chapter is organized according to the gender relations displayed in those utopias and explores the choice of gender concepts used in each variant. It then also gives an introduction to depictions of gender relations in economic and feminist economic theories which it also discusses, and it concludes with a vision of gender relations in queer economics.

Innovative feminist literary utopias are a source for reconsidering gender in a free and creative way. I will concentrate on a few examples and their specific take on gender interactions. Regarding the issue of whether it is scientific or even acceptable to draw economic theory form feminist literature, Irene van Staveren argues that fiction does have epistemological value for the social sciences, and also for the analysis of economic behavior (Staveren 2003), and van Staveren "suggest[s] some ways to use feminist literary texts as possible epistemological sources for feminist economics" (Staveren 2003: 56). An example for this technique is given in Staveren's historical analysis of efficiency, in which she carefully extracts the economic background from Perkins Gilman's literary works, an approach which I will discuss more on pp. 105–107.

From a multitude of feminist utopian works of fiction, I concentrate here on a few titles I find most appropriate and which I believe to be the richest concerning considerations related to feminist economics. Those include Marge Piercy's *Woman on the Edge of Time* (1976), Joanna Russ's *The Female Man* (1975), Charlotte Perkins Gilman's *Herland* (1915), Gerd Brantenberg's *Egalia's Daughters* (1977), and Donna Haraway's *A Cyborg Manifesto* (1980) (although this is not a work of fiction in the general sense). I will mention other works as examples regarding certain issues, but I will mostly focus on those five pieces. The reasons for choosing them are based on their originality in proposing different organizations for various aspects of economic life, specifically work, reproductive work, and their depiction of science and technology, amongst other issues. Additionally, their very different concepts of gender relations are an important reason for choosing these examples for closer scrutiny. The first option for gender relations is equality.

Gender equality

Tineke Willemsen classifies writers oriented towards gender equality as "feminists who emphasize that women and men are basically equal. [They] tend to describe a society in which women and men have equal rights and opportunities and, as a consequence, probably expect that they live in the same situations" (Willemsen 1997: 5). Willemsen gives an example for the sphere of working life, namely the song writer Joke Smit who in 1967 proclaimed that everyone, men and women, would have to work in a paid job five hours a day as a means to attain this goal.

Woman on the Edge of Time

A good blueprint for gender equality is designed in Marge Piercy's novel *Woman on the Edge of Time*, which is a prime example of a radical feminist utopia and contains a very detailed model society. Most astonishing is probably the environmental consciousness displayed by Marge Piercy already in the mid-1970s. Her utopian world is completely sustainable, all energy is renewable and all leftovers are recycled, toxic materials are avoided, rural farming is complemented by high-tech production in which machines perform all the boring manual labor on their own. People live in small villages, as it had been found that large systems do not work, since people lose their sense of responsibility and hierarchies replace a feeling of communal existence. On a large scale, it is interesting that Piercy establishes ideas for a parliamentary system in which villagers are chosen by lot to be temporary representatives for an overall government. This aims to avoid power concentration, policy frustration, and corruption. Piercy draws a lot of her ideas for communal conflict management and self-guidance from the extinct Native American tribe of the Pony Indians, who lived in a "technologically backwards" way from a modern Western European point of view, yet had an amazingly advanced social system. Regarding gender roles in *Woman on the Edge of Time*, maternity takes place in breeders, which are machines that grow children for nine months in aquarium-like devices. With medical aid, breast feeding can then be conducted by men and women. Every child has three parents of various gender and race, where diversity is most preferred. The nuclear family is therefore completely impossible, and friendships and sexual partnerships are non-monogamous, as is the case in nearly all feminist utopias.

An interesting aspect is that, in the tradition of many utopias, Piercy opens *Woman on the Edge of Time* with a critique of the status quo. Like Hélène Cixous, Piercy uses the metaphor of the insane woman as the starting point for her excursion into a better world. One of the most interesting aspects of *Woman on the Edge of Time* are the power relationships between men and women, i.e. gendered portraits of power and disempowerment. These issues are experienced through Piercy's main protagonist, a poor New York Chicana named Connie, who gets locked up in a mental hospital by her brother. Jennifer Burwell interprets this turn by relating it to the Foucauldian network of power operating against the female protagonist (Burwell 1997). Given this adverse starting point for the *Woman on the Edge of Time*'s heroine, Burwell characterizes the feminist relationship between utopia and dystopia as formed by porous boundaries, such that what distinguishes utopia from dystopia is not the relative level of harmony; instead it is the relative distribution of power. In Piercy's work this is illustrated by the parallel existence of a utopian and a dystopian world that Connie can travel to. Neither of the two worlds is described as a utopian "given," but rather as an option depending on Connie's decisions in her present scenario of power struggle. It is the individual's access to self-empowerment (Connie becomes a feminist in the mental institution and also an assassin; she manages to kill the doctors who are ready to lobotomize her and her fellow patients) and not the individual's level of self-integrity that distinguishes the utopian from the dystopian in *Woman on the Edge of Time*. It is the radicalization and not the unification of Connie that motivates the feminist moral code in that utopia (Burwell 1997: xv–xvii). Given the setting of the status quo in one of the most powerless situations possible (a mental asylum for the poor inhabitants of a 1970s New York), utopia and issues of power are woven together profoundly:

> As a projection of Connie's desire, utopian space initiates the cognitive alienation that allows Connie to redefine her position within contemporary society and perform the strategic function that permits her to politicize the medicalizing discourse of the welfare system and to expose this discourse as neither natural nor inevitable, but rather as something that is imposed upon her.
>
> (Burwell 1997: xv)

Connie may be crazy but she is able to mind-travel to a utopian future world that supports her now and teaches her how to overcome her powerless situation in her present. *Woman on the Edge of Time* is also a fascinating example of feminist utopian thinking because of its strong ties to the theoretical work of Shulamith Firestone and the radical roots of the second women's movement, which are closely related to the utopian impulses of feminist strategies:

> The need to change things radically, not just continue to "make do," was the impulse out of which grew the various movements for women's liberation in the United States and western Europe in the late 1960s and early 1970s. Their common premise was that since the historical oppression of women was grounded, conceptually and materially, within the structures of patriarchy, an alternative future for women could never be built within the confines of those structures. Therefore, these new feminisms envisioned a transformation of patriarchal culture

> so all-encompassing that not only the political, economic, and ideological structures, but the structures of human identity, relationships, and language – of consciousness itself – would be fundamentally reorganized. Taken together, they were as radically utopian as they were revolutionary.
>
> (Bammer 1991: 53)

Connie's reliance on the help of an (imaginary?) utopian world is embedded in a context in which the second women's movement follows the insistence of theorists on the Left (such as Bloch and Marcuse) that "utopianism – the belief in a radical alternative" (Bammer 1991: 54) – was not escapist, but historically imperative, and for feminists it was axiomatic. In Adrienne Rich's words:

> We need to imagine a world in which every woman is the presiding genius of her own body. In such a world women will truly create new life, bringing forth … the visions, and the thinking, necessary to sustain, console, and alter human existence. … Sexuality, politics, intelligence, power, motherhood, work, community, intimacy will develop new meaning; thinking itself will be transformed.
>
> (Rich, in Bammer 1991: 54)

These urgent political needs are perfectly well integrated into the suspenseful adventure of Connie on her journey from insanity to empowerment.

The Dialectic of Sex: The Case for Feminist Revolution

Shulamith Firestone's radical feminist proposals resonating in *Woman on the Edge of Time* were published in *The Dialectic of Sex: The Case for Feminist Revolution* (1970) one of the early texts of the second wave of US feminism. Firestone realizes that there is a lack of feminist visionary thinking. On utopia she comments:

> We haven't even a literary image of this future society; there is not even a utopian feminist literature yet in existence.
>
> (Firestone, Lefanu 1988: 57)

Firestone's theories were then groundbreaking for the utopian works of the most recognized feminist writers; thus her theoretical background is at the heart of many feminist alternatives and visions. Without her groundbreaking theories the utopias of Piercy, Russ, Charnas, and Gearhart could not have been written as such (Lefanu 1988). Firestone also first verbalized the thought that men's utopias might actually be women's dystopias and men's dystopias might actually bear some good for women. An example is Huxley's *Brave New World*:

> Huxley wanted to point to the absurdity of rejecting our biology; Firestone wants to show the necessity for doing so in order to gain true equality. She is on the side of his conservatives rather than his rebels.
>
> (Shafi 1990: 44)

What Shafi is referring to is that in *Brave New World* Huxley describes the mechanistic reproduction technology as dehumanized and views it as a horrendous development for manhood; while, on the other side, Firestone demands similar reproduction technology to free women from their role as mothers:

> Firestone gave primacy of place to the question of reproduction, seeing the oppression of women as inextricably related to their work as child-rearers as well as child-bearers. And it is this insistence on that central question 'who looks after the children in our brave new world?' that is the hallmark of the feminist incursion into science fiction.
>
> (Lefanu 1988: 57)

Firestone strongly believed that women needed to give up their biological "privilege" of being able to bear children to enable true equality between the sexes, an idea which has been incorporated in Piercy's novel and fleshed out to allow to imagine the practical application in a utopian everyday setting. Firestone developed her demands within a wider context of libertarian politics. She was inspired by social utopianists such as Charles Fourier and the Owenites. She incorporated Simone de Beauvoir's analysis of the oppression of women as described in *The Second Sex*, as well as the radical race politics of the US Black Power movement of the 1960s and Ronald Laing's theories of family. Firestone rejects the nuclear family as the norm of communal living and instead opts for units, such as loosely constructed households. Her beliefs are with the collectivist politics of the Left of the 1970s. Firestone was also strongly opposed to schools, which she saw as prison houses for children. This view has clearly not developed into mainstream thinking since. Firestone was strongly criticized for her psychology-based analysis and for her insistence that class is based on biological sex (Lefanu 1988: 58). In her works Firestone violently demanded a feminist revolution. The following list offers an overview of her most basic demands:

1. Women should be freed from the tyranny of reproduction through the use of technology;
2. The rearing of children should be the responsibility of society as a whole, men as well as women;
3. Through 'cybernetic communism', that is, the use of machines for all drudgery work and the elimination of wage labor, there should be economic independence and self-determination for all, including children;

4 Women and children should be completely integrated into the larger society;
5 With the elimination of the nuclear family's stranglehold on the individual, and thus the end of the Oedipus complex and the incest taboo, there should be sexual freedom for all untrammelled by unequal relations of power and freed from the primacy of genital sex;
6 Sex should be allowed to be expressed as in Freud's 'polymorphous perversity';
7 Last, and absolutely not least, Firestone demands the possibility of love.

(Lefanu 1988: 58)

All of Firestone's proposals are included in Piercy's literary work. Unlike during the first women's movement, when Gilman provided both theory and utopian fiction herself, the second wave developed clear cooperation between theory-building writers and literary workers. Firestone provided the theory and Piercy wrote a novel that spread utopian thought and feminist theory to readers in an easily digestible format. Many theoretical stances in Piercy's *Woman on the Edge of Time* are directly adopted from Firestone's theories. On the one hand, this shows a very interesting utilization of theoretical work. Piercy not only elaborates on the theories and implicates them into a literary model of utopia, thus exploring the workings of the different parameters of feminist theory in the framework of a literary model. On the other hand, Piercy explores in great detail how Firestone's demands could work in a model "real-life" setting and thinks about the psychological, political, economical, and sociological consequences of Firestone's ideas, offering various examples of how adjusting individual parameters – *ceteris paribus* – might influence the utopian model's outcomes. (This very much compares to the strategies of economists who create mathematical, dynamic models, in which different scenarios are calculated with various input factors.)

In *Woman on the Edge of Time* Marge Piercy chose gender equality as the most preferential of gender relations for a future society. Gender equality here is based on utopian socialization: education, reflection, and maturity of characters. A great deal of the gender equality is certainly connected to Piercy's/Firestone's solution of eliminating difference in the reproductive process based on technological progress and also regarding the category of work. Piercy solves the issue of gender discrimination by making the distribution of work independent of gender.

Gender inequality

The second category of gender relations can be subsumed under the heading "gender inequality." Willemsen describes gender inequality in utopias as some feminist utopias emphasizing the differences between women and men. These utopias consist of ideal worlds in which women's positions are better than men's:

> There are various forms of matriarchy, or even a utopia that resembles the Greek myth of the Amazons, the tribe of women warriors. Another possibility within this general category which stresses gender differences is a society in which traditionally feminine qualities are valued more highly than traditionally masculine qualities. They describe a society where emotionality reigns instead of rationality, or where love is more appreciated than status.
>
> (Willemsen 1997: 6)

[Another option for gender difference] consists of feminist utopian worlds which exclude men – they have done away with men altogether. They portray a world fashioned after women's desires – usually a world free from war, violence and competition, based on peace and harmony. These works fail to satisfy women who do not want to do away with men altogether, but who would like to see a world in which women and men live together with dignity and equality. In fact, "because feminism seeks to promote social change in the real world, some feminists may find that the all-female utopias have little to say to them."(Gupta 1997: 87)

A matriarchy replacing the existing situation in patriarchy is seen by some theorists and authors as a welcome alternative to better conditions for all. The three examples I have chosen for discussing separatist strategies in utopian visions each realise this visionary goal in very different ways. The character Janet in *The Female Man* describes her planet Whileaway, which is a world populated by women unbothered by males and their violence where the women themselves have developed some forms of ruthlessness that do not comply with Gupta's idea of a very harmonious (in the sense of boring and friction-free) utopia. In *Egalia's Daughters* gender inequality is expressed through power inversion and in *Herland* through abolishing the male sex. In a final example I will briefly discuss separatist organizing in current ecofeminist streams. This last example is not based on a utopian literary work per se, but I am discussing Mary Mellor's manifesto *Women, Work and the Environment*. I think that the theories of ecofeminism need to be considered at this point, since many ecofeminist ideals are based on essentialist beliefs placing women on top of a gender hierarchy and there is an array of feminist science fiction works following that line of thought. I am also introducing the ecofeminist discourse at this point as a means of contrast, because, unlike *Herland*, Marge Piercy's utopias (which are working with gender equality rather than inequality) are also concerned with environmentalism but are offering different solutions rather than essentialist ecofeminism.

The Female Man

In *The Female Man* utopia and dystopia coexist: patriarchy, matriarchy, and gender war are all in one "little book." The storyline therefore becomes very complicated; it interweaves parallel worlds and alternative stages of feminist struggle and the world's gender-related fate in general. The protagonists are "the 4 Js": There is Janet from the utopian world of Whileaway, which has been separatist for some centuries, who comes to another probability dimension as an explorer. There she meets Joanna, who is a feminist of Russ's contemporary 1970s, who finds herself with a rising consciousness in a patriarchal world, but still lacks radicalism and options for taking action. Jeannine lives in the USA of the 1960s in which World War II never took place and the economic depression was never overcome. Jeannine works in a precarious job as a librarian, has very little money, and her only hope is to marry a man to slightly improve her economic status but greatly improve her social status. Finally, Jael is a cruel man-hating assassin from a future world of gender war. In the course of the book the realities intermingle when the characters encounter one another.

Egalia's Daughters

In *Egalia's Daughters* all gender roles are reversed and women rule over a class of intimidated, effeminate men, who are economically and sexually exploited, the reversed world being very close to any "typical" white, middle-class, Western woman's experience in the 1970s. The most fascinating facets of Brandenberg's novel are the institutional structures designed for maternity benefits and reproductive work, which will be discussed in greater detail in Chapter 5. *Egalia* is not a typical example of gender inequality in the sense that a vision of a desirable matriarchy is created; *Egalia* is more a caricature of male hegemony by twisting gender hierarchy but not really offering a "better world."

Herland

Charlotte Perkins Gilman's *Herland* is one of the feminist utopias of the first wave. Perkins Gilman wrote three utopian novels, *Moving the Mountain* (1911), *Herland* (1915) and its sequel *With Her in Ourland* (1916), of which *Herland* is most well known. She was a contemporary and friend of Edward Bellamy, and together they edited the magazine *The American Fabian*, but "where his *Looking Backward*, set in Boston in the year 2000, posits the advance of technology as the prime mover of social change, Charlotte Perkins Gilman centralizes human agency, and in particular, that of women" (Lefanu 1988: 56–57). In *Herland* men have died out, leaving behind very peaceful, asexual women, whose main goal is to collectively be the perfect mothers and create a better species in an all-women society. The novel is set at the moment when three men from Gillman's contemporary world discover the women's land (which is set in a remote, inaccessible mountainous region) and learn about the women's culture. From my perspective the most fascinating thoughts in *Herland* concern scarcity and priorities in the economic system.

Because the women's land is situated on a small plateau secluded from the rest of the world, the women have to set very strict priorities and avoid any waste whatsoever. The improvement of human capital is equated with the belief in better technology, greater efficiency, and a better life for future generations.

Ecofeminism

While *Woman on the Edge of Time* concerns itself very much with ecological issues it does so in a non-essentialist manner. All genders are equally responsible for preserving the planet for future generations. A separatist version of environmentalist concerns can be found in feminist strategies subsumed under the heading "ecofeminism." Utopia has always been about land, creating in theory and practice physical places for alternative ways to be. (Examples of direct practical thinking about land are Morgan's *Christian Commonwealth* or Fergus O'Connor's land plan.) The *Garden City Movement* pushes for a return to the land and establishes the ideal of a new cooperative ecological community, influenced by the emergence of landscaping and planning in the early 20th century. Central is a belief in the regeneration of people and society through contact with the land (Tod and Wheeler 1978: 119). As a separatist movement ecofeminism has been highly influential in feminist movements, particularly those in the US and Europe that follow the idea of setting up "Women's Lands" free from patriarchy and in contact with nature and the land. These have been practical experiments that have shaped the discourse, as they have demonstrated possible spaces for practicing a lived utopia. An example of the theoretical reasoning of ecofeminism can be found in Mary Mellor's work on "Ecofeminist Economics" in *Women, Work and the Environment* (Mellor 1999). Mellor claims that the modern economic system is based on a "dualistic hierarchy of values," mainly expressed through money and profit. External to these mainstream values, there are unvalued and unaccounted-for givens of work, such as the ecosystem and the unpaid and unrecognized domestic and care work:

> The unvalued economy is the world of women, of women's experience – a WE-economy. The valued economy, on the other hand, is male-dominated, representing men's experience – a ME-economy. ... ME-economy is thus a DISEMBEDDED system, which bears no responsibility for the life cycle of its environment. It is disengaged from ECO-LOGICAL TIME – the time it takes to restore the effects of human activity, if there is even the possibility of renewal and replenishment within the ecosystem.
>
> (Mellor 1999, online)

Regarding solutions, Mellor believes that looking to women or nature for the answer is not the right way. If women clean up the ME-economy's "mess" (it is assumed that women are able to do so) that will not resemble a break with the existing division of labor. Rather, it should be the decision makers' responsibility to recognize the false base upon which historic systems have rested. Mellor lists what she considers necessary precautions for an ecofeminist economic vision to become true in nine issues. Amongst them are: sustainable production and consumption patterns; concentration on local production and waste reduction; local basic food provisioning; direct sale of farm produce; self-sustenance instead of profit; meaningful work; reduction of pollution; interactive workplace and living base; communal living; non-gendered work distribution; emphasis on cultural rather than economic trade; and social security in creation of social ties instead of money.

Ecofeminist thinkers like Mary Mellor, Mary Daly, Vandana Shiva, and Maria Mies have been widely criticized for operating with essentialist assumptions and for their beliefs that women are somewhat closer to nature than men and can therefore be expected to be more predestined for saving the planet. The next section exemplifies some of those criticisms:

> Where to begin? Ecofeminism is essentialist, biologist and it lacks political efficacy. Ecofeminism is inconsistent, intellectually regressive and it lacks rigour. Ecofeminism is the fluffy face of feminism.
>
> (Sargisson 2001: 52)

After stating the above, Lucy Sargisson turns around and delivers a strong pledge of the ecofeminist idea not as a scientific, profound, and political program but as a powerful utopian vision. She argues that "what's really wrong with ecofeminism is that it denies its full potential" (Sargisson 2001: 52). In her view, ecofeminism, like any effective utopia, has the potential to create a transformative opposition. She also finds that ecofeminism is extraordinary in its diverse forms and therefore forces upon the scholar similar challenges. Sargisson looks at Starhawk's work (which I will discuss in Chapter 7), who in *The Fifth Element* presents a utopia where women are leading societies but are doing so with the consent of men. Sargission comes to the conclusion that the ecofeminist, spiritual approach Starhawk takes is not a good political program, but nevertheless offers an inspiring impulse:

> The strength of this utopian expression is *not*, I suggest, in its potential to found a program of political action. In this ecofeminism is lacking. Rather, it adds creativity to feminist critique. Much feminist thought is angry, critical, and relentless. There is, I suggest, a need of an extra dimension that is provided by the dreamers who combine pragmatism with expressions of barely imaginable desires.
>
> (Sargisson 2001: 57)

Another example Sargisson looks at in her essay "What's Wrong with Ecofeminism" is Mary Daly's *Gyn/Ecology*. An interesting example of her toying with language is Daly's take on the essentialist view of women's concepts of work as opposed to men's understanding: "Wild Crone-centering is rigorous play/work, which is utterly Other than the rigor mortis of gamesmanship exhibited in phallocratic plays and works" (Daly, in Sargisson 2001: 57). Sargisson also attests that ecofeminism offers a very clear and complex analysis of oppression in her critique of the status quo. She finally finds that ecofeminism "enables other forms of feminism to be reflective and cautious about their claims" (Sargisson 2001: 57) and that ecofeminism helps the ecological environmental ethics to see their missing critique of rationalism.

But another important aspect when reflecting on essentialist ecofeminism is the aspect of the history of the land one aims to free by settling a utopian enclave on it. The famous US American utopian experiments were all established on land unrightfully gained from their former landowners. When starting a utopian enclave it should be essential to consider the ethical rights related to property issues. This postcolonial viewpoint can be expanded to ecofeminist thinking. The assumption that women may be by nature more inclined to understand and defend nature is often easily expanded to assumptions of certain races or tribes being better in touch with their surroundings. This kind of reasoning is highly critical; specific care needs to be taken by Western and Northern feminists when happily applying examples of "earthy" tribal people to their alternative scenarios. Further along in the text I will be illustrating how Marge Piercy has tried to deconstruct racial prejudice in her *Woman on the Edge of Time* (see pp. 183–189).

Fluid, non-binary conceptions of gender

A third category of gender relations in feminist utopias, based not on equality between the sexes, nor on being exclusive of men, nor on women being better than men, are the utopias in which gender no longer exists as a binary opposition, based on only two sexes. This kind of thinking is currently being established in deconstructive feminist theory or "queer theory," which claims that genders (and therefore also sexual desires) are more complex than commonly assumed and also more fluid than the binary rigidity implies.

Already in the 1960s and 1970s, literary feminist utopias began to toy with fluid non-binary gender concepts, as the following examples show.

Rad van avontuur, Triton, and androgyny

Rad van avontuur by Alkeline van Lenning (1995) is a utopian design where race and gender are made non-permanent. As Willemsen points out, here the Rawlsian veil of ignorance is used symbolically. In the novel this functions with the aid of a biomedical technology where everyone is forced to change their bodies once in their lifetime to an unforeseeable but completely different persona, changing skin color and gender etc. Willemsen supports the utopian vision that this might theoretically eliminate all racism and sexism, hoping that people expect themselves to be in different positions, therefore leveling out all conditions, but on the other hand Willemsen criticizes the element of coercion in that work and states that this might make this utopia rather dystopian (Willemsen 1997: 8).

Another possibility is the imagination of a multitude of sexes. An extreme is Samuel Delany's planet *Triton* (1976), where about 40 different sexes exist and therefore maleness and femaleness as we know it have completely disappeared. What Poldervaart describes as interesting in that regard is that people can change their sex when they want; they live in communities, either mixed or unmixed with different sexes (Poldervaart 1997). Parenthood, including breastfeeding, is shared by all members of the commune. The utopian society described in *Tritron* is nevertheless situated in a context of war, and the gender fluidity does not necessarily result in the happiness of their bearers. Still, the work allows a broader sense of differentiation, considering issues of race, class, and gender.

Poldervaart then researches a different approach, namely the idea of making fathers into mothers by supposing the existence of only one sex: The earliest example Poldervaart lists is Gabriel de Foigny's *La Terre australe connue*, which dates back to 1676. The androgynous fantasy is the key to sexual equality. Another extended example of this "one-sex idea" is Ursula Le Guin's *The Left Hand of Darkness* (1969), where the unisexed people temporarily morph into another sex to allow mating and reproduction:

> Our entire [terran] pattern of socio-sexual interaction is non-existent here. [The Gethenians] cannot play the game. They do not see another as men or women. This is almost impossible for our imagination to accept. What is the first question we ask about a newborn baby?
>
> (Le Guin 1969, online)

> Yet you cannot think of a Gethenian as "it." They are not neuters. They are potentials; during each sexual cycle they may develop in either direction for the duration of that cycle. No physiological habit is established, and the mother of several children may be the father of several more.
>
> (Le Guin 1969: inside front cover)

Poldervaart concludes her list of examples of non-dualistic gender/sex societies as follows: "In most feminist utopias, fixed relations between men and women are rejected. The norm of such exclusive relationships is seen as a crippling and unsatisfying construction" (Poldervaart 1997: 186–187).

A Manifesto for Cyborgs

Within feminist studies, Donna Haraway's *A Manifesto for Cyborgs* is a famous example of a vision that fits into this category of beyond-gender utopias, although its form hardly relates to the classic utopian narrative. *A Manifesto for Cyborgs* is not a piece of literature; it is considered feminist theory, but has been chosen anyway to represent this section of differently gendered utopias.

A Cyborg Manifesto is the most well-known article in Donna Haraway's *Simians, Cyborgs, and Women* (1980). The manifesto defines a cyborg as "a hybrid of machine and organism, a creature of social reality as well as a creature of fiction;" it aims to deconstruct all other types of binary givens in theory and social reality, such as self/other, mind/body, nature/technology. Haraway thereby criticizes current feminist theory and practice, and shows that alternative ways of thinking are possible. She argues that technology can be used to expand feminist goals. Both of these aspects, the criticism and the presentation of an alternative, are characteristic of utopias, while Willemsen states that Haraway takes the ingredients currently present in our culture and uses them in a revolutionary way (Willemsen 1997: 6), literary feminist utopias had already employed the cyborg image before Haraway's theoretical text.

The Female Man

In *The Female Man* the cyborg is alive in the personae of Jael, the men-hating assassin:

> Her real laugh is the worst human sound I have ever heard: A hard, screeching yell that ends in gasps and rusty sobbing, as if some mechanical vulture on a gigantic garbage heap on the surface of the moon were giving one forced shriek for the death of all organic life. Yet J likes it, this is her *private* laugh.
>
> (Russ 1975: 159)

Jael, who lives in a world of gender war, is very much a cyborg in Haraway's sense. She is a fighting machine with imbedded weaponry, razor sharp cybernetic claws that may extend if needed, steel ribbons implanted to replace weak human teeth and other more mysterious features:

> The grafted muscles on my fingers and hands pulled back the loose skin, [on my fingers I have] Claws, talons like a cat's but bigger, a little more dull than wood brads but good for tearing. And my teeth are a sham over metal. … I always carry firearms. The truly violent are never without them. … You have to build up the fingers surgically so they'll

> take the strain. A certain squeamishness prevents me from using my teeth in front of witnesses – the best way to silence an enemy is to bite out his larynx.
>
> (Russ 1975: 181)

Another example of cyborgs populating feminist dystopias is found in *Trouble and Her Friends* (Scott 1993), where a more likable cyborg character than Jael, called India Carless, a professional computer hacker who sports neural implants, is apt to attach to computers and the virtual web. Many science fiction novels (the most famous of which is *Matrix*) have developed ideas of merging humans with computers. Rarer are feminist or GLBT (gay, lesbian, bisexual, or transgender) plots in those novels.

From Frankenstein *to android*

The idea of artificial life is another issue relevant to this stream of thinking. From Mary Shelley's *Frankenstein* (1818) to Marge Piercy's *He, She, and It* (1991) the archetypical story of the artificial man is repeated. Whether the artificial life is created from the dead, computers and robotics, or magic and clay in the case of the Golem, who was the protector of the Jewish inhabitants of Prague's Ghetto around 1600, is a question of timely fashion. Piercy places the story of the future artificial man, the modern Golem, as a protector in the fictive 2050s, where a humanoid computer with artificial intelligence watches over a utopian enclave threatened with being overrun by an aggressive corporate world which has just about devastated the whole planet and impoverished nearly everyone. Feminist utopias and dystopias therefore not only toy with gender roles, they also question what separates humans from machines and reflect on the consequences of "cyborgization."

Gender relations in economics

After considering gender relations in feminist utopias I want to turn to the model worlds of economic and feminist economic theory. Interestingly, gender relations in "rational science" look, from this perspective, rather removed or utopian themselves.

Men-only worlds

Economic theory in a scientific setting describes model worlds of economic relationships between a certain set of economic agents. Interestingly, the model worlds populated by these agents are usually worlds of men-only adventures. Ulla Grapard is one of the feminist economists who has examined the life of the model economic protagonist, the archetype of the *homo oeconomicus*, Robinson Crusoe.

> It is clear, that [Robinsons] escape is ruined if you mix the family, or even women into the story. . . . [Crusoe's] island remains for us an Eden uncomplicated by the wiles and distractions of an Eve.
>
> (Walter De La Mare, in Grapard 1995: 44)

Robinson Crusoe, the adventurer, is the typical economic textbook agent. His (economic) relationship with his partner Friday becomes the model relationship in economic theory, where at first glance gender and invisible work do not seem to be an issue in this two-person set up. In larger models women are taken for granted and their reproductive work is seen as an endless trouble-free supply, including the production and maintenance of the labor force. For instance, Paul Samuelson's exemplary concept of the Overlapping Generations Model of 1958 establishes basic assumptions about gender relations by setting up the following condition for *all* agents in the model (and nothing more):

> Men enter the labor market at about the age of twenty. They work for forty-five years or so and then live for fifteen years in retirement. (As children they are part of their parent's consumption and we take no note of them.)
>
> (Samuelson 1958: 468)

Women are subsumed among either the workers or the parents; we do not know, a differentiation of genders is not made. Indeed, the model only looks at the labor market and the problem of retirement for a uniform male agent. We never really find out if women are considered part of their husbands' consumption, and are thus not taken note of, or if it is assumed they are just like the male agents. Another example is the invisible woman, as can be seen in Adam Smith's analysis of the dinner provision:

> It is not from the benevolence of the butcher, the brewer, or the baker that we expect our dinner, but from their regard to their own interest.
>
> (Smith 1776, online)

(Notice that paid professionals are cooking here; no wives are visible.) Only with the engagement of Mary Reid, Hazel Kyrk, Elizabeth Hoyt, and then later on the School of the New Home Economics, most prominently Gary Becker, did specific thought start to be given to gender relations and the division of labor. The neoclassical view in this case states that a man and a woman will form a household with a common utility function, trying to maximize household utility by specializing in reproductive work versus work in the labor market. Due to biology, women will realize that they need not invest as much as men into education as they are expecting breaks in their professional career for childbirth and care. Therefore, their wages will be lower, which makes it even more sensible to specialize in the unpaid work segment. Feminist economists have criticized Becker's model in the last decades; bargaining power theorists have expanded the assumptions and proven that this specialization is not all that rational for women since it only increases their dependency on the male breadwinner (Ott 1992). Michèle Pujol has summarized neoclassical economists' prejudices towards women in the following five implicit assumptions: all women are married and have children or will do so, they are or ought to be dependent on a male relative, are or ought to be housewives, are unproductive in the workforce, and they are irrational and cannot make economic decisions (Pujol 1995). The man in the market community will be fully rational, egoistic, and independent. Becker nevertheless states that his behavior in the household will take on altruistic forms: if he is away from the marketplace, then the so-called *homo oeconomicus* will operate as a benevolent patriarch sharing with his wife and children. This is still the status quo in most mainstream economics' thought on gender relations.

Gender relations in feminist economics

Feminist economists have protested the mainstream models and their depiction of gender relations, exposing wage disparities and unequal work burdens as unfair, demanding that the representation of women in theory should change and that practical cooperation between men and women should improve. In the first instance, a lot of this work has been related to pointing out gender biases and injustices, documenting incomes forgone in the marketplace and exploitation in private homes. Radical changes in the system, i.e. challenges of the nuclear family, questioning the nature of work per se, have not become a focal point in the discipline.

The next section will point out differences in feminist economic thought and their relatedness to the question of sex and gender.

Essentialism

Julie Nelson acknowledges a desire for a gynocentric, possibly separatist, strategy from the position of a feminist economist as such:

> This wish for an ideal society with gynocentric economics has been explored in numerous works of utopian literature and has also been mentioned by most feminist economists as one possible alternative, even if it is not the one alternative they wish to take.
>
> (Nelson 1995)

Where most feminist economists hesitate to ground their work on the basic assumption that one gender is better equipped to take on a certain position in economic life, essentialism is the core of "feminist" empiricism (i.e. the School of New Home Economics). In the early 1900s, Anne Wheeler and

William Thompson, with their critique of the concept of the benevolent patriarch, probably would not have imagined that the same concept would resurface in the New Home Economics of the Chicago School over a hundred years later. Ideologies as expressed by Becker in a scientific context are hardly new, yet the ongoing critique around them has been quite interesting. Another aspect in the course of this analysis is that when viewing the issue of the New Home Economics' family structure through the filter of a quest for utopia, one can clearly see that Gary Becker's economic world does not include any utopian vision. Instead, it relies on the status quo of gender roles created during the past decades and centuries. Hewitson states that feminist empiricism might have some potential for change in a feminist sense simply by raising issues, but she still dismisses that approach as not useful for changes demanded by feminist economists (Hewitson 1999: 49).

Another example for essentialism in feminist economics, yet with a gynocentric point of view, is displayed in Deidre McCloskey's "Some Consequences of a Conjective Economics" (1993). McCloskey starts her piece with Arjo Klamer's parable of squares and circles as representing hard and soft approaches of science. She explains how economics has entered an era of modernism or positivism since the 1940s. My critique of McCloskey's view is that she does not depart from binary concepts of male and female, and, even more, she associates certain attributes to maleness and femaleness. For instance, she writes that

> a conjective economics would use a more higher figure than masculine economics would, interfering more with the devil-may-care attitude of males, especially young ones, zooming about helmetless on their Kawasakis. Consequently, though a feminine economy would need spontaneously less interference, the interference that did take place would be more thorough – one might say more motherly.
>
> (McCloskey 1993: 80)

A feminine economics is not the same as a feminist economics. While Margaret Thatcher's economic policy is not typically "feminine," it is certainly not "feminist." Thatcher's femaleness per se has nothing to do with her economic vision. Nor does maleness necessarily lead to being on a motorbike without a helmet. McCloskey's argumentation is truly inspiring – I would certainly like to live in a better, feminine world – but I believe the argument is still too essentialist, trusting sex stereotypes for social change and picking up on Pujol's example of the assumption that all women are mothers or at least should be motherly. McCloskey's call for utopian visions – "Economists better equipped than I am to see the economy with feminine eyes will think of twenty other ways in which an economics amended by women would differ from the male-centered version we now have" (McCloskey 1993: 81) – makes sex the program necessary for change, which does clearly speak against the sex and gender distinction made by most feminist thinkers. McCloskey's utopian desire is an interesting version of feminist envisioning; it leaves one to ask whether she is one of the few Julie Nelson has mentioned who would indeed opt for a matriarchy, a world and economy run by wise and motherly women.

Feminist constructivism

Another feminist economics approach regarding gender is "feminist constructivism," which is currently the most popular feminist economics approach, and it entails much utopian potential. Feminist constructivism, or "gender feminism," reasons that the two sexes are fundamentally similar and that gender differences are not deeply rooted, but superficial and based on social control. Political implications are to avoid social conditioning that creates sexual difference. Feminist economists have largely adopted the view of the social construction of gender. Social equality can therefore be created via a process, which Hewitson describes as "degendering society," in which all gendered aspects would be eliminated (Hewitson 1999: 10). The result would be the creation of "the new androgynous men," or, better worded, the "androgyn." This would be a feminist version of "*der neue Mensch*" (the New Man), who is ever present in (socialist) utopias and dystopias. Here, feminist economics can be seen as part of the feminist process of creating the androgynous inhabitants of utopia.

> Not only will the patriarchal distinction between men and women disappear but with it also the distinction between the private and the public sphere of paid and unpaid work, or the domains of the – masculine – market and the – feminine – domain of the family.
>
> (Pateman 1987, in Hewitson 1999: 11)

Instead of spending time envisioning the "new world," as Francis Bacon did with his mechanistic approach, it seems as if feminist economists have chosen to focus on envisioning and thus creating the new inhabitants of that other world, whatever that world might look like. This goes along with the notion that many feminist economists work in the education sphere. The theoretical quest, even though not focused on the first-wave feminist strategy of creating a new world, instead emphasizes on creating new people, and is thus related to their very practical work and the decision to spend their life energy on teaching and thereby promoting alternatives.

When measuring the progress in the process of creating androgyny, Dianne Perrons, in "Measuring Equality in Opportunity" (1995), proposes a way of constructing a single scalar index of gender equality in the labor market. Perrons makes a distinction between radical utopian strategies (the long agenda) and changes for women within the system (the short agenda). An example of the feminist economics (non-utopian) short agenda regarding women's opportunities in the labor market would be affirmative action, allowing women to break through the glass ceiling more easily. The utopian approach of the long agenda would be, for example, to replace traditional hierarchical employment structures where the skill profiles of all workers could be raised by the use of human-based technologies and world practices and where the contributions of all workers would be more appropriately rewarded. Although Perrons goes to the trouble of making this distinction, her indicator remains a little shortsighted. (Unemployed women are not included, for instance.) Perrons finds that "all citizens could spread their time more evenly between these activities in order to obtain a more equitable distribution of the costs and benefits of social reproduction" (Perrons 2000: 105).

Gender bending

A very creative idea is embedded in Esther Redmount's 1995 piece titled *Toward a Feminist Econometrics*, in which Redmount introduces gender as a choice variable to econometric modeling. Redmount's approach is rather fascinating. Even though she remains in the field of econometrics, which has been deemed rather non-radical and anti-utopian, she manages to give her agenda an interesting twist. She builds an option into her model which assumes that gender can be chosen. That sounds very much like the literary utopia discussed on pp. 23–24 where gender becomes fluid and humans are then thought to interact with each other very differently than today. If gender could be chosen for biological men and women, much economic thought as we know it today would cease to make sense. For example, studies by Nancy Folbre and Doris Weichselbaumer regarding differences in earnings for differently gendered men and women, such as feminine men and masculine women, showed that feminine men indeed earned less than masculine men and vice versa. The idea of incorporating such a radical concept in an econometric model is surely intriguing.

Heterocentrism

Suzanne Bergeron (2007) and Drucilla Barker (2007) have recently written about the heteronormativity displayed in feminist economics, and Bergeron looks into examples of heterocentrism in the most progressive works of feminist economics. Normative sexualities are considered a given and promoted by most feminist economics; gay and lesbian economics is, at best, accepted as a distinct entity on the margins of the discipline, and basic insights, such as the constructedness of gender and sexualities, have largely not been taken on board in the feminist economics agenda. Contrarily, feminist economics – probably in order to establish a scientific character within the realms of mainstream economics – has focused on empiricism, as I have demonstrated in a piece of small-scale research on the journal *Feminist Economics*, which is discussed in Chapter 6. Liberal feminist stances, such as that suggested by Barbara Bergmann, often advise women to try to "pass" as men in the economic realm, thus un-leveling the disadvantage Simone de Beauvoir has pointed out, and enabling women to become the ones policy makers respond to. From the vantage point of this type of theory building, policy implications, i.e. the underwriting of an assumed heterosexual dualism which ensures women's caring labor, have been incorporated, for instance, in development discourse in which men and women are seen as essential counterparts for enhancing development (Bergeron 2007). The problem does not necessarily lie in an inherently ill intention, as Drucilla Barker has argued, but more in loyalty to a certain idea of science:

> Although feminist economists are highly critical of mainstream economics, most are committed to the notion of scientific inquiry. That is, they are committed to transforming economics by using gender as a category of analysis while at the same time retaining the scientific character and status of feminist economics.
>
> (Barker 2005: 2,190)

Queer economics

In the view of queer theorists such as Antke Engel or Hanna Hacker, Foucault's regulatory notions of sexuality not only refer to heterosexual cultures, but can also include gay and lesbian conservative desires for normativity. "Queer" is then seen as a term divergent from any forms of sexual normalizations. In a paper given in 2006, German philosopher Antke Engel applies queer theories and ideas of homonormativity to a neoliberal shaping of society. She puts forward a proposition she calls "projective integration," which she describes as a process that creates a new consensus in a society that does not regard only certain forms of homosexuality as worthy of integration, but also regards them as role models for consumption-oriented citizens. This process is interesting, because in the queer tradition a strict hetero/homosexual binary opposition is questioned and replaced by an alliance of majority and minority groups established around political acceptance and support for the neoliberal project. This process is especially useful to explain the simultaneous occurrence of liberal pluralization and discrimination/violence against gays, lesbians, and transgender people. While production methods are changing (Donna Haraway calls this the *New Industrialization*), diversity concepts within large companies seem to proclaim a wonderful and healthy mix of different people working together under the rainbow. Engel explains these processes of a tolerant capitalist system in regard to non-normative sexualities as one that doesn't only rely on similar characteristics in market behaviors (markets may also inhibit abnormalities) when striving for profit or regarding a modernization of capitalism that relies on more flexible, individualist laborers. Engel focuses on explaining how sexual pluralism and freedom may function as an analogy for market pluralism and freedom, but based on the notion that sexuality is connected to the private sphere. Engel shows us that gay stereotypes can be regarded as the ideal models for neoliberal economic agents. Stereotypically, gays not only exhibit a desire to keep up with a gay lifestyle and can therefore be considered avant-garde consumers, but also, as with liberal feminism, some queer politics seem to embrace a strategy of empowerment that is filled by a desire to fully belong to the *free market*. In *The Rise of the Creative Class. And How It's Transforming Work, Leisure and Everyday Life*, Richard Florida (2002) discusses this as a collective effect of a conglomeration of gay residents in certain urban areas who help improve the neighborhood by pushing local economic development. Furthermore, gay and lesbian couples have become role models for creating small circles of friends or family instances as support groups and as pioneers in replacing state-provided social security with private networks. Sexual emancipation is connected to values of commitment and therefore becomes exemplary for the individual discourse of freedom and private responsibility. A weakening of solidarity within a society goes along with the recipe that one is allowed to live as one pleases as long as one is successful and operates at one's own risk. Lisa Duggan calls this process "new homonormativity" when she analyses the politics of the Independent Gay Forum, where she sees the privacy of the home, freedom in the market economy, and patriotism as interlinked. Engel furthermore connects the new homo-normativity, which considers itself politically neutral and which also states that it does not aim at posing "threats to social morality or the political order," as a specific constellation of governmentality in the sense of Foucault – i.e. attempting to explain the self-government of subjects. An interesting part of the process is to integrate minority demands into the hegemonic discourse, yet these become severed from their contextual struggles for political justice and against economic exploitation. The hegemonic consensus is enabled by allowing minorities to see themselves as an avant-garde of much-needed creativity and flexibility in the mainstream. As a solution, Engel offers concepts like Shane Phelan's "queer citizenship," based on political participation and alliances formed along different axes of "strangeness." She finally calls for a process to initiate a discussion on how gender/sexual existences may be able to propagate alternative forms of society and what the effects on contemporary power structures may be (Engel 2006).

Until the April 2007 issue, the journal *Feminist Economics* lists only one paper with the term "Queer" included in its title and/or abstract. This paper is Richard Cornwall's "A Primer on Queer Theory for Economists Interested in Social Identities" in issue 4(2), 1998. In his paper, Cornwall aims to provide a primer on queer theory for feminist economists. He states that his "goal is to queer the temptation for economists to use 'identities' uncritically" (Cornwall 1998: 73). In doing so, Cornwall reviews Foucault's contemporary meta-narrative that describes how "Western discursive structures since late antiquity have very slowly evolved to make the male–female *couple* the social–civic atom" (Cornwall 1998: 75). I find one of the most interesting statements in his article the point when Cornwall says:

> Following Foucault's queerly bold hypothesizing means we would do well to find analytically tractable ways to grapple with (i) the impact on markets (and other institutional manifestations) of changes in discursive systems and (ii) how markets affect discursive systems. I conjecture that we must marry institutional and theoretical (mathematical) analysis to understand this circle of interdependence between how perceptions of the body – these constructed, overlapping differences (by sexuality, gender, race, and class) – affect markets and, in turn, how markets affect our perceptions of the body. . . . Queer political economy shares with feminist and race theory interest in the social articulation of cognitive codes (what in psychology are termed schemas) which stigmatize bodies and so amplify inequality. This interest in the perception of bodies differs from both neoclassical analysis and classical Marxian analysis which have constructed analytical methods which ignore "desiring bodies" and instead model the interaction in markets of bodiless actors whose "desires" have been largely erased.
>
> (Cornwall 1998: 78 and 81)

This anticipation clearly echoes in what Antke Engel has compiled in her 2006 essay in addressing her example of the neoliberal society. I feel this research is a great enrichment for all of feminist economics, and not only for a "queer" or "gay and lesbian" margin of the discipline. While borders and strategic barriers between marginalized groups in political theory and practice have long been shifted along the new demarcation lines of "good and bad neoliberal citizens" regardless of their status of sexual dissidence or of other minority identity virtues (race, class, religion) they might inhabit, Engel points out the new construction of insiders and outsiders. I find it essential that feminist economic theory reacts to these changes and adopts concepts which incorporate these changes into theoretical analyses. "Women" or "mothers" have long since ceased to be useful categories, for instance, in analyzing discrimination or gendered pay gaps. In an age of "diversity management," other more complex categories of dominance and suppression have come to replace outmoded essentialist structures.

Feminist economics is, however, not solely responsible for negating queer theories. When researching for publications on "queer economics," in nearly each case the term "queer" is confused with "gay and lesbian economics." Currently, presumably "queer" research issues include gay and lesbian consumer behavior, the "pink dollar," gays and lesbians in the working place, discrimination and its costs, gay and lesbian business owners and pink business guides, marketing to gays and lesbians, and the like – all issues that can be subsumed as "add queers and stir." A more promising analysis can be found in Elizabeth Whitney's article "Capitalizing on Camp: Greed and the Queer Marketplace," in which she contemplates whether the cooptation of queer identity and cultural practices is liberating or oppressive. She looks into "the camp element that is so appealing to heterosexist efforts to reframe queer cultural practices ... [and] ... the role that capitalist economics plays in leading to a potentially false sense of civil liberties for queer individuals and communities" (Whitney 2006). Mostly, however, where economics (or business studies) is concerned the term "queer" is considered a handy abbreviation for "gay and lesbian" or sometimes for "gay, lesbian, bisexual, and transgender." In economic analysis the more political use of the concept/term "queer," as is the case in queer studies, is usually forgone, and in discourses led by gay and lesbian movements there is also no unified use of the concept "queer". In my view, this distinction is particularly important for political economics as well as for feminist economics, as I have stated above, since the new structures of the social networks of *homo oeconomicus* (formerly the nuclear family) must be correctly depicted in order to reshape theory.

In closing, let me briefly give an example of why it may lead to different results when a queer perspective on economic theory is employed. Neoclassical economic theory sees economic man as a self-sustained individual in possession of full information and as acting upon egoistic impulses to increase his personal utility. Feminist economics has stepped in and pointed out the invisible recourses the *homo oeconomicus* has taken for granted, which his wife provides in the realm of the nuclear family. While the economic man is working in the marketplace, his wife is providing at home for him and the family. It has recently been accepted that there are alternative family structures, that there are singles, mothers, and lesbian-double income earners, who face discrimination when trying to buy a house. From a queer perspective, it instantly becomes apparent that *homo oeconomicus* is not really a family man, but he truly is a closet queen! This can easily be discerned as such because from a queer perspective it is apparent that *homo oeconomicus* in his model shape is not as far from a real-life character as feminist economists might have been thinking: *Homo oeconomicus* is really much more an impersonation of the neoclassical role model than we could have ever dreamed of. It is not an omission, but a fact, that he is truly self-sustained! There is no wife (or even a same-sex partner) doing the reproductive work in the home for him. Gay marriage is still not legal in many places, but private health and retirement plans make up for a possible utility loss in forgone social relationships. *Homo oeconomicus* (who is white, or of another "respectable" ethnic minority) is working with a high salary, in a white-collar job, or perhaps in the creative industry; he is well educated, flexible and has access to the Internet, i.e. "full" information. He aims to maximize his utility; he certainly needs to keep up his gay lifestyle; his taste and allowance are clearly superior to that of the single, heterosexual mother. He possesses some social capital; he is embedded in a group of friends and sexual partners, thus forming a network that could enable him to become the mayor of any liberal European capital city, now that he has been outed. Certainly this toying with the queer lens does not mean to imply that all economic actors are gay. But considering the notion of heteronormativity which I have been discussing it seems interesting to see how the model ideal of *homo oeconomicus* can more and more be recognized in the independent, well-off gay consumer, or maybe at least in the stereotypical image of such a person.

Considering economic realities, Lee Badgett has analyzed the pay gap between gays and lesbians and heterosexual men and women and has found that there still is a financial penalty for homosexuality (Badgett and Jefferson 2007). I wonder whether this penalty is now slowly removed in accordance with the new homonormativity and whether wage discrimination will only remain when based on, for instance, the gender performance of the specific profession, i.e. when gay men work in female-gendered professions (such as hairdressing, care and health work, etc.) and thereby bring the pay average down for the group of gay men; and whether there really is not that much discrimination left for gay men who perform in the homonormative realm and in male-gendered jobs. Certainly, these considerations are made for urban or semi-urban areas in Western Europe or the US; however, *homo oeconomicus* cannot be interpreted from such a queer perspective in other areas, such as in north-eastern Europe, or even other contexts. The concept of homonormativity certainly does not hold true everywhere: Legislation that actively punishes homosexual behavior certainly prevents the establishment of a New Homonormativity.

3 The Cartesian Turn in utopia

This chapter examines realms in the history of epistemology and science. Gender roles and scientific paradigms, for example the establishment of the concept of scarcity in economics, are not ahistorical givens. The concept of scarcity, current gender perceptions, and scientific methodology as it is known today emerged from the last great paradigmatic shift in scientific thinking, the "Cartesian Turn." I aim to talk about this change from an "organic" to a "mechanistic" worldview, but rather than lamenting a lost pre-witchhunt past here, I seek to show that paradigms do change and what consequences and opportunities that brings. This realization broadened my horizon in terms of the possibility for a radical version of feminist economics that replaces not only the greedy fear of scarcity but also the conceptions of a hierarchically binary science as we know it.

My starting point for this line of thought was Hella Hoppe's first comprehensive German-language book on feminist economics (*Feministische Ökonomik*, 2002). Hoppe describes in great detail the paradigmatic change from the organic to the mechanistic worldview. The organic worldview saw men and women as equal parts of one whole organic being, the world; the mechanistic worldview replaces this medieval notion with hierarchical dualisms and an idea that man must control and tame nature. Maleness was associated with the attributes of the new-born science; it was rational, virile, and not connected to the subjects of research. The idea thus became that all knowledge can be derived from basic axioms and that knowledge is accumulative. As a scientific discipline, economics was created as a "second nature," strongly influenced by Isaac Newton's physics. Hoppe states that the mental division of the world into hierarchical dualisms (e.g. masculine/feminine, objective/subjective, rational/emotional, etc.) led to a narrowing of the methods and contents in modern science (Hoppe 2002: 27).

Changes in gender and nature perception: mechanists escaping a female cosmos

Why did this paradigmatic shift occur in the first place? Hoppe sees the transformation from the heliocentric to the geocentric worldview as a catalyst to cause this overall paradigmatic shift in science. She explains this perception with a metaphorical studies analysis and posits the idea that metaphors are not merely ornaments of speech, but also constitute knowledge. In the heliocentric world, the sun circles the moon, yet more essential to understanding what the collapse of this worldview meant was that the sun was metaphorically associated with "the male principle" while the earth was viewed as "the female principle." The change in astronomical thinking not only was relevant for astrophysics and astrology, but also collapsed the construction of gender relations and, moreover, everything related to "male and female spheres." This meant great insecurities for those times, given that the earth, mother earth, the "female principle," was known not only as the nurturing giving mother, but also as a potential danger, who could bring natural catastrophes over the inhabitants of the planet. Driven by insecurity and fear, new metaphors were sought to replace the void the lost idea of the harmonious cosmos had left behind. The mechanistic worldview set out to restore order in the world. Since the earth and the female principle turned out to be small and nearly insignificant in the larger realm of things, it seemed a logical conclusion that one would search for new potential forces to lean on. The belief in mechanics, logic, and order posed a solution. Binary hierarchical pairs were introduced as the element of thinking. Hoppe quotes Pieri V. Mini, who argues that these dualisms put an end to

> [the] balance which underlies true science: the balance between thinking and observing, deduction and induction, imagination and common sense, reflection and action, reason and passion, abstract thinking and realism, the world within and without the mind. Under the impact of Cartesianism the second element of the equation was sacrificed to the first.
>
> (Mini, in Hoppe 2002: 35)

René Descartes's (the Cartesian Turn is named after Descartes's Latin name Renatus Cartesius) new perspective during that time included cognition and the idea of a machine-like order to a dualistic worldview. The scientific concept of positivism and the foundation for modern sociopolitical systems, such as governance, were established. The mechanistic metaphor replaced "Mother Earth." David Hume's and John Locke's later classical empiricism sought to free science from the innate ideas of Descartes's deductive method, but in the end their approach is still based on cognition, since it assumes that reality exists independently of its observer. In the 19th century, all streams of epistemological individualism were incorporated in positivism, which has remained greatly formative for economic theory until today.

Hella Hoppe claims that feminist economics rejects positivism, since it has been incorporated from the natural sciences into neoclassical economics as an expression of "masculine" values. As I have said, the explanation

Hoppe gives for the cause of the paradigmatic shift is grounded on the importance of metaphors and their constituency of knowledge and effects on thought at the point where metaphors break down. In another light, Hoppe's explanation of the end of a "harmonious worldview" can be also seen from an ecofeminist point of view:

> Ecofeminist practice claims to "dig at the roots" of oppression. ... Oppression, they say, is not a simple matter. Lori Gruen identifies four connecting narratives that comprise frameworks of legitimate oppression. The objects of oppression are, she says, women and animals. The narratives are: (1) evolution stories in which male humans are characterized as developing hunting skills and being or becoming in some way significantly the stronger sex; (2) evolution stories that locate a moment of significance in the shift from nomadic to sedentary living which brought a further sexual separation of roles; (3) religious narratives that construct nature as a source of fear and man as its conqueror; (4) an empirically based belief system in which mechanistic and (a certain kind of) scientific world views further separate man from nature. Each narrative – and most so called emancipatory discourses (liberal feminism, Marxist feminism, socialist feminism, radical feminism, animal liberation theory) all "accept normative dualisms that give rise to a logic of domination" ... They are thus trapped in (and complicit with?) a world view that constructs the Other in opposition and responds to it with violence.
>
> (Sargisson 2001: 60)

I find the consideration of feminist economics very interesting in relation to point 4 in Gruen's categorization. Hoppe claims that feminist economics rejects positivism; Sargisson picks up the argument here that all emancipatory discourses nevertheless still accept normative dualisms and are trapped within that epistemology. I agree with Hoppe that feminist economics is highly critical of positivism and I believe that the discipline has not yet managed to replace those dualisms that trap it in the same realm as neoclassical economics. Nevertheless, I see the emergence of a few levers that may aid in escaping this trap. Some are new arguments brought forth by postmodern, postcolonial, and queer theories; others are lessons from utopia that allow for new options of thinking, although they remain strongly connected to their historical and epistemological contexts. Nonetheless, utopias provide steps which allow one to transcend a given status quo. However, there is one danger that remains in terms of utopia's embedment. It remains essential to ask, for each and every utopia, whom does this ideal world benefit and who loses out? An example of this problem which I find particularly interesting regards the Cartesian revolution and its implication for gender roles, which can be closely observed in the changes in utopian thinking during the Renaissance.

Paradigm shift reflected in the gender roles of Renaissance utopias

The following section explores the changing gender relations shortly before and after the Cartesian Turn within the utopias of that era. Whereas women could have improved their status in the earlier utopias, this opportunity disappeared in the later utopias. Utopian modeling became a coercive tool that completely lacked moments of freedom for women as an oppressed group.

Previous to the Renaissance, utopian thought was mostly shaped by a multitude of groups who propagated thoughts on how to realize the Christian utopia of amity and egalitarianism, bridge class and gender differences, and communalize all goods. This version of utopia and its implications for people's everyday lives convey an inherent critique of the hypocrisy of the often corrupt lives of those in the clergy that had been strongly supported by the teachings of St. Thomas Aquinas, who pledged that the "real" good life for everyone would only begin in heaven, hereby stabilizing the inequalities inherent in the existing status quo. The heretics desired to do away with the socioeconomic structures of the family and argued that no one was to be the property of another. Many such utopians practiced either celibacy or free sexual relations among "brothers and sisters." Saskia Poldervaart claims that the important role women played in all heretical movements was one of the most important reasons why heresy failed, as "contemporaries saw it as a dangerous feminist movement" (Poldervaart 1997: 178).

The utopias of the early Renaissance

The 16th and 17th centuries were eras in which utopian theories and movements reflected the change in thought paradigms and the struggle over epistemology in science. In his work on feminist literary theory and the utopian discourse in the Anglo-American novel, Mario Klarer also describes the Renaissance as the turning point for the utopian discourse. In most utopias of the ancient world and the early modern era, nature is depicted as a caring organism. First, nature is still described as a nourishing mother who takes care of the living creatures in the universe. The break is reflected in a different view of this personified caring nature. It turns into a violent, uncontrollable force, one that causes horrific storms, draughts, floods, and chaos, yet still both aspects of nature are depicted as female personae. The most famous works on utopia, which describe nature as the ideal, well-meaning mother, are the pastoral visions in Philip Sidney's *Arcadia* (1593) and Edmund Spenser's *The Shepherd's Calendar* (1579). In these works, nature is passive and boundlessly giving, easily exploitable and manipulated. The historical context is provided by the spirit of the successful "discovery" of America by Columbus and Vespucci, who described their findings using very utopian language. The archetypical description of the

Golden Age (compare to Homer, Hesiod, Horaz, and Ovid) can be found in most of those travel journals. The tradition of describing the new found land as a fertile woman is celebrated; Columbus describes the shape of the globe not as a perfect sphere, but as a giant female breast (Columbus, in Klarer 1993: 30). In another vein, the newly discovered worlds are often depicted as deceitful female identities, sporting unknown dangers and catastrophes; i.e. the mythical image of the Amazon is restored in Vespucci's journals; in historical plates *America* is either described as a lusty seductress or an Amazon monster (Klarer 1993: 31). Klarer concludes that

> the passive benevolence of the organic conception of nature practically invites resources to be exploited; the chaotic mischievous element again legitimizes submission and regulates intervention. Colonial discourses form the basis for both approaches and they especially shape the great utopias of the Renaissance, which are set in the frameworks of journeys of discovery. Organic and mechanistic approaches become visible as opposing conceptions of the world in the utopias of the early modern era ... the ambivalence of gender is a key issue for the realization of each utopian vision.
>
> (Klarer 1993: 3, author's translation)[1]

Well-meaning nature, the well-meaning mothers, the well-meaning lands to be conquered usually form the backdrop necessary for the functioning of society in modern economic models. Interestingly, even though the Cartesian split with all its misogyny has occurred and shaped all scientific thinking, a thoroughly organic worldview is often assumed in neoclassical economic models (i.e. Samuelson's 1958 Overlapping Generations (OLG) Model); for instance, the functioning of female provisioning and recreation is never questioned, i.e. is taken for granted, the inhabitants of the happy land are free from their social contracts in addition to the existing basic care and support system women provided. Utopias in which the very same organic perception of nature is included in the setup are, for example, Tommaso Campanella's *The City of the Sun* (1602) and Valentin Andreae's *Christianopolis* (1619). Both works can be considered organic philosophy, because a friendly, trusting balance and cooperation between inhabitants and the nourishing background are considered as the ideal.

City of the Sun

In Campanella's tale, the harmonic interaction between nature and the cosmos expands to some extent into the gender relations of the utopian society. Campanella strives for an egalitarian integration of women, as his book is one of the earliest works that points out such demands. Therefore, Elaine Hoffman Baruch describes Tommaso Campanella's *City of the Sun* as a refreshing chapter in the history of utopia (Rohrlich and Hoffman

Baruch 1984: 213). Women are trained in arms and exercise; they are thought to have many but not all of the same occupations as men:

> There are occupations, mechanical and theoretical, common to both men and women, with this difference that the occupations which require more hard work, and walking a long distance, are practised by men, such as ploughing, sowing, gathering the fruits, working at the threshing-floor, and perchance at the vintage. But it is customary to choose women for milking the cows and for making cheese.
>
> (Campanella 1602, online)

In the *City of the Sun*, beauty norms are androgynous in a revolutionary way radical feminists might today still envy; the sex/gender division seems to have completely disappeared:

> When the women are exercised they get a clear complexion and become strong of limb, tall and agile, and with them beauty consists in tallness and strength. Therefore, if any woman dyes her face, so that it may become beautiful, or uses high-heeled boots so that she may appear tall, or garments with trains to cover her wooden shoes, she is condemned to capital punishment.
>
> (Campanella 1602, online)

Even though at first glance this may seem extremely humorous to some feminists, it is notable that free choice is lacking and uniformity is secured by the death penalty, which may be used against all gender deviants, which is certainly not a desirable state of feminist affairs. There is also only limited choice concerning marriage and childbearing, as male and female magistrates work on planning the perfect population. Nonetheless, Campanella longed for a community of solidarity and sharing. Everything should be honestly divided among the male members and private property would be abolished. Housework and relationships between the sexes were regarded as political, and thoughts of alternatives for the family existed, yet forfeiting the male privilege of receiving women's care and reproductive work was not part of his utopia: while domestic work was to be carried out collectively, it was still only to be done by women (Poldervaart 1997: 178).

The man who saw through time

While my analysis of Campanella's utopia is located on a more socio-theoretical level, Bacon's utopia offers the perfect opportunity for discussing changes in epistemology's history. Where Campanella describes an organic world with a caring, giving nature and endeavors to revolutionize gender relations, Francis Bacon has swung around to present a mechanistic world, in which (male) technology is needed to overcome the dangers of nature's adverse and chaotic properties. Bacon's contemporaries praised him; he is described as "the man who saw through time," as someone who, "more fully than any man of his time, entertained the idea of the universe as a problem to be solved, examined, meditated upon, rather than as an eternally fixed stage, upon which man walked" (Eiseley 1973: 4). From a feminist point of view, Bacon seems like a pretty unpleasant man: he expresses his personal views on women in his writings, as they are manifested in statements such as "He that hath wife and children hath given hostages to fortune; for they are impediments to great enterprises, either of virtue or mischief." (Note the similarity to Walter De La Mare's take on the Robinson adventure.) He expresses another very clear view here: "Wives are young men's mistresses, companions for middle age, and old men's nurses" (Bacon 1601). This again seems to be somewhat similar to Paul Samuelson's standpoint in his OLG model when he regards the issue of old-age provision. Certainly, this comfortable insurance is not abandoned in utopias created by thinkers such as Bacon, as his misogyny is clearly mirrored in his utopian work. It was, however, the metaphors that Bacon managed to install into the scientific discourse in the course of the Cartesian paradigm change that were even more important than his personal view on men and women. For instance, in *The Feminist Science Question* (1986), Sandra Harding reports that a huge wave of misogyny came to be associated with Renaissance thought. Through various examples, Harding elucidates that Bacon was one of the prominent scientists who established misogynist metaphors of rape and torture of females in order to illustrate the necessity for science to control and penetrate nature. During Bacon's era, science became institutionalized and the new paradigm along with its core misogyny became the foundation for all established knowledge production. This serves as a further explanation of the persistent reluctance to allow women into scientific realms.[2] The change in women's image was the normative basis for modern science to control and suppress nature. Francis Bacon's unfinished critique of philosophical traditions is appropriately called *The Masculine Birth of Time* (around 1603). Interestingly enough, apart from promoting the new paradigm and the hatred of women through his new metaphors, *The Masculine Birth of Time* also conveys his proclamation of the wonders of homosexual love for boys; for instance, when an older male speaker instructs a younger man, pleading, "My dear, dear boy ... from my inmost heart ... give yourself to me so that I may ... secure [you] an increase beyond all ... ordinary marriages," Joseph Cady presents an account of Bacon engaging in homosexual practices, as he cites letters from his mother that complain about Bacon keeping a "bloody Percy ... as a coach companion and bed companion." Bacon's turn to misogyny can sadly be regarded as another example in which essentialism becomes the dominant paradigm, instead of a mode of thinking that takes into consideration the restrictions posed by gender roles and heteronormativity for men and women alike.

Bacon not only functioned as a philosopher and statesman in his utopian works, but he also described his ideas of a better world. *Nova Atlantis* (Bacon 1627) is written in the context of the "evil" conception of (female) nature. Nature is considered chaotic and hostile and becomes the catalyst for a new ideology that strives to dominate and rule over nature, which is in stark contrast to the former organic views of utopia. Bacon's utopia is set in a world where mechanization becomes the key to its inhabitants' well-being. The principles categorized as female have now been completely exploited, as he replaces the imagination of a natural paradise with a perfectly technocratic society. The male ratio is necessary in order to overcome the chaos of nature; technological inventions replace the idea of kind mothers. In *Nova Atlantis'* Feast of the Family the "tirsan" (the male head of the family and clan) is honored by a feast paid for by the state. The family must respect and obey him, as it is "the order of nature." Mothers and partners of the tirsan are not honored equally; they do not join in the celebration, but are hidden away.

> On the feast day, the father, or tirsan, cometh forth after divine service into a large room where the feast is celebrated; which room hath a half-pace at the upper end. Against the wall, in the middle of the half-pace, is a chair placed for him, with a table and carpet before it. Over the chair is a state, made round or oval and it is of ivy; an ivy somewhat whiter than ours, like the leaf of a silver-asp, but more shining; for it is green all winter. And the state is curiously wrought with silver and silk of divers colors, broiding or binding in the ivy; and is ever of the work of some of the daughters of the family, and veiled over at the top, with a fine net of silk and silver. But the substance of it is true ivy; whereof after it is taken down, the friends of the family are desirous to have some leaf or sprig to keep. The tirsan cometh forth with all his generation or lineage, the males before him, and the females following him; and if there be a mother, from whose body the whole lineage is descended, there is a traverse placed in a loft above on the right hand of the chair, with a privy door, and a carved window of glass, leaded with gold and blue; where she sitteth, but is not seen.
>
> (Bacon 1627, online)

There is an extremely troublesome implication that lies in Bacon's words "if there is a mother." Certainly, Bacon never regards the question of sexual equality. No sexual pleasure is mentioned in *New Atlantis* and it seems as if the repression of the natural and bodily (heterosexual?) instincts is considered a prerequisite for civilization to dominate untamed nature and women: "Bacon felt that the pursuit of progress was a male endeavor that women would impede" (Rohrlich and Hoffman Baruch 1984: 212).

Nova Atlantis' most symbolic example of the change in perspective from an organic to a mechanistic worldview in Bacon's thinking is in regard to mining: in Greek and Roman mythology the formation of minerals was explained as a cooperation between female earth and male sun, and ores were regarded as a fetus that needed to grow before being given birth to. Mining was seen as an artificial process that shortened the time of ripening. In *Nova Atlantis* scientists can artificially construct mines and imitate the mythological reproduction of earth and sun. Not only are the soil and the earth artificially constructed, but sunshine is artificial, too. Klarer argues that the mythological reasoning of sun and earth, who, as sexed beings, give birth to ores, has become more and more embedded within science's subconscious. Thus, these structures remain subconsciously present: the scientific male spirit is forever considered as possessing the ability to create any number of givens out of the earth's *mater*-ial (Klarer refers to a Mary Daly-style pun by Alice Jardin from 1985; Klarer 1993: 36). In Bacon's *Nova Atlantis* not only is natural creation imitated by male scientists, but even the creation of life as well as the birth of human beings takes place without the participation of women.

Feminist and feminist economic reflection

In reflecting on the notion of paradigm shift as it occurred in the Renaissance, Angelika Bammer says:

> utopias tend to appear in response to a world in transition. For what may in form be a fantasy, is by design an historical need. When the coherence of a familiar and ordered universe is disrupted and established boundaries no longer respected, the horizons of the possible shift and the previously unimaginable suddenly becomes thinkable. It is then that "utopian thinking becomes conscious of itself."
>
> (Krauss, in Bammer 1991: 21)

Utopian thinking creates new metaphors and, in turn, new metaphors create new realities in thought, thus enabling a transformation to take place within science. Those disadvantaged feel the real-life implications of the new ontology based on the new project. For women the Renaissance was

> not a period of empowerment or infinite possibilities. On the contrary, for women this period which in utopian history is often hailed as the Golden Age was a time of unprecedented repression. Universities barred their doors to women just as they were opening them to men; throughout Europe hundreds of thousands of women were persecuted and executed as witches. It was not a time in which visions of a better world for women were likely to be written or made public. As the feminist historian Joan Kelly summed it up, "there was no Renaissance for women – at least, not during the Renaissance" . . . . Things were changing, but not for the better for everyone. From the perspective of

> women's history, therefore, the history of utopia must be charted differently. For if utopias appear when people's consciousness of possibilities are changing, women's utopias appear when women realize that times are changing, i.e. getting better for them. Therefore, while men's utopian visions flowered in the period known as the Renaissance, it was not until late in the seventeenth century, when the witch hysteria had finally run its course that utopias by women began to appear.
>
> (Bammer 1991: 22)

An exception to the barren landscape of women's utopian thinking in the Renaissance was Margaret Cavendish's *The Description of a New World, Called the Blazing World* of 1666. Her extravagant science fiction utopia was very progressive for her times in the sense of involving fantastic creativity. She envisioned a parallel world inhabited by odd animal-like species, which was thought to be connected to our North Pole and of which she herself becomes the empress. In her utopian world she establishes schools and generally consigns herself to thinking about women's exclusion from the education system of her times, and she also plays with paradigm changes in thinking, giving a premonition of the postmodern puzzlement with "squares and circles" (McCloskey 1993):

> The Empress having hitherto spent her time in the examination of the bird-, fish-, worm- and ape-men, etc. and received several intelligences from their several employments; at last had a mind to divert herself after her serious discourses and therefore she sent for the spider-men, which were her mathematicians, the lice-men, which were her geometricians and the magpie-, parrot- and jackdaw-men, which were her orators and logicians. The spider-men came first, and presented her Majesty with a table full of mathematical points, lines and figures of all sorts of squares, circles, triangles, and the like; which the Empress, notwithstanding that she had a very ready wit, and quick apprehension, could not understand; but the more she endeavoured to learn, the more was she confounded: whether they did ever square the circle, I cannot exactly tell, nor whether they could make imaginary points and lines; but this I dare say, that their points and lines were so slender, small and thing [*sic*], that they seemed next to imaginary. The mathematicians were in great esteem with the Empress, as being not only the chief tutors and instructors in many arts, but some of them excellent magicians and informers of spirits, which was the reason their characters were so abstruse and intricate, that the Empress knew not what to make of them. There is so much to learn in your art, said she, that I can neither spare time from other affairs to busy myself in your profession; nor, if I could, do I think I should ever be able to understand your imaginary points, lines and figures, because they are non-beings.
>
> (Cavendish 1666, online)

Cavendish is concerned with the exclusion of women from knowledge; she obviously saw an imaginary world populated by non-human beings as a more likely place for her to gain knowledge and learn than her contemporary surroundings.

The witchhunts and violent injustices in the paradigm shift of the Renaissance and its effects resurfaced during the second women's movement. One of the main issues during the era of the witchhunts revolved around women's ability to control their own bodies and their independence from men. This is certainly an issue that continues to reappear like an archetype within feminist utopian and fantasy literature, particularly regarding the discussion on "feminine magic versus masculine science." Some examples of this are Starhawk's work or Andre Norton's *The Witch World Series* (1963), Marion Zimmer Bradley's *The Darkover Series* (started in 1978), Suzette Elgin's *Coyote Jones Series* (starting in 1970), Vonda McIntyre's *Dreamsnake* (1978), etc. Other novels furnish examples of utopias set in the slot between utopia and dystopia. They describe worlds where men and women engage in battles of the sexes and struggle over power being held by one of the genders.

Despite its stance as critical of positivism, feminist economics has only rarely reflected on the paradigm shift and the resulting challenges for feminist economics as a discipline. There are, however, some examples of this reflection process.

In "Toward a Feminist, Post-Keynesian Theory of Investment" (1995), Lee B. Levin starts her work with two premises. One is that epistemology is of great importance in economics and the second is that feminist contributions to the epistemology of economics would be beneficial to the discipline if they were seriously taken into consideration. Levin's piece is a synthesis of feminist, postmodernist, post-Keynesian, philosophical, and psychological insights. It is a good example of the "negative hermeneutics of exposure," which is discussed in the introduction of this volume (see Chapter 1). Levin's finding on the feminist, post-Keynesian theory of investment is that investment knowledge is socially and emotionally mediated. Levin rejects the Cartesian epistemology of economics for the same reasons that Deirdre McCloskey does. Like McCloskey, she also gets caught in the trap that feminist economics will then offer the second part of epistemology; similar to the principle of yin and yang the dichotomy here is that male economists think rationally and women think emotionally. The strategy here is to combine the two to form a complete, enriched discipline. Julie Nelson criticizes her turning toward the "old dualistic opposites," quoting Martha Nussbaum, who said:

> When we get rid of the hope of a transcendent metaphysical grounding for our evaluative judgments . . . we are not left with the abyss. We have everything that we always had all along: the exchange of reasons and arguments by human beings within history.
>
> (Nussbaum, in Kuiper and Sap 1995: 123)

What Nussbaum says here is that matters are more complex than a simple black-and-white worldview would suggest. Not all women are emotional, just as not all men are rational. Feminist economics does not have a common, complete answer; neither does any other stream of economic thought. This is an issue that also appears in feminist utopian literature. Both *The Female Man* and *Woman on the Edge of Time* describe a complex system of possibilities that exist simultaneously. Their approach is not dualistic but leaves the readers with an array of gender-related non-linear issues to consider. (I will be discussing this in greater detail.)

The myth of scarcity

Imagination

Another example of the reflection on the Cartesian is based on Julie A. Nelson's "The Study of Choice or the Study of Provisioning? Gender and the Definitions of Economics" (1993). She begins by pointing out that economics has more and more become the science of choice, rather than the science of provisioning. She goes back to 1935, when Lionel Robbins defined economics as "the science which studies human behavior as a relationship between ends and scarce means which have alternative uses" (Robbins, in Nelson 1993: 25). She claims that since then this definition has somehow come to limit the scope of economic theory by narrowing it to a "gendered Cartesian ideal." This means that economics is removed from the material world or real persons who interact within a material world, but is concentrated on the detached *cogito*. Here, there is (only) one subject of economics who makes individual rational choices in a world of scarce resources:

> Nature, childhood, bodily needs, and human connectedness, cut off from "masculine" concern in the Cartesian split, remain safely out of the limelight. The emphasis on the "scarcity of means" suggests that nature is static, stingy, and hostile, a view of nature perhaps still based on a conception of man as dominating feminine nature, which, while dominated and passive, is still able to frighten.
>
> (Nelson 1993: 26)

Nelson does not directly relate this finding to the history of thought as reflected in the utopian discourse; however, Eveline Forget does so when she traces the origin of the establishment of doctrine in Jean Baptiste Say's work on the French Revolution (see Chapter 6). It is in a footnote that Nelson retells and revokes the story of the well-meaning nature:

> Contrast Robbins's definition with an alternative: "the science which studies how humans satisfy the requirements and enjoy the delights of

> life using the free gifts of nature." One can appeal to no evidence outside of human prejudice whether this or Robbins's view of the relation of humans to nature is "correct."
>
> (Nelson 1993: 26)

It may have helped to point out the historical background in explaining how this prejudice came into being, yet this may have also been in need of incorporating ecofeminist ideas concerning the origin of suppression. Provided that one subscribes to the view that the whole history of science and economics has come to a turning point with the shift of thought from the idea of a well-meaning to an adverse nature, one would conclude that Bacon's view has triumphed over the subject of economic science to such an extent that no one would seriously consider a definition of economics as playful as the alternative Nelson provides. It is unthinkable and unimaginable, certainly harmful to one's scientific reputation, even though there is no evidence that this alternative definition might not be as true as the common focus on scarcity. This is, in my opinion, certainly a turning point in feminist economist thought. With the aid of a utopian approach, and the way Julie Nelson employs it, the entire discipline of economics could be viewed based on a radically different assumption, and thus if this were applied to policy it would lead to thoroughly different results.

Nelson does not continue her thoughts in this regard; moreover, she resumes her work with a study of epistemology in economic theory, which mostly criticizes the emphasis on mathematics and mechanical analogies in science, i.e. what McCloskey has referred to as "masculinsm." However, a few pages further on Nelson does address the utopian:

> When all we know is masculine economics, it is hard to imagine an alternative. The common way of thinking about gender suggests that the only alternative to macho economics must be emasculated, impotent economics.
>
> (Nelson 1993: 28)

Nelson describes the difficulty of leaving the staked-out realms of dualisms in science, but she still tries to leave the binary dichotomy of gender bipolarity intact. This becomes clear when she states:

> Envisioning an alternative that is not simply weak and mushy requires a new view of gender, value and knowledge.
>
> (Nelson 1993: 29)

This is clearly a call for the imaginative power of the utopian vision. What Nelson then says may seem like an extension of Sandra Harding's constructionism at first glance:

> A better economics would neither be purged of all its distinctively masculine characteristics nor simply have feminine-associated characteristics tacked on indiscriminately; in a better economics we would choose carefully from both "masculine" and "feminine" approaches those that result in the best science.
>
> (Nelson 1993: 29)

Another reading of that quotation, however, shows that a world as described in *Woman on the Edge of Time* may be possible: A world where all economic agents can choose their gender and actions from an array of non-hierarchically judged alternatives and act solely based on their liking rather than on social constraints. Assuming that the gender pay gap does not result from market-based crowding (Bergmann 1986), and from a new evaluation of traditionally female-connoted jobs, female professions, e.g. haircutting, would thus pay just as much as male professions, and men who choose employment assigned to the wrong gender would not be punished through curbed financial rewards and women would not be kept outside male professions. Julie Nelson calls for a new approach to science in the following:

> The impression fostered by the Cartesian view that only theorems that can be proved (à la geometry) constitute knowledge; tends to block from view alternative kinds of knowledge.
>
> (Nelson 1993: 29)

In the following, Nelson does something very interesting. She looks into the theory of epistemology, feminist theory, and studies of cognition and language as well as economics for the "thing" that might provide an outlet from the Cartesian block she adds as an element that has been missing in the story of Arjo Klamer's square-and-circle analogy. Here, she adds a concept, which she describes as "imagination," to the elements of scientific rationality. She claims that Einstein defined this as "intuition, resting on sympathetic understanding of experience," or that it is what economist Nicholas Georgescu-Roegen referred to as "dialectical thinking." Howard Margolis used the term "seeing-that," linguist George Lakoff and philosopher Mark Johnson called it "imaginative rationality," feminist Evelyne Fox-Keller named it "dynamic objectivity" (Nelson 1993), and Jane Flax calls for the creative (Flax 1990). Another example is Charles S. Pierce's analysis of metaphors, in which he states that metaphors are the source of all creativity. He believes that the methods of induction and deduction were insignificant in establishing mental innovations. He favors the so-called method of "abduction." He says that only this method is capable of creating new perspectives in thinking through facilitating the congregation of originally separated areas of knowledge. It is the metaphorical transfer of an idea into a completely different context which may create mental innovations (Hoppe 2002: 45):

> The abductive suggestion comes to us like a flash. It is an act of *insight*, although of extremely fallible insight. It is true that the different elements of the hypothesis were in our minds before; but it is the idea of putting together what we had never dreamed of putting together which flashes the new suggestion before our contemplation.
>
> (Pierce, in Hoppe 2002: 45)

From a utopian perspective, Nelson's idea of expanding economics as a science through adding a conceptual imagination still has a few shortcomings. While Nelson starts out with the definition of "imagination," she ends up with definitions of knowledge based on intuition or insight, which are, in my view, two very different things. Intuition does not go beyond its designated sphere; it merely makes different connections than those assumed; in other words, it creates sparks but not the flames of a fully innovative alternative or envisioned utopia. Yet maybe a spark is not as scary as a fire, so the strategy of creating sparks could possibly be more successful in the long run. Smaller fires are less easily discerned and put out less quickly; sparks all around the positivist paradigm may finally ignite a fire so large that it cannot be extinguished before destroying the entire epistemological building. I understand my last comment as critically reflecting on the horrid images of burning witches on stakes to destroy heathen knowledge; or Nazi practices in the Reichskristallnacht of 1938 when book burning was thought to be effective in eradicating unwanted knowledge. But these are not quite the flames I am envisioning here. Rather than trying to burn and destroy, I believe in a warming, cozy and attractive fire that people might want to gather around to sing and feel comfortable with each other; rather than hunting for pleasure in air-conditioned super-malls, that is the kind of effect a successful utopian fire in an era of a neoliberal mainstream should have on people.

Climate change

Susan Feiner's "Reading Neoclassical Economics. Toward an Erotic Economy of Sharing" (1995) is an example of interdisciplinary feminist economics. An interesting aspect regarding utopian visions is that Feiner (similar to Julie Nelson's *Beyond Economic Man*) picks up on the conflicting worldviews personified in Campanella's and Bacon's work. The most important postulate of scarcity of nature becomes Feiner's analogy of a child's fear that her mother might not nourish her. This is also represented in Bacon's pessimistic view of nature, which, in his opinion, must be controlled by male technology. Feiner ponders:

> How is it that this approach which counterpoises an assumed scarcity of nature (mother) to the insatiability of Homo oeconomics (manchild), and then elevates this tension to the guiding principle of economic

> science, is able to attract adherents while drowning out most voices of dissent?
>
> (Feiner 1995: 162)

Campanella and his optimistic belief in nature were replaced by Bacon and the sole belief in mechanics, technology, and control. This replacement has not been successfully countered until today. Reading Feiner's piece leads one to inquire how it could happen that people have all been conned into a collective fear of starvation and depletion that can only be countered by never-ending shopping sprees. An explanation I managed to find is related to climate analysis. The climate changed around 1550 and a miniature Ice Age took place in Europe. Food became scarce, and morale related to the climate change came to dominate political thinking, economics, and social relations; scapegoats for natural disaster were sought in the witchhunts (Behringer 1999, online).

Efficiency in Herland

Finally I will turn to *Herland*, the feminist utopia by Charlotte Perkins Gilman (1915), to demonstrate an option for undoing the scarcity problem which was established in the paradigm shift as the most problematic, unsolvable category and became the core issue of all economic thought. This is precisely the most intriguing problem Charlotte Perkins Gilman endeavors to counter with a practical solution in *Herland*: scarcity. By placing her utopian world in a tiny mountain area, Gilman does not allow economic growth, in the sense in which mainstream economics praises it, to be the only solution to creating employment and increasing wealth for all. The solution Gilman offers is population control, which is related to her second concern: efficiency. In her publication "Feminist Fiction and Feminist Economics: Charlotte Perkins Gilman on Efficiency," Staveren (2003) analyses Gilman's work while focusing on the issue of efficiency. She claims that not only Gilman's theoretical work but also her literary piece strongly criticize the definition of efficiency used in welfare economics, most prominently the concept of Pareto optimality. Staveren points out that Gilman names two major sources of inefficiency related to gendered labor division: market production, where the concern is waste, and also the non-market production, inefficient due to lack in human capital (Staveren 2003).

Gilman's most important observation in relation to efficiency is a counterargument to Gary Becker's belief in the efficient division of labor within the family, in which women forgo much of their education because they are expected to waste their human capital during career breaks: Gilman believes that the sex/gender division of labor leads to great inefficiencies and that "the lack of proper education for women reduces their efficiency as housewives" (Staveren 2003: 60). Staveren thoroughly demonstrates Gilman's depth of analysis of household production and the nature of caring labor, which through duty, love, and necessity creates an efficiency removed from Pareto's market view. Gilman's analysis is groundbreaking and already foresees what is later re-established by Reid and Kyrk in the 1930s and 1940s and also by thinkers like Nancy Folbre in the 1990s.

Gilman not only points out what she perceives to be errors in economic theory and real life, but also offers possible alternatives in her use of utopian literature. Staveren analyzes Gilman's model economy as described in *Herland* regarding its stance on efficiency and comes to the conclusion that

> [*Herland*] effectively makes the case for a holistic understanding of efficiency. The *Herland* economy exhibits both allocative efficiency through specialization and economies of scale, and distributive efficiency through intrinsic motivation rather than the profit motive, ensuring that what is wanted and needed is what is produced. Moreover, the *Herland* economy expresses dynamic efficiency to a much larger extent than market economies, since the diversification of production reduces uncertainty and risk and the high levels of trust and responsibility among producers and consumers reduces the occurrence of economic crises while it is limiting the incidence of negative externalities such as pollution.
>
> (Staveren 2003: 65)

So far, feminist economics has not created many new alternative concepts to replace the criticized concept of Pareto efficiency. Julie Nelson (1996) has proposed one alternative of appraising economies based on the notion of provisioning. She suggests a complete shift in priorities, very much like Marilyn Waring. Nelson argues that economics should be concerned with how humans try to meet their needs for goods and services:

> Economic provisioning and the sustenance of life becomes the centre of study, whether it be through market, household, or government action, or whether it be by symmetric exchange, coercion, or gift.
>
> (Nelson, in Staveren 2003: 60)

The most interesting issue and a core revelation in this research is that Gilman, by means of a creative technique or a tool that is a current standard in neither economic theory nor feminist economics, manages to explore scarcity and efficiency from a very different angle. Approaching theory in this manner points to the paradox that is otherwise eclipsed when it is described via a standard economic text that utilizes the standard tools available: The utopian vision Gilman installs to describe her economic model of an efficient society with a very different system of labor organization is an opportunity to solve dilemmas that cannot be overcome with the tools in a regular economics toolkit. In *Herland* Gilman manages to solve the paradox of caring labor, which I will discuss at length in Chapter 5.

I hope I have been successful in demonstrating how the establishment of new powerful paradigms can function; how these new paradigms can affect gender relations beyond the realms of science and socioeconomic realities; and how they are reflected in coercive utopias.

On the more optimistic side I have attempted to imply that utopian models, such as Gilman's *Herland*, represent opportunities for feminist theory to undo predominant paradigms. Nevertheless, I am proposing that as a discipline feminist economics needs to strongly consider options for following up on its criticism of positivism through creating strategies and methodologies to launch opportunities for new modes of thought, possibly with the aid of thinkers like Charlotte Perkins Gilman and others that might still need to be rediscovered.

4 Nuts and bolts

Methodology

A lot of this research is about how the methodology of feminist economics could open up more options and space within feminist economics discourse in order to allow feminist economics to give more creative impulses to a public debate, (scientific) discourse, and practical policy recommendations. My base theory is that feminist economics may, in that regard, advance by learning from feminist utopia a certain inclination to dream, to envision, imagining a radical change, and I am assuming that this may help to make feminist economics more flexible and sleek. I also propose that feminist theory will benefit from opening up more to postmodern stances that question knowledge production and power, but more important for this project is that feminist economics, as a theory, should allow itself to stride away from the predominant Enlightenment methodological goal of providing a more objective and therefore "better" truth. Instead, I am subscribing to pleading for a more creative discipline, allowing for input of feminist desires and fantasies. Epistemologically, I inquire whether certain realities are eclipsed from economic theory's vision, which may only become visible by making use of the visionary, the unthought-of, and the utopian. The disruption of the discourse with new or old stories from "nowhere" could function as a boost for a creative modeling of possible feminist realities.

Sharp boundaries: the scientific and the babble

> He must not dismiss as ridiculous what was, after all, of tremendous importance here. He tried to read an elementary economics text; it bored him past endurance, it was like listening to somebody interminably recounting a long and stupid dream. He could not force himself to understand how banks functioned and so forth, because all operations of capitalism were as meaningless to him as the rites of a primitive religion, as barbaric, as elaborate, and as unnecessary. In a human sacrifice to deity there might be at least a mistaken and terrible beauty; in the rites of the moneychanger, where greed, laziness, and envy were assumed to move all men's acts, even the terrible became banal.
>
> (Le Guin [1974] 2001: 109)

Feminist economics' proximity to mainstream economics versus the possibility for a radical break with mainstream concepts and solutions is a key issue for feminist economics; more generally speaking, "radicalism" in thought is often a crossroad between feminist economics, feminist theory, and utopias. Specifically when discussing the subject of utopia, the question of radicalism regarding methodology becomes another area of conflict: For instance, a science fiction work which carries feminist theory and a utopian critique of real-world patriarchal economic systems is usually regarded as unscientific/not fitting for scientific purposes and too unconventional an approach regarding (economic) science. Nevertheless, this chapter seeks to indicate the need for a radical feminist methodology, something that is at least as radical as econometrics, but on a very different level. Radical methodology should not be confused with radicalism in thought; those two do not necessarily go together: radical policy can be carried by conventional methodology and vice versa.

Economic and utopian models

A question arising at this point is: aside from the difference in genre, what makes a model a model and a utopia a utopia? Could one conclude that the models of the discipline of economics are equivalent to the utopian thought experiments of, e.g., the social sciences? The definition offered in this work describes utopia as follows:

> The idea of "Utopia" was named by Thomas More's Utopia, published in 1516. (Utopia is a pun on two Greek terms, "ou topos" meaning [1] no place and "eu topos" meaning [2] good place.) [3] A utopian vision can be seen as a thought experiment for philosophers, social scientists, economists and other theoreticians, whether feminists or not. [4] Utopias reflect beliefs of what an "ideal" society should be like and also imply a critique of the current state of affairs.

When applying these four points to my question, I find the following responses:

1 Is an economic model set in a "no place" situation? It is likely that the simplifications, i.e. perfect information, infinite timeframes, isolated economies, uniform agents, have distorted reality so much that economic models have diverged into a collection of clearly unreal situations; thus whether one should or could call them "no place" is to be questioned.
2 Does the economic model represent a "good place"? Are socially optimal (Pareto optimal) outcomes in a model world a "good place," better than that reality with its eternal faults of incomplete information and irrationality?
3 Clearly, economic models serve as thought experiments.
4 Regarding "beliefs," certainty is less easily established. From a position of feminist critique, which basically assumes that mainstream models

function on the basis of androcentric bias (a belief in a system of any sort where everything is connected to men), it seems rather easy to also agree to the fourth part of the definition above.

To summarize this argument, it seems clearly rational to conclude that an economic model can also be a utopian vision in a mathematically coded form. Yet, could form be the key issue for rendering one concept a utopia and another a model, *not* a utopia? Sargisson asks the following question on the form of the utopian genre:

> Does form represent the best approach to utopianism? The answer must be 'no', because approaches that take form as the primary defining characteristic of utopianism tend to assume that the form in question is that of literary fiction. The assumption that utopianism is a literary genre is common in utopian studies and is perhaps dominant in colloquial understanding. This approach, I suggest, results in an unnecessarily restrictive definition of utopianism and of utopias (constructions of utopian thought). . . . Definitions exclude that which is not the subject of the definition in question; this is their primary function. But it is possible . . . that definitions may be constructed in such a way as to exclude that which should be induced.
>
> (Sargisson 1996: 14)

Sargisson furthermore toys with the rigidity of definitions and offers an alternative approach, suggesting that definitions should be open-ended or have "porous boundaries." She argues that this restriction would otherwise be too narrow a starting point for a comprehensive analysis of utopianism. She strongly argues that utopias not be reduced to "verbal constructions" or "speaking pictures" – utopian thought is not restricted to these terms. She claims that the literary genre is only one particular manifestation, and thus cannot be taken as the "definitional point of departure for its other forms" (Sargisson 1996: 15).

Sargisson's argument that form is not a relevant criterion for defining utopia is strongly supported by Donna Haraway's findings regarding the construction of knowledge and science. Haraway analyzes the natural sciences and argues that sciences can be seen as a specific form of storytelling (see also Grapard 1995 and McCloskey 1993), as a cultural activity producing meaning. In this sense, Western sciences can be regarded as powerful traditions of narration, which can distinguish between fact and fiction. They carry the key for accepting one matrix of explanation as one creating Truth and others as not. Haraway describes each scientific discipline as a genre of narration, which means that each science forms a structure of tales, including rules for telling those stories. Scientists are the only ones who are authorized to develop streams of narration and declare objects of research (Haraway 1995: 17). Furthermore, Haraway explores the issue of genre-creating status. Haraway describes the question raised above whether economic models simply evade the label of utopia because of their genre as follows: She says that the depiction of the world is always embedded in a context of approaches or apparatus, without which we are unable to relate to the world, also depending on the power relations between the individual agents. The perspectives and partiality of knowledge are put into the following metaphor. Haraway compares knowledge to the image of an embodied vision in a final underground room. This image is a contrast to the belief in knowledge independent of space (the claim for a perspective from nowhere). It is also a counterpart to the cynical and militaristic conception of the world as a hyper-real simulation space or a fully automatic battleground on which the only goal for the production of knowledge concentrates on remaining a player as long as possible. Haraway offers the alternative of a topographically visual metaphor of space as a heterogeneous room, criss-crossed by power relations of the practices lived by the embodied agents populating that space. This image does not omit dominance or discrimination; it also does not exclude possible political intervention. Using this metaphor Haraway highlights the surrounding diversity of real and possible perspectives, and their respective distances from each other, which are always tied to a certain place in the world due to their embodiment (Haraway 1995: 23). The answer to the question whether economic models could be regarded as utopian in that context is "yes."

The trouble with economic models is that from those very simple model settings large-scale policy conclusions are designed. Examples are, for instance, the policy implications especially for women drawn from Paul Samuelson's OLG model or the importance the Lucas model has had for policy making. If models were deemed "utopias," maybe policy makers would be more cautious with their generalization practices. Certainly some economic theory, such as welfare economics, tries to differentiate black-and-white conclusions drawn from simple model assumptions to make economics more inclusive.

In this instance, it might be interesting to regard the use of the utopian terminus in its historical tradition. First, from a scientific perspective "utopia" has always had a negative connotation as being soft and highly unscientific daydreaming. Whether the term can be positively reclaimed is highly questionable. Second, and more importantly, whether "utopia" in Thomas More's sense is indeed the same wishful thinking as so-called feminist "utopias" describe should be considered.

Historical annihilation of feminist knowledge production

On the path to rediscovery

Having considered the form of utopias versus scientifically accepted models as sites for experimental knowledge creation, this section is also concerned with the issue of space, here the storage space of information, of the process of keeping archives versus using "living" knowledge in a discursive canon.[1] In this process, I will rely on Jane Flax's idea that epistemology should predominantly be conceived as genealogy that aims to study the social and unconscious relations of the production in knowledge. Zillah Eisenstein describes the starting point for such a process as follows:

> History resonates in the present even if unconsciously. So the present is always rooted in its earlier forms. And people continue these beginnings in and through daily life. History is made while old histories are simultaneously reproduced, without most of us ever owning the story told. And we also remember and forget and never know.
>
> (Eisenstein 2004: 25)

Luise Pusch, the most distinguished feminist linguist for the German language, in a public reading of her newest book *Die Frau ist nicht der Rede wert*[2] in Vienna in November 2006, started me thinking about the eradication processes destroying feminist knowledge production from one feminist generation to the next. Frustrated with the lack of awareness regarding the need for gender-sensitive speech patterns[3] in some of my women's studies students and young lesbian acquaintances, I hoped Luise Pusch would explain why gender-sensitive speech, which seems granted in many activist circles and in feminist academic contexts, is obviously completely irrelevant in the lesbian mainstream of an *L-Word* adoring crowd and also among young gender studies students. Luise Pusch explains by saying that it seems that every generation of women (and men) has to reinvent feminism anew, all the processes and struggles have to be re-fought, all once-gained terrain is lost again for each generation of newly established feminist thinkers and practitioners. A new generation of feminists some deem the "third wave" are proudly explaining their findings to an older generation of feminists who may sometimes feel tired when their often painfully discovered knowledge from the 1970s has not simply been passed on but has already been forgotten and is now, only 30 years later, "newly discovered." Pusch claims this is due to a lack of archives, i.e. feminist institutionalized knowledge, such as within universities. While other non-feminist, mainstream knowledge becomes institutionalized, feminist knowledge cannot sustain itself and is not established once it has been gained, therefore making it necessary to reinvent and rediscover the knowledge for each generation. An explanation supporting this claim is the insufficient institutionalized marketing of feminist knowledge; even worse, feminist thought is often not even organized in the existing archives of the large institutions – especially if it is marginalized or grey literature, it is often considered as inappropriate form according to scientific standards. Every major city has autonomous feminist or lesbian and/or gay archives, run by poorly paid staff or volunteers who are trying to conserve what has already been done, but are usually unable to reintroduce what has been stored into the mainstream or even feminist discourse. A good example of this problem is the very late publication of Charlotte Perkins Gilman's *Herland, a lost feminist utopia* (written in 1915), which only appeared in the early 1970s. In the so-called first wave of the women's movement, *Herland* had only been printed as a periodical in one of Gilman's own magazines. Hanna Hacker's metaphor for unemployed feminist knowledge is "Camilla, the lesbian vampire," who replaces Foucault's specter in haunting the archives (Hacker 2006). Part of the reason for the marginalization of this kind of knowledge is the price of streamlining that needs to be paid when alternative knowledge is lifted to enter the mainstream discourse. Another part of the problem is that knowledge, which is only very rudimentarily available through the mainstream discourse, will need to be resituated in ever-changing new contexts to become applicable for research and activism and/or feminist theory. I believe that old material is highly valuable, since I find that even more important than the precise solutions offered in "lost feminist utopias" is the fact that it offers examples of ways of thinking.

A recent example of rebuilding feminist history and recollecting early feminist thought and theory for a broader audience can be found in Marge Piercy's latest novel *Sex Wars* (2005a), which describes the complicated interwoven issues and players in the fight for women's suffrage in the late 1800s. Another example is Sarah Dreher's mystery novel *A Captive in Time*, in which her heroine is time-warped into the meeting at Seneca Falls. No matter how entertaining these attempts at broadening knowledge via electrifying novels might be, they can surely not be accounted for as a method of institutionalized knowledge setting as has been recommended by Luise Pusch.

In *What Are We Fighting for? Sex, Race, Class, and the Future of Feminism* Joanna Russ describes the same phenomenon. Her introductory chapter "Advancing Backward" opens with the following questions:

> Whatever happened to male supremacy?
> Women's oppression?
> The women's liberation movement?
> Matilda Joslyn Gage?
> Who?
>
> (Russ 1998: 1)

Russ's introduction exemplifies how women's achievements have been "edited out of history" (Russ 1998: 1). Matilda Joslyn Gage was "one of the most brilliant theorists of feminism in the United States" in the so-called first wave of the women's movement, a "feminist movement that in numbers and sheer duration equalled and surpassed our own" (Russ 1998: 1). How is it possible that an important thinker like Matilda Joslyn Gage is widely forgotten? How is it possible that her contemporaries, like Elisabeth Cady Stanton, Susan B. Anthony, and Victoria Woodhull, at best draw faint recollections among students of the history of women's movements and are not by any means part of common knowledge? Another example is the omission of African-Americans from official, white[4] history. Audre Lorde describes her disturbed recollection in her autobiography *Zami*, when she realizes that she, as a highly educated college graduate, has never heard of the Black man Crispus Attucks, who became the explosive personified reason for the start of the civil war, the "shot that was heard world wide" (Lorde 1986: 158). Martin Luther King, Jr. referred to Attucks in "Why We Can't Wait" as an explicit example of a man whose contribution to history has been ignored by standard histories.[5] Zillah Eisenstein explains the process not only through a lack of institutionalization, but with a reference to power and purposeful eradication processes of those in power in order to stabilize the status quo. In Eisenstein's words:

> The tools of thinking are always in part tied to the repressive regimes they wish to challenge. I therefore continue to look for what I do not already know. But each colonial visor is wrapped and already embedded. It is extraordinarily hard to think about what we see and don't see when progressive ways of thinking are continually being stolen and redeployed for the purposes of the preserving power systems. Oppression and repression, deception and silences, stunt our viewings of the present, with no before or after.
>
> (Eisenstein 2004: 39)

Eisenstein formulated these thoughts in a discussion on colonization and its effects, but I am arguing that a similar process may take hold for feminist thought. Feminist researchers and activists are constantly forced to rediscover the knowledge already produced by their predecessors and this is related to an often painful process of a struggle for women's rights as equal rights, often not even that, but simply an acceptance of women as human beings worthy of respect.

Christine de Pizan in her famous *Le Livre de la cité des dames* (*The Book of the City of Ladies*), written in 1405, is most likely the first to be credited with rediscovering and newly creating a *her*story of strong and positively connoted female role models. She wrote her famous widely read book, which can be considered as a first feminist utopia, in an attempt to counter the deeply ingrained misogynist stances in her (literary) society's discourse with a creative moral stance:

> Christine de Pizan's *The Book of the City of Ladies* could be seen as an originary text in the history of utopian thought. Not only is it, structurally and conceptually, utopian; it situates the question of gender at the very heart of the quintessentially utopian debate over what a better world might look like.
>
> (Bammer 1991: 12)

Pizan establishes a metaphorical city of women out of historical archetypes of women's strength. With the help of three personified female virtues she tries to prove that women are depicted wrongly by male social scientists and the clergy; what she is not trying to do is to prove that women are equal to (or better than) men. She does not demand that women and men be equal, nor does she challenge the status quo of the gender relations of her time. She inhabits her city by glowing examples of women from the past and present (mostly saints) in order to correct the misogynist views of her contemporaries. Pizan is the first to reclaim lost feminist worlds, such as the Amazon myth, the archetype of the Xanthippe, the seducer Circe, etc. These are all reclaimed as positive figures and integrated into the architecture of the city of women. All those lost (anachronistically considered) feminist worlds have thus turned into the utopian, situated in the past, and out of reach. The process of reclaiming is a creative act that thus provides a new livable utopia, the *City of Women*, built out of the bricks of the neglected archive, formed from women's achievements of the past. Angelika Bammer concludes that by breaking with and challenging prevailing ways of thinking about women, (their) history, and the "myriad possibilities of both, which is an exemplary instance of reality-transforming thinking," Pizan enables a thinking that aims to bring about changes in the real world by breaking with the traditions in the space of the text (Krysmanski 1963, in Bammer 1991: 12).

In Austria today, feminist economists have barely started the process of rediscovering lost feminist economics' history but still they are applying their findings with a utopian stance. All of Austria's more progressive knowledge has only recently been destroyed and banned in the most violent way possible. Gabriele Michalitsch and Christa Schlager initiated a project of rediscovering the works and findings of Austria's female economists before 1945. Due to the country's horrific modern history of fascism and genocide, none of the 1920s and 1930s women economists are still found in Austria after 1945; none of those who survived in exile have returned with their knowledge, and their ideas were purged from the country and never replaced. In Austria, women were first allowed to attend universities in 1919. (Curiously, the first person to graduate in the then newly established discipline of national economics was a woman.) Women quite actively participated in Austria's strong tradition of economic theory building. They were associated with Ludwig von Mises and the Viennese School or with Otto Bauer and the Austro-Marxist School and, finally, some were associated with the Austro-Fascist tradition. Mises was relatively liberal towards teaching women and was therefore a very popular teacher. His students were mostly devoted to economic policy creation and they were not associated with the women's movement of their times. The most famous of the socialist school were Käthe Leichter, Emmy Freundlich, and Helene Bauer; all were forced to flee Austria. Freundlich managed to emigrate and find employment with the United Nations, Bauer migrated to the U.S. in 1941, but

Leichter was gassed in a cattle train in Germany in 1942. Now Michalitsch and Schlager are explicitly trying to rediscover women's history in Austrian economics to open up new perspectives in contemporary feminist economics discourse. They are trying to travel "back to the future" for new ideas and strategies, feeling that the process of rediscovering is not an unnecessary repetition of epistemological processes but an exciting way to rediscover the past to enhance present thinking (Michalitsch and Schlager 2007).

But let me return to my line of thought regarding feminist utopian works: Pizan's book was granted a prominent place in the discourse of her time and it is also still quite prominent today. Other feminist utopian writers engaged with imagining better economies for women (and men) to live in were disregarded and not given a voice, such as Gilman, with *Herland*, or were simply denied publication at all, as feminist researchers are discovering today:

> There are utopias so private that they border on schizophrenia. The Description of a New World, called the *Blazing World* (1666) by Margaret Cavendish, Duchess of Newcastle, has much in common with the delusions of Dr. Schreber analyzed by Sigmund Freud in a famous paper.
>
> (Shafi 1990: 75)

(More about the *Blazing World* can be found in Chapter 3.) Some feminist strategic methods from the French feminist philosophers are to play with the forgottenness of those disempowered through employing utopian strategies. For example, Hélène Cixous toys with the notion of "Paradise." She uses the concept of a "Paradise" that has been lost to measure the shortcomings of the contemporary world. Cixou realizes that "Paradise" cannot be regained, but has to be reinvented; it needs to be reconstructed via "a different subjective economy" (Shiach 1997: 11 and 12). Shiach lists *Limonade tout était si infini* (1982) as the work where Cixous regards "Paradise" as an individual construct of imagination, therefore dealing with an existential rather than a social form of utopia. Creating a paradise involves a kind of imagination that "thinks and understands on the other side of forgetfulness and of things neglected by thought. In this alternative economy, there will be an undoing of hierarchies, a remembering of things that have been culturally marginalized" (Shiach 1997: 11 and 12).

Different waves or different issues?

Maybe it is not true that feminist thinkers are constantly rediscovering ideas from their forgotten past, maybe these are not the same phenomena that are being brought up, maybe the times and discourses have changed so much that the first wave of feminist thought is really a completely different matter than the second wave. Rosalind Delmar (1994) examines this idea, which interestingly also appears to be of significance for feminist economics, whether the new women's movement of the 1960s is simply a "second wave," a continuation of a dormant struggle, which started over a century ago. While Delmar points out that it is not quite clear whether feminism had been dormant between the first and the second wave or whether the second wave is actually a completely new phenomenon, Gillian Hewitson states in *Feminist Economics* (1999) that the use of the term "Feminist Economics" as a label for a recognized field of research within economics is only fairly recent. She sees the emergence of "feminist economics" as a rather new phenomenon, dating back only to the second wave of feminism, the 1970s, where – in her opinion – "the terms 'women' and 'economics' started to be linked" (Hewitson 1999: 5). Hewitson explains that in the mid-1980s scholars first started to refer to themselves as "feminist economists," and a more largely institutionalized, explicitly organized form of "feminist economics" only started with the foundation of the International Association for Feminist Economics (IAFFE) in 1991. Hewitson utilizes this recentness, as she states that on the one hand it makes the discipline "new and exciting" and on the other hand "just keeps it in check," before the whole complex of diversity subsumed under the umbrella term of "feminist economics" breaks apart. Herein Hewitson's strategy follows Delmar's of extending the definition to a plurality or an umbrella term. Hewitson is certainly right when she states that feminist economics only became a discipline when scholars employed the definition themselves; nonetheless it is not true to say that the terms "women and economics were only started to be linked in the 1970s." Most prominently, Charlotte Perkins Gilman titled her economics volume *Women and Economics* in 1898, and there are countless other examples from that era. Although Hewitson's argument is certainly correct if one places this linkage in a certain historical context, Hewitson's historical restriction might prove to be insufficient for the course of the research into utopian visions of feminist economics. I argue that some important keys lie in those long past considerations of feminist economics, which might prove to be essential for the new discipline of feminist economics. The problems of continuity and discontinuity are connected to the question of the links of historical time and space that feminist economic knowledge may inhibit: resituating already existing knowledge within new historical contexts is an ongoing process and a difficult endeavor for feminist theorists.

Delmar also proposes one reason that can explain also Hewitson's tight construction of the timeframe. As mentioned above, she suggests the possibility that the two different waves of feminism (and feminist economics) are so substantially different from one another that they should not be viewed as a unique phenomenon, which simply had a dormant phase. Hewitson writes that 19th- and early 20th-century theorists worked with a whole different conception of sexual difference and understanding of sexual subjectivity. Hewitson also considers that deeming feminist economics a legitimate field of economics is possible only within the historically specific moment of the second-wave feminist movement. This also entails all its theoretical ramifications, especially around sex and gender, concepts which have had completely different meanings and theoretical underpinnings in first-wave feminism (Hewitson, personal communication), which I will expand on in just a moment, particularly the connections between sex, gender, and race. Beforehand, I will briefly consider the phenomenon of waves in social movements from a feminist utopian point of view.

Regarding feminist utopian thinking, Dutch feminist Saskia Poldervaart creates a theory of waves for feminist utopias. In her line of thinking, she claims that certain eras are cohesive to utopian envisioning while others are not. And the possibilities for dreaming up new worlds are different for different groups. While the Renaissance proved to be highly fruitful for men envisioning better lives for themselves, utopias written by women are not accounted for at that time (apart from a few exceptions such as the *Blazing World*). Poldervaart develops a seven-tiered system of periods to categorize utopian periods historically:

> People always may have dreamt about a better world, but as far as we know, they have done so in some periods more than in others.
>
> (Poldervaart 1997: 178)

Generally, after Plato's initial utopia, Poldervaart plots the next wave in utopian thought during the 12th and 13th centuries. This period is one comprising a multitude of groups thinking to realize the Christian utopia of harmony and egalitarianism, bridging class and gender differences, and communalizing all goods. The next wave she lists is the Renaissance, specifically the paradigm change from an organic to a mechanical world design. A next peak time for utopia is early Socialism, coinciding with the "first wave" of the women's movement, followed by the period between the great depression and the 1960s, a time in which mostly anti-utopias (dystopias) were written, including Huxley's *Brave New World* (1931) and Orwell's *1984* (1948). Poldervaart finally locates the 1960s and 1970s as the latest utopian period. Poldervaart states that it is no coincidence that this period again coincides with a feminist wave, namely the second wave. She points out that Linda Gordon observed in 1980 that a women's movement usually arises when other movements have created a climate in which it is possible to be critical of society. However, she has also recently claimed that in order to have some attraction, the place utopia has changed in a radical way. It no longer is a good place to be or to describe; instead it is a place not to be or to be in a completely different way. As Joke Hermsen puts it, utopia has, properly speaking, become more utopian than ever before: it has become an "indescribable 'no-man's land' "[6] (Hermsen 1997: 21)

Jane Donawerth's and Carol Kolmerten's (1994) anthology on feminist utopias takes a position contrary to Hewitson and Delmar. They consider feminist utopias' connection to the first and second waves of the movement as a category that has existed since the first women's movement and which functions as a common thread that was established once and now holds for all time. Monika Shafi counters that

> a totalizing sense of tradition and a linear sense of continuity underlie ... Donawerth and Kolmerten's work *Utopias and Science Fiction by Women: Worlds of Difference*. They argue that women's utopian fictions "historically speak to one another and together amount to a literary tradition of women's writing about a better place." They also suggest that studying such works from the vantage point of "estrangement" enables them "to piece together the squares to see the design of this history as a whole."
>
> (Shafi 1990: 78)

Shafi strongly objects to this generalizing theory, very much in the same way Hewitson argues when she rejects the idea of including Gilman within the category of "feminist economics." Shafi lists four problems with this historical connection:

> (a) the assumption that alienation is resolved with the retreat to a "home," (b) neglecting how women authors cite and rearticulate spatial designs from patriarchal culture, (c) essentializing historically specific representation of female creativity, and (d) conflating the conventions of a genre with historical parameters.
>
> (Shafi 1990: 79)

I have been considering Shafi's issues and have interpreted and integrated them into feminist economic theory as such: The first issue Shafi lists, that utopia creates a new place, a new home, is most interesting for feminist economics since it deals with the household, a space, for instance, focused on by the Chicago School's "New Home Economics." When women retreat to their homes not only are they usually the ones to keep them, but, Shafi argues, the problem is that "utopian designs involve the quest for a new place but also the newness, estrangement and displacing effects of the educational experience." What is searched for is usually not a home, but the displacement from that home (i.e. personal freedom).

The second issue she raises states that recovering patterns of continuity among such utopian authors sometimes overemphasizes thematic similarities across generations of authors and undermines how "women authors negotiate and re-signify spatial designs from contemporary discourses, even patriarchal ones" (Shafi 1990: 80). This would point towards neglecting different strategies developed during different eras and leveling historical and current discourses, thus narrowing the utopian spaces for finding solutions. The third issue is in very close relation to McCloskey's discussion on rhetorical shapes in the scientific discourse. Shafi argues that Donawerth and Kolmerten's attempt to "piece together the 'squares' of a women's tradition … could inadvertently valorize certain 'squares' as universal feminist forms and neglect how women authors at specific historical instances are able to claim authorial authority exactly by appropriating rhetorical shapes from other dominant discourses" (Shafi 1990: 80). This is an interesting argument, as it brings up the other side to McCloskey's pledge for working with squares and circles where Shafi now argues for working with various shapes (i.e. methods) regarding the techniques in feminist theory.

Nevertheless, given the discussion of continuity versus a completely new emergence of feminist utopia (and the waves of feminist thinking), it is necessary to mention that mainstream utopian studies theorists usually disregard feminist utopias. Shafi, for instance, strongly critiques the renowned utopian theorist Krishnan Kumar for ignoring the long utopian history of feminist theory:

> Not only does Kumar derogatorily equate the "revival" of the utopian novel by feminists with the decline of utopia as a social vision but he also, as his use of the term "revival" suggests, either ignores or deliberately dismisses a long history of utopian writing by women. He both taints and contains women's modern utopian writing within a narrow and homogeneous "tradition": "There is a tradition here going back to Charlotte Perkins Gilman's 'Herland.'"
>
> (Shafi 1990: 58)

Based on my personal experience, I have to sadly relate that my proposal to present my brand new dissertation *Utopian Visions of Feminist Economics* at the Economics and Utopia[7] conference at the Vienna University of Economics and Business Administration in 2005 was turned down without any reason being given. I found this a surprising decision, as I felt I had an interesting contribution to make that also very much fitted the theme of the conference.

I think that it can be concluded that feminist theorizing related to feminist utopias needs to urgently recognize its historical roots, but without trying to equalize different historical strands in regard to contemporary standards. Another example of this conclusion is the importance of the historical contexts regarding biological classification that lead to the developments of concepts used by the two waves of the women's movement and which shaped the discourse at different times. The following thoughts were established by Hanna Hacker in her lecture series in 2007: according to Hacker the historical contexts of the women's movements differed in great complexity: in 19th-century Europe (here Hacker is specifically considering France and Germany) the constitution of "woman" as the subject striving for liberation occurred chronologically parallel to the establishment of the "homosexual" as a (pathological) category. Women advancing to change their roles from their designated place in society needed to worry about being categorized as pathologically lesbian, insane, criminal, oversexed, or racially inferior. In some instances people formed alliances across categories; the French feminist movement, for instance, consisted also of upper-class sex workers, whereas in Germany that was not the case. In the U.S. many streams of the first-wave women's movement were at least in their origins closely interlinked in solidarity with the emancipation movement for African-Americans (Davis 1982), but the women's movement per se was always far from a united pressure group in considering the hierarchies of race, class, and other privileges. In Europe, and particularly in Germany, the first women's movements were working with the movements for sexual reform. Especially the more radical wings of the German women's movement were proclaiming the ideas of eugenics and racial hygiene; the evolution theories of a necessary predominance of more advanced races served as the theoretical background. The influence of racist (under)tones in Northern first-wave thought were reflected in the well-intended practices of white emancipated women who aimed to help their disadvantaged sisters in the South or to spread women's superior moral standards. Josephine Butler set out to help female sex workers in India from a position of dominance, aiming to help her helpless, victimized, dirtier sisters by pushing them into the position of the subaltern. Florence Nightingale established niches for unmarried single women working as nurses, but at the same time she was a patriot, working at colonial war sites, providing morals, morale and hygiene, which the male soldiers lacked (Hacker 2006). These problematic ties are also apparent from the racism inherent in early feminist utopias (while feminism and anti-racism usually go together in contemporary feminist utopias):

> The racism of these utopias cannot be dismissed merely as the unfortunate myopia of texts that were written in pre-civil rights, i.e. less enlightened, times. Their attitude toward race, rather, is already implicit in, because it is no different from, their attitude toward gender: they assign both to nature (which is seen as inherent and given) rather than to culture (which, in contrast, is seen as constructed and thus subject to change).
>
> (Bammer 1991: 34)

Proclaiming "The End of Innocence"[8]

Less colorful feminist utopias

As mentioned on p. 7, just the notion that a utopia is feminist does not make a feminist utopia a perfect world for all. Unfortunately, feminist knowledge and utopian production do not necessarily open up better science or a better model world for all. Whereas colorblindness or issues of heterocentrism in feminist utopian thought are largely found in early feminist utopias, such as *Herland*, modern feminist utopias usually reflect on those issues somewhat, as I mentioned earlier. Gilman does not address the issues of (homo)sexuality or race but perceives women as asexual beings. (In a single-sex environment there had to have been some attraction towards other members of the community.) By literally equating parthenogenesis with "virgin birth," Gilman reproduces the heterosexist norms in her own culture, associating female sexuality primarily with childbearing and reproduction, thus opposing the capacity of women to live sexuality independent from men (Clemons 2000: 5). Regarding race, Gilman assumes the women in her utopian world are white; she makes references to the fact that the women appeared to have "descended from the noble Aryan stock." She also assumes that civilization was necessarily coupled with whiteness, though she never explicitly states this. Regarding this issue, Shafi recalls:

> Besides the metaphysics of voice that underlies the metaphorics of the 'wild zone' I see another problem in feminist utopian criticism. The emphasis on the voice obscures how the 'wild zone' of female utopia can be re-mapped through exclusions of others. Such exclusions are effected not only by stereotyping 'others' but also by failing to narrativize others' agency in the travel or passage to the utopia. ... Gilman's scenes of nurseries are filled with rosy white babies. Both Bradley and Gilman valorize the mobility of the female subject across borders but also silence or police the passages of others. ... In *Moving the Mountain*, Gilman not only eclipses historical liminal 'others' from her new world, but the inauguration of utopia requires that immigrants are 'cleaned'.
>
> (Shafi 1990: 74)

In her dissertation, Zelia Gregoriou also researches early feminist utopias and their treatment of race and she describes the fairly widespread criticism prevalent in the feminist community as follows:

> Let us attempt to reread this highly re-cited and worn-out manifesto for utopia. This time though let us re-insert the modifiers that writers such as Mannheim and Kumar eliminate from their grand narrative – the distinct rhetoric of imperialism: the excessive use of synecdochy [*sic*], the empire's prerogative to erase others or its own internal difference in its historical self representations. How would such a revised script read? [Western] man would lose his will to shape [World] history and therewith his ability to underhand it, i.e. ... rationalize the control of the World, identify its "distinctive historical" understanding of itself as a world "mission." We start to see that definition of utopia as the "reality transcending" principle is neither a-historical nor transcendental but

> instead resonates with the rhetoric of imperialism. Utopia, I will argue here, is not an epiphenomenon, a mirror that reflects the West's sense of its historical destiny. Instead, it is a discourse that participates in the ideological and rhetorical construction of imperialism in two ways: First as the machine of West-making, this discourse produces and rationalizes the unique identity of the West as missionary; second, as a discourse of othering, utopia constructs others as unimaginative and historically inconsequential.
>
> (Gregoriou 1998: 59)

The critique of feminist utopias is also still prevalent in the critique of feminist thinking per se: Currently, Noam Chomsky's, Howard Zinn's, and Michael Albert's zmag is one of the (few) places where an interactive discussion between feminist thinkers in "non-Western" countries and the U.S. takes place. Sayantani DasGupta, a U.S. American of Indian origin, responds to Gloria Steinem's writings by stating:

> As a woman of color, I take particular umbrage to the historically racist and exclusionary nature of the mainstream women's movement. By fashioning itself as the one monolithic feminism, rather than one of many different feminisms, the movement left a legacy of marginalization on the bases of race, class, language, sexuality, age, and ability. In the 1990s, mainstream feminism seems to be attempting to rectify its historic homogeneity. However, this process appears nothing more than an assuagement of white privilege since inclusion (in numbers only) is its corrective method of choice. Rather than critiquing its exclusionary ideologies and methodologies, mainstream feminism is merely subsuming "other" women into its pre-existing agendas.
>
> (DasGupta 1999)

This discussion is particularly important, since it not only criticizes white feminists' colorblindness, but points out that certain issues are deeply intertwined and that it is necessary to recognize them as connected. Racism, sexism, classism, colonialism, negative effects of globalization and Neoliberalism, violence against women and other minorities, i.e. expressed as homophobia, can only be overcome when abolished as a connected complex. On that issue bell hooks, one of the most well-known speakers of African-American feminism, states:

> This 'version of Sisterhood was informed by racist and classist assumptions about white womanhood, that the white "lady" (that is to say bourgeois woman) should be protected from all that might upset or discomfort her'. The 'white lady' who participates in this version of feminism has not stopped to question whether all women are oppressed in the same way and to the same degree, whether her

> liberation is purchased at the cost of the further oppression of other women.
>
> (hooks, in Elam 1994: 31)

Not only does the "white lady's" feminism exclude "non-white" or other "non-lady" feminisms, it offers a good chance for right-wing backlashes harmful to all feminism, as "Susan Faludi alludes to ... when she remarks that 'examining gender differences can be an opportunity to explore a whole network of power relations – but so often it becomes just another invitation to justify them'" (Elam 1994: 44).

In *zmag*, Third World Viewpoint interviews bell hooks in an article called "Challenging Capitalism & Patriarchy," in which hooks explains the issues from her point of view and offers an insight into what the European/U.S.-American-centered view might leave out:

> I would disagree that my political standpoint begins with feminism. My political standpoint begins with the notion of Black self-determination. In order for me to engage in a revolutionary struggle for collective Black self-determination, I have to engage feminism because that becomes the vehicle by which I project myself as a female into the heart of the struggle, but the heart of the struggle does not begin with feminism. It begins with an understanding of domination and with a critique of domination in all its forms. I think it is, in fact, a danger to think of the starting point as being feminism.
>
> I think we need a much more sophisticated *vision* of what it means to have a radical political consciousness. That is why I stress so much the need for African Americans to take on a political language of colonialism. We owe such a great debt to people like CLR James and the great thinkers in the African Diaspora who have encouraged us to frame our issues in a larger political context that looks at imperialism and colonialism and our place as Africans in the Diaspora so that class becomes a central factor.
>
> (hooks 1995)

Note that this last sequence offers examples of who bell hooks regards as visionaries among African-American thinkers. C.L.R. James is probably unknown to most white academics, a voice of people of African descent; while trying to pick up the broken social pieces fragmented by centuries of deportation and slavery is an enormous issue, it largely takes place in unknown and invisible spaces, with audiences who are not directly compounded by it, even though the U.S. economy has mainly depended on slave labor in the past and still relies on labor services provided by poor and non-white working classes.

A main focal point of *zmag* is taking into consideration issues of colonialism in rethinking economics, since phenomena such as neocolonialism can only be recognized if the history of colonialism has been processed and dealt with. Imperialism and wars for economic control dominate a huge proportion of *zmag* issues. Noam Chomsky's analysis is particularly important in that regard. *Zmag* is one of the few sources in which American foreign policy is discussed outside the mainstream media, a perspective sorely needed given that Chomsky's lectures at the Massachusetts Institute of Technology (MIT) draw audiences in the tens of thousands. An alternative voice to the American mainstream seems to be in high demand, although it may seem impossible for *zmag*'s visions to compete with popular culture.

In this regard, one of the most fascinating insights into the quest for feminist utopias is also the most difficult one. Outside of Europe and the USA it was nearly impossible for me to find material. An exception is Rokeya Sakhwat Hussain and her work (1860–1932). She is described as one of the pioneers of women's emancipation in Bengal. She wrote *Padmarag* (1925), a novel in which she created "Tarini Bhavan," her vision of a utopian household and a place where "bhagini" (so-called sisters) have united to escape the oppression of patriarchy (Gupta 1997: 93) Nevertheless, a vital project to undertake would be to research the utopian desires of women and men living outside the matrix of Western dominant culture, gender norms, and backgrounds. I think that views unthought of in Western premises would emerge, thus allowing the unthinkable to arise. If this sounds as if I am assuming the exotic "other" will set out to save the rotten world order of the West, perhaps I shall rephrase this. Leaving the narrow margins set by Western culture frames may provide a utopian space for Western thinkers to envision more freely and beyond Cartesian dualisms, despite Foucault's claim that there is no possibility for escape.

The colorful experience in science?

Joanna Russ[9] endeavors to show that women of color's active participation in the process of knowledge production will tremendously enrich the options for thinking for white feminists. She very carefully phrases her statements so that they do not sound like that very idea that "women of color were put in this world to benefit White feminists . . . such ideas are one of the most ghastly forms White racism takes" (Russ 1998: 353). However, Russ does argue that the end of a limitation to a narrow, white worldview may nevertheless aid white people in learning to look at the world in a way that is "more accurate, complex, multi-layered, multi-dimensioned, more truthful to see the world of overlapping circles, like movement on a millpond after a fish has jumped, instead of the courthouse square with me at the middle" (Russ 1998: 353). Therefore, a break in the dualistic view of Black and white and replacing that view with many more different shades of colors and cultures would serve to enrich knowledge production and utopian visions. As I have mentioned, I wonder whether this is actually the case; I wonder whether this wonderfully enriching process is experienced as enriching by the people of color concerned and whether Joanna Russ and myself are not completely trapped in that "ghastly form of White racism" Russ (and I) wishes to avoid. The problem sounds familiar to me from my own contexts, e.g. in which a queer movement demands that lesbian-only spaces are opened and immersed into queer culture, which includes men and straight people, in order to create a strong, colorful and enriched counterculture that questions, for instance, neoliberal family norms. Personally, I feel highly ambivalent about the idea of making other people's lives "more colorful" and even more open-minded through my personal existence or my ideas. The history of displaying difference at freak shows or the Viennese upper class keeping Black slaves as "pets" a few hundred years ago is a looming shadow from the past, which is only critically explored today, when in mid-2007 an exhibition called "Let It Be Known," on the African Diaspora of Austria's last 300 years, opened in Vienna. Certainly, it is wonderful to share different experiences to open up windows in the thinking of people who have not had a chance to think outside of the framework society has dictated for them. The question then is: What does one get in return?

When talking to mostly heterosexual schoolchildren about prejudices against gays and lesbians within the Viennese Lesbian Counseling Center's education program we try to explain how prejudice works and how it is a disadvantage for everyone, for one reason or another. We also try to point out that there is more than one way of realizing a happy family life. In turn, we hope to contribute to creating a less homophobic, sexist, and racist society. We are pleased to see that children and young adults leave our Center and training programs with some transcending thoughts. Sometimes it still does not seem as if it is enough. (Our educational work is strictly on a volunteer basis, since there is no (state) funding for it.) As activists, we teach the kids the knowledge and experiences which we developed in an autodidactic fashion, mostly from thin air, as there had not been much exchange or passing down of knowledge from earlier generations. But where can *we* get the possibilities to learn? This is probably what is missing when white feminists profit from women of color enriching their thoughts: what do the Black feminists get in return for their knowledge, insights, emotional support? To continue with my example from the Counseling Center: after working with 20 homophobic kids for two hours you may think you have done a good deed, but it is extremely hard work. Everything you learn within that process comes from yourself, your own strategies and those of your peers – very rarely do the kids give something back in return. I wonder if that is what it is like for Black feminists and thinkers who share their thoughts with white feminists. Russ quotes Lorraine Bethel, who writes:

> Dear Ms Ann Glad Cosmic Womoon
> We're not doing that kind of work anymore

> educating white women
> teaching Colored History 101
>
> (Bethel, in Russ 1998: 303)

Russ clearly states that she does not want women of color to teach white feminists, unless they are clearly invested in an exchange on a specific issue, but where does teaching begin, and where does it end? I am clearly in favor of teaching groups of kids for two hours and then sending them home to reflect and decide what they will use in their lives, but teaching straight couples in queer housing projects on a daily basis on the life realities of the sexually oppressed is not what I would consider personally enriching. However, it may be possible to create an exchange on another level, assuming nobody wants to be a saint forever, engaging in non-reciprocal giving. One of the problems with handing out free knowledge from a minority position is that knowledge often leaves the places where it originated and is then used by those formerly taught to establish their own careers and material lives. This is a critical aspect that unfortunately quite frequently occurs in areas of "critical whiteness studies" or researchers of migratory backgrounds, when white, privileged scientists "sell" the knowledge provided by marginalized groups on the knowledge market. (I will also be talking about this in Chapter 7.)

Still, from a utopian perspective, teaching is in itself an interesting prospect. In *Towards a Feminist Pedagogy in Economics* April Laskey Aerni quotes bell hooks, who says:

> But learning is a place where paradise can be created. The classroom, with all its limitations, remains a location of possibility. In that field of possibility we have the opportunity to labor for freedom, to demand of ourselves and our comrades, an openness of mind and heart that allows us to face reality even as we collectively imagine ways to move beyond boundaries, to transgress. This is education as the practice of freedom.
>
> (hooks, in Aerni *et al.* 1999: 41)

An idea I find rather useful has been formulated by Donna Haraway in *A Cyborg Manifesto*, in which she suggests that it is necessary to overcome the crisis in feminist consciousness regarding the problems of representation with Chela Sandoval's model of political identity called "'oppositional consciousness', born of the skills for reading webs of power by those refused stable membership in the social categories of race, sex or class" (Haraway 1980, online). Sandoval's concept can overcome the postmodernist construction of otherness and difference by providing "contradictory locations and heterochronic calendars, not about relativisms and pluralisms" (Haraway 1980, online).

In a disturbing essay, "The End of Innocence," Jane Flax (1992) appeals to feminists to leave their claims of innocence as the better, less biased (social) scientists behind. Sandra Harding's idea that deconstructing gender bias in economic theory connected to an altering of the discipline by a feminist perspective (Harding 1995) leads to a more inclusive and correct knowledge in economic theory is here dismissed. Flax claims that this incorrect assumption results from a failure to leave the realms of the Enlightenment meta-narrative. Instead of "growing up" and taking responsibility for their own needs and desires, for their will to seize power, in Flax's analysis feminist theorists are still trying to construct better, objective "truths." We are hoping that these better, more rational arguments will convince others of the more correct, more truthful position they should be in, which could function as an emancipatory concept, ignoring the fact that the best arguments can be dismissed by those who disregard what is right or wrong as long as they profit in certain, often material, ways. Flax challenges feminist theorists who dismiss postmodern approaches as politically incorrect. She claims that this process could be a reflection of racism in feminist thought based on the disappointment that the global sisterhood has not worked out after all, and that important power differences are overlooked in disregarding difference and relations of domination within the group of "all women."

Flax recommends that feminist scientists finally leave the Enlightenment meta-narrative that endlessly seeks to design hierarchical binaries as explanation models. Instead, she calls for a "radical shift of terrain" (Flax 1990: 457). Since she argues that truth and force or domination are not necessarily antinomies, she calls for a rethinking of conceptualities and she "would like to move the terms of the discussion away from the relations between knowledge and truth to those between knowledge, desire, fantasy, and power of various kinds. Epistemology should be reconceived as genealogy and the study of the social and unconscious relations of the production of knowledge" (Flax 1990: 457). This thought has also been established by Lucy Sargisson in her considerations on the possibilities posed through ecofeminism. (See Chapter 2.)

Emotional science

Another slippery slope for (white) feminists regards the next issue, the problem of "emotional science." Many theories developed throughout the feminist movement have been regarded as unscientific due to their "emotional" or even "hysterical" qualities, a theme which resounds in Marge Piercy's *Woman on the Edge of Time*, as her main character is imprisoned in a mental institution for presumably being mad, crazy, too emotional, and hysterical. Some theorists and writers confronting those accusations have reclaimed emotion as a valid tool for feminist modeling and utopian visions:

> Yet, even anger, of course, has a utopian dimension. Indeed, as feminist theorists, prominently among them Audre Lorde, have pointed out, change and anger are inseparable. Thus, Lorde argued that women's anger 'expressed and translated into action in the service of our vision

> and our future', has a powerful, transformative potential. For such anger, consciously expressed, maintained Lorde, is a sign of 'our power to envision and to reconstruct. . . . a future of pollinating difference and the earth to support our choices'. The politicized, anger – even 'painful anger' – was recast in a utopian mode. . . . Both feminism and utopianism set themselves as antitheses to the existing order of things. This order, they insisted, was constructed and maintained as much by what we – and others – think as what we 'actually' do. In this sense, they argued, the immaterial (desires, fantasies, needs) must also be considered real; it has merely not (yet) materialized. Change begins with a vision of what could be.
>
> (Bammer 1991: 56–57)

This accusation of being irrational and emotional has been directed towards all women, but more so toward Black thinkers, such as Audre Lorde, who are additionally faced with the notion of eroticizing and exotifying themselves and also their own ideas. From the perspective of enriching knowledge, Russ discusses some feminist epistemological solutions with the help of Audre Lorde's thoughts. She quotes her, saying:

> When we view living in the European mode only as a problem to be solved, we rely solely upon our ideals to make us free, for these were what the white fathers told us were precious. But as we come more into touch with our own ancient, non-European consciousness of living as a situation to be experienced and interacted with, we learn more and more to cherish our feelings, and to respect those hidden sources of our power from where true knowledge and, therefore, lasting action come. . . . I [do not] speak here of the sterile word play that, too often . . . cover[s] a desperate wish for imagination without insights.
>
> (Lorde, in Russ 1998: 358)

From my point of view, based on the above quote it becomes relatively easy to see the similarities between white and Black feminists: both were oppressed and taught by the same white fathers; their thoughts were shaped and bound by the same positivist, dualist notions. Unfortunately, white feminists (myself included) are usually stuck only with a European consciousness; nevertheless, a core of hidden sources of personal power exists within each one of us. Russ continues by quoting Lorde on "the erotic," and nursing the deepest knowledge that can be gained:

> Lorde uses 'the erotic' broadly: emotion, pleasure, 'what feels right', including sexuality itself. Thus: *'The erotic is the nurturer or nursemaid of all our deepest knowledge.'* Such thinking – the erotic as knowledge – not only points to the splits in living caused by industrial capitalism. It heals the splits precisely by the way it speaks of them. It is emotional and learned, lyrical and analytic, personal *and* historical, indivisibly so.

> Asked about such statements by Adrianne Rich in an 1979 interview, Lorde defined reason as a way of getting from one place to another but not capable of choosing what place to go to, saying, 'The white fathers told us, "I think, therefore I am," and the Black mother within each of us – the poet – whispers in our dreams, "I feel, therefore I can be free."'
> (Russ 1998: 358)

At first glance, this seems really problematic. Joanna Russ bases her theories on a Black woman writer saying that the erotic is the foundation for knowing, i.e. a Black woman is the one who can tell us what real erotic power is; this rings so thoroughly racist. However, it is quite fascinating to look at that particular quotation again. Audre Lorde, Adrianne Rich, and Joanna Russ, three lesbian women, in a dialogue on the power of the erotic and knowledge – this alone sounds like a plot for a feminist utopian witch guide seeking to upset the notions of power and rationality as we know them. And then there is the notion that there is a Black mother within each of us, a poet, who tells all of us that feeling is more advanced than thinking. If one takes this advice seriously, all knowledge production would need to be measured by whether it is related to feeling, to emotion, rather than rationality; the art of scientifically weaving quotations, previously established facts, and "big words" or fancy mathematical models into a carpet of a new paper, a new publication, a new theory – all this would be questioned. In *A Cyborg Manifesto* Donna Haraway credits Audre Lorde and Adrienne Rich with profoundly affecting our political imaginations. At the same time, she points to the restrictions established through their insistence on the organic. She says that their "symbolic systems and the related positions of ecofeminism and feminist paganism, replete with organicisms, can only be understood in Sandoval's terms as oppositional ideologies fitting the late twentieth century" (Haraway 1980, online). Another argument to prevent throwing the baby out with the bathwater when disregarding outmoded theory, such as Adrienne Rich's early works, is that those theorists who are still alive will work with their old theories and reshape them, so that they may fit with what we have come to know today.

This brings me to contemplate economics as a knowledge-producing discipline. Is mainstream economics devoid of emotion? What about the theory of the free market? What about Gary Becker's *Treatise of the Family*? The basic ontologics sound biased, given that one group will certainly lose and another will win due to the existing system. The methodologies applied in addition to ontology seem strictly rational. What about the emotion behind all this? Is Gary Becker happy that the man in the household can win away some advantages from his wife in the bargaining process? If so, is that enough to make New Home Economics an emotional science? At this point, I am willing to conclude that not only female or non-white thinkers make use of emotion in their epistemology, but I will elaborate more on the emotional components in economic theory. They are analysed with the example of "work" in mainstream, Marxist, feminist, and utopian theories in Chapter 5, on "Work."

Donna Haraway's *Cyborg Manifesto* is another example of utilizing an emotional science. It is written in order to "contribute to the socialist-feminist culture and theory in a postmodernist, non-naturalist mode and in the utopian tradition of imagining a world without gender" (Haraway 1980, online). Haraway claims that writing, power, and technology, with the aid of new miniaturization technology, which has changed our experience of mechanization, are "old partners in Western stories of the origins of civilization" (Haraway 1980). She states that the process of shrinking the technical devices makes their power harder to perceive that those "floating signifiers moving in pickup trucks across europe [*sic*] [are] blocked more effectively by the witch-weavings of the displaced and so unnatural Greenham women, who read the cyborg webs of power so very well, than by the militant labour of older masculinist politics" (Haraway 1980, online).

When Haraway describes a woman's place in what she calls the "integrated circuit," she lists a few idealized locations (Home, Market, Paid Work Place, State, School, Clinic-Hospital, and Church) and concludes that "there is no place for women in these networks, only geometries of difference and contradiction crucial to women's cyborg identities" (Haraway 1980, online). The interesting part about the *Cyborg Manifesto* is that Haraway does not stop short in analysing the existing structures of oppression. On the contrary, she comes forth with a vehicle, a strong concept to overcome the undesired conditions in epistemology:

> If we learn how to read these webs of power and social life, we might learn new couplings, new coalitions. ... The task is to survive in diaspora. ... From the point of view of pleasure in these potent and taboo fusions, made inevitable by the social relations of science and technology, there might indeed be a feminist science.
>
> (Haraway 1980, online)

Haraway lists storytellers, who she describes as "theorists for cyborgs," amongst whom are Joanna Russ, Samuel R. Delaney, Octavia Butler, and Monique Wittig, partly utopian writers, partly feminist theorists. Her conclusion for a utopian future is that the possibility for regeneration needs to be part of a utopian dream of a world without gender. She says that cyborg imagery

> [may] suggest a way out of the maze of dualisms in which we have explained our bodies and our tools to ourselves. This is a dream not of a common language, but of a powerful infidel heteroglossia. ... It means both building and destroying machines, identities, categories, relationships, space stories.
>
> (Haraway 1980, online)

The Cartesian view from nowhere

I presume that not only is emotion a factor in existing scientific thought, but another interesting idea Flax describes is related to the person, the researcher herself based on the concept of the Cartesian ego, who is thought to operate from a general, legitimate, unquestionable "view from nowhere." Nowhere is where utopia is located in a context of utopian studies. Therefore, this proves what Irigaray also describes in her concept of the "utopian mirror" that the Cartesian view is really a mental placement of the observer in a perfect mental world, a world in which knowledge-based rationality and justice can exist, a world in which pure, objective facts can be established without the danger of unclean supernatural horrors destroying the organized laboratory setting. As I have previously stated, Flax points out the need for scientists and feminist scientists to leave this virtual, white-coat, utopian "nowhere" of thinking and to admit their human embeddedness into the subject of their research within the net of power relations, injustices, biases legitimating oppression, science used as means for rationalization, and so on. This leads Flax to point out the problem of fearing to create another void: one of feeling the need to newly create when old contexts are disrupted, as postmodernism claims to. Flax says that feminist theorists like Sandra Harding

> assume that domination and emancipation are a binary pair and that to displace one necessarily creates new space for the other. They conceive disruption of the given as entailing an obligation to create something new. The legitimacy or justification of disruption depends in part on the nature of what is offered in place of the old. They fear what will emerge in disrupted spaces if they are not in feminist control. In order for the new to be secure and effective, it must be located and grounded within a new epistemological scheme. Like other Enlightenment thinkers they believe innocent, clean knowledge is available somewhere for our discovery and use.
> (Flax 1990: 457)

I agree with Flax that feminist thinking must leave the presumed "view from nowhere," which proves to be the Enlightenment's mental utopia of the clean laboratory, and deconstruct the binaries set up, contrary to Harding's argument that

> the notion of objectivity is useful in providing a way to think about the gap that should exist between how any individual or group wants the world to be and how in fact it is.
> (Harding, in Ramazanoglu 2002: 72)

Aside from the notion that it is difficult to state how the world in fact is, it seems more fruitful to escape from the restrictions of objectivity and the associated Cartesian dualism, for instance through employing Donna Haraway's notion of “situated knowledge” or the “privilege of partial perspective.” In accordance with Flax’s argument against remaining in the objective realm, I cannot quite follow Flax’s criticism of the logical fear in feminist theory of not being in control of the opening void. In Flax’s theory a new epistemology seeks to fill a void that is opening before “something really bad” replaces that gap. For this reason, feminist theory’s task is to prepare a new, alternative meta-narrative to fill it; that is, a new paradigm that accommodates a more just and better world and proclaims that happiness is brought about by sharing and caring rather than by rationally maximizing utility for an egoistic self or nuclear family. It may sound naïve here to argue for responsible individuals who look out for themselves, others, and the planet without the intervention of a central government while doubting that the deconstruction of old paradigms will be followed with a philosophy which reflects on past and current discourses to understand knowledge construction and conflict. However, Flax argues that no secure, nonconflictual common ground exists for an effective knowledge and action to rest upon. Flax claims the feminist theorists she critiques hope for harmony and unity and privileges consensus over conflict, i.e. a sense of “rule following over anarchy” (Flax 1990: 459). This claim that there is no harmony in a society of differing interests is intriguing. For most feminist utopias reflect this revelation. Unlike most utopias written by men, feminist utopias are frequently disrupted. There is an absence of an all-engulfing harmony, the forces of those with different interests always threatening to overpower the feminist version of a better world. In *Woman on the Edge of Time*, different realities are in conflict with one another and various parallel realities exist, ranging from the moderately bad to the horrible, in which women are bred purely to function as prostitutes. Piercy claims that everyone must fight for their beliefs in a better world to enable its emergence:

> So that was the other world that might come to be. That was Luciente’s war and she was enlisted in it.
>
> (Piercy 1976: 301)

This is also the case in Russ’s *The Female Man*, where four women of four different probable realms of gender relationships meet and the evil world has just found a way to enter the good world via space travel. Here, Russ implants a careful optimism, that the women who populate utopia will be able to defend their world. Thus, Flax may be right: instead of worrying what will happen if feminist theory will allow old paradigms to dissolve, theorists must try to be honest about their wishes and incorporate them in knowledge production in a responsible way while considering the effects this has on power constellations as well as who profits and who loses.

Some interesting strategies which could be helpful in establishing a new epistemology include creating fluid categories and groups of researchers, as Gayatri Spivak recommends with the use of her *strategic essentialism.*

Another option lies in Foucault's argument that it is less important *who* speaks (i.e. produces knowledge), and more significant which rules bestow authority, what is said, and the effects that knowledge has. In that regard utopia might prove to work as a window for methodology and ontology, allowing desires and fantasy to enter the realm of power and knowledge and reality.

A multitude of feminist economics' methodological tools ... but still no cat

An example of the shortcomings of feminist economics' theory is Lisa Jo Brown's attempt in "'Gender' und die Wirtschaftswissenschaften"[10] (1994) to explore the male approach towards gender issues in economics, concentrating on the example of the development of New Home Economics. She chooses an empiricist stance and demands that a feminist economics should be created that clearly leaves behind the framework of neoclassical modeling. She argues that economics should allow a multitude of methodologies, since one and only one tool is never suitable for solving all problems. She quotes an example by Mary Hawkesworth, who said that, for instance, hermeneutic methods are efficient at interpreting human actions, but unsuitable for structure analysis; statistical methods are absolutely necessary for pointing out discrimination, but are unsuitable for explaining ideological oppression. Therefore Brown concludes that only a multitude of tools is a key for a more gendered economics. Her arguments are reminiscent of Deirdre McCloskey's[11] work regarding the issue of both squares and circles as necessities for more objectivity. She concludes by saying that including gender will lead to economists becoming more scientific than speculative. The problem with this critical approach, which assumes that the inclusion of both genders' views will make economics richer and more objective, can be found at the start of McCloskey's paper titled "Some Consequences of a Conjective Economics," in which she quotes Virginia Woolf, who reminds us that we have forgotten about the cat:

> Let a man get up and say: "Behold, this is the truth," and instantly I perceive a sandy cat, filching a piece of fish in the background. Look, you have forgotten the cat, I say.
>
> (Virgina Woolf, *The Waves* (1931), in McCloskey 1993: 69)

Even if the category "women" is added, even if a gender perspective is added, even if all androcentrism has been deconstructed, even if all signifiers and all etymological backgrounds have been exposed, even then economics will not yet have left its position. The emperor will be standing in the center of the room without any clothes, but no one will have told him whether to get dressed again or not, what to put on, and where to take his newly discovered beauty. It is likely that this is what the cat stands for: a completely different realm must be imagined, not just one in which a cat exists, but one in which the cat must be drawn into the picture as an agent with certain goals and desires. The cat wants a fish, the fish comes from a river, the river should be clean and not polluted, cats should have the option of going outside instead of being locked in a cramped city apartment, etc. It seems rather easy to imagine a perfect world for a happy cat. To imagine a perfect world for people regarding gender issues is far more complicated. Not only does one need the tools to build this world, but without an image of what to build the whole situation will remain static and theoretical discourse will spiral to ever more advanced levels without ever reaching any real-life conclusions.

Marketing of ideas

While Flax has argued that it is necessary to accept voids opening and not to try to replace old paradigms with "better feminist knowledge," given my discussion on archives and lost knowledge I stress that it is very important to display feminist findings and make them accessible to those who want to know. Unfortunately, and as horrible as it may sound, good marketing strategies for knowledge are an essential issue, without which Neoliberalism would never have become the predominant theory in economic thought. The decision whether knowledge remains safely stored in an archive haunting the archivist as a specter or whether knowledge becomes part of the active discourse is a result of scientific marketing. In *The Archeology of Knowledge* Foucault defines the archive as the set of rules defining the things that are allowed to be said. Given my discussion on the colorblindness of feminist utopia and science it is worthwhile considering Foucault's ideas on archives and reflecting the issue of whiteness. Foucault speaks of *the* archive, which is certainly European centered in a geopolitical way, and indeed it is highly problematic to imagine a history without a center. What about archives in the periphery? What do we know about them? Do white, Western feminists ever research there? Or have those archives been burned down in some kind of conquest or in another catastrophe, such as the library of Alexandria? Or has storing knowledge taken on different forms in different cultures?[12]

The opposite of the closed, void, and dusty archive is the ultimately open and large space of the marketplace. In "Not a Free Market: The Rhetoric of Disciplinary Authority in Economics," Diana Strassmann researches core ideas on how economic research is shaped, which can be interpreted from a marketing angle. Strassmann states that the models of economic theory "highlight certain aspects of a situation while suppressing others" (Strassmann 1993: 55). This is certainly necessary to simplify a situation in order to model it. Strassmann then provides four examples for pointing out that the partial nature of mainstream economics is a form of storytelling, which is not objective from a gendered point of view. Her first example is the *story of the marketplace of ideas*. She claims that "the story of the marketplace of ideas is a classical example of economic imperialism" (Strassmann 1993: 56). In standard economic theory it is assumed that "in the marketplace the best ideas bubble up to the top ... ideas are exchanged as in a marketplace, their worth ascertained in a competitive process of bidding and exchange" (Strassmann 1993: 56). Nevertheless, Strassmann deems this to be untrue, as she claims that this story implies that cultural values or institutional configurations have no role in the exchange of ideas in the market of the story. She raises the question of who the judges in the economy of intellect might be. Just consider this book. Undoubtedly, this work will not be hailed by the mainstream economic community (hopefully not due to lack of quality, but) due to the absence of free entry into the marketplace of economic ideas. Ideas are never equally valued at the start of the bidding process; cultural, geographical, racial, and gendered preconditions determine their value way before they become admitted to the forum. Strassmann does not point out solutions to this problem, but it seems clear that feminist economics must try to get into the marketplace for ideas much more. Consider Bacon's mechanistic worldview: the idea became a bestseller in the last century and still has not lost this status. Feminist economics thus needs to look for better, alternative marketing strategies for the ideas it develops. An example is Donna Haraway's call for "more noise" in *A Cyborg Manifesto*, where her strategy is to limit the impact of the loudest voices by creating a chorus of alternative voices.

Another example for a story that sells really well in the marketplace for ideas is that of the *benevolent patriarch*, who makes choices in the best interest of the family. The story is, as Strassmann claims, partial, as are all stories. Amartya Sen, for example, points to how the benevolent patriarchs system is dysfunctional and thus causes hardship for women and children in India. He states that male family heads indeed behave so selfishly that women's mortality and poverty rates become much higher than those of men. The next example Strassmann lists is the *story of women's leisurely existence*. Women are retold as creatures who stay at home and play with the children all day, decorate the house, and go shopping. (That is also why their work is not paid.) Strassmann's final example is that of the *story of free choice*. Strassmann wonders whether mainstream economic theories can be repaired. She thinks that this depends on the extent to which the stories created are linked to core assumptions of economic theory. Strassmann argues that an increase in alternative stories within the discipline of economics might be a way to improve or extend economic theory, which is basically the same argument Haraway uses. The story or the utopia of the free market is not an example given in Strassmann's text which would have been interesting. I develop further thoughts on this in Chapter 8.

Generally, it can be said that utopian writing was not only a leisurely pastime when historical contexts were not as severely repressive, but was also used as a window of opportunity for critique and radical change. An example of women using the utopian tool is that "during the French Revolution, Olympe de Gouges . . . couched her vision of full citizenship rights for women in political terms: her utopia took the form of a manifesto, the Declaration of the Rights of Women and Female Citizens (1791)" (Bammer 1991: 23):

> American suffragists and feminists like Victoria Claflin Woodhull, Elizabeth Stuart Ward, and Charlotte Perkins Gilman all couched their political visions in utopian form.
>
> (Bammer 1991: 24)

Also the strategy of hiding powerful political thought marketed in utopian wrappings continued throughout the history of feminism, which will be explored in greater detail in Chapter 5.

Tools, insights, and questions

This chapter's discussion of the methodology of feminist economics has resulted in the following themes, which may prove helpful for the analysis I will engage with in the following chapters. Along the introductory guidelines of *time, space, knowledge* and *action*, I will consider the following insights:

> *Time*: Feminist theorizing related to feminist utopias needs to urgently recognize its historical roots, while being aware of the necessity of re-adapting theories to contemporary contexts.
>
> *Place*: Metaphors establish knowledge; metaphors are marketed, and therefore knowledge is power. Feminist economics needs to urgently establish more space for taking forgotten knowledge out of the archives and opening up attractive feminist stalls in the marketplace of ideas. However, too large concessions to the mainstream when aiming to become part of the canon must be avoided.
>
> *Knowing*: Feminist economics has the potential to become a fully transdisciplinary project, replacing the current hierarchical inter-disciplinary approach and thereby relying on mainstream economics as its most dominant discipline. This would be instead of radically shifting knowledge production from the realm of hierarchical binaries to a terrain of relations between knowledge, desire, fantasy, and power of various kinds. Hence, the relevant questions here are what the emotional components in mainstream economic theory are and how they can be used in a more constructive way. New insights and utopian visions may be drawn from deconstructing, e.g., the racial dualism of white /non-white, and by replacing this dualism with the insights from a wider spectrum of races, cultures and ways of thinking, including the question of genre in science. (Another example of a broadening of the view is queering economics.) Nevertheless, it is necessary to bear in mind a

reciprocal distribution of the benefits of pooling knowledge and experience.

Action: Feminism, and hence feminist economics, represents a partisan standpoint. Instead of worrying what will happen if feminist theory allows old paradigms to dissolve, theorists should try to be honest in formulating their wishes and incorporating them in a responsible way into knowledge production. This entails looking at the effects this has on policy implication and power constellations and considering who profits and who loses with each theory. Finally, for this reason, feminist utopian models serve as excellent indicators for standard economic models in providing cues for which direction economic policy should take.

5 Work

> "Production" and "reproduction", work and the family, far from being separate territories like the moon and the sun or the kitchen and the shop, are really intimately related modes that reverberate upon one another. ... [The] model of separate spheres distorts reality. ... It is every bit as much of an ideological construct as are ... "male" and "female" themselves. ... Matters such as birth control and abortion, or definitions of "illegitimacy", are political in the highest degree. ... There is no "private" sphere.
>
> (Petchesky, in Russ 1998: 354)

In this chapter, I will focus on the issue of work: paid and unpaid, and the theoretical discourse contesting the sex- and gender-based differentiations associated with the issue of work. First of all, I will look into the history of an envisioned improvement of working conditions in utopian thought and classical Marxist thought. Second, I will consider utopian ideas. Finally, I will connect the struggle for working women's rights in the first women's movement with theoretical backgrounds of feminist economics as well as with work-related utopian ideas on changes in reproduction and technology.

Work in utopia

Utopian thinkers have been looking into repairing exploitative structures on the labor market for the last centuries, but the question on radically improving injustices related to gender-based work have not been their core concerns. One of this project's main purposes is to look into gender relations as they are displayed in utopian thinking in order to draw some insights from those visions and develop ideas for more just gender relations in current givens and also feminist economic modeling.

Ian Tod and Michael Wheeler claim that the earliest recorded journey in search of a utopia on earth was made by Gilgamesh, the legendary king of the city of Uruk, in ancient Sumeria. Stone tablets dating from around 2000 BC tell of his travels (Tod and Wheeler 1978: 9). Tod and Wheeler also say that this was the earliest recorded finding of an "ideal world," depending on the perspective of the beholder, since it was founded on discovery and colonialism. Certainly no women served as active protagonists in this enterprise. Another early form of an ideal world is Cockaygne; it is an archetype of peace and tranquility, of freedom from labor, of eternal life and bountiful nature. It reappears throughout history in popular legends of a promised land, either past or future. Tod and Wheeler describe it as an "earthly paradise [which] is the perpetual response to perpetual hard times, the dream of people, from the Israelite slaves in Egypt to the American hobo, who want a break" (Tod and Wheeler 1978: 10). Notice that women as a class are not listed as suppressed people who might want to have a break. Tod and Wheeler continue their chronological list with the Peasants' Revolt of 1381. It was directed against serfdom and the heavy taxation of its times, but it was also sustained by the belief that England, before the Norman Conquest, had been a free country with equal rights for every peasant, where everybody was cultivating his own plot in peace. They are quoting John Ball, one of the spokesmen, who summed up this attitude when he asked, "When Adam delved and Eve span, who was then the gentleman?" (Tod and Wheeler 1978: 11). While he questioned class, the household with its division of labor is not an issue in those times.

More's *Utopia* (1516), even though influenced by Plato (his *Republic* will be discussed in Chapter 8), is much more conservative than its predecessor's work at least in regard to women's positions. Not only is the sharing of work and equality of opportunity restricted to men, but hierarchy in the patriarchal family remains also firmly rooted and is taken for granted. Even though *Utopia* offers a pathbreaking alternative, it still portrays "a microcosm of the hierarchical structure of Renaissance political life" (Rohrlich and Hoffman Baruch 1984: 209). More's family is lead by the undisputed authority of the oldest male. Women are first subordinated to their fathers as children and later to their husbands as wives. Corporal punishment by male family members is a given. Unlike in Campanella's *City of the Sun*, slaves do the more laborious work of the kitchen and it is the women who prepare the meals in the common dining halls. Women's caring work is noticeable in the typical family sitting arrangements: while men are settled nicely, wives sit on the outside of tables so that they may quickly run to nurseries when they need to breastfeed their babies. No communal nursing takes place in More's utopia, as is the case in Plato's vision. Overall, the well-being of the utopian society depends on slave labor and the unpaid labor of wives and mothers. (Rohrlich and Hoffman Baruch 1984.) Clearly, leaving issues of sexism and classism out of More's famous utopia, it is made into a place where "women would not want to live" (as Joke Smit, the Dutch song writer would say).

Early socialists

The utopian-socialist period (1820–1850) was the first time when it was broadly thought that utopian designs could be put into practice. The so-called

"Utopian Socialists" (e.g. Robert Owen and the Owenists in England, Charles Fourier and his followers in France, and Saint-Simon with his followers the "Saint-Simonians"), like the preceding utopianists and their movements, attacked private property and prevailing family structures, and aimed at redesigning working conditions in their utopian models and societies.

The "social utopia of the family"

Robert Owen's most famous project was the "New Lanark Mills" in Scotland. They were examples of the possibility of cooperative factory communities. Many industrialists visited Owen's "model factories" and some even adopted parts of Owen's system. There the minimum working age was raised to ten and the hours of actual work were reduced. Community stores sold inexpensive good-quality food and each week a contribution was made from wages to cover sick pay and retirement. During a slump in the cotton trade, Owen still paid wages after three months of no production. Although wages were slightly lower than elsewhere, the social provisions were unique and precious to the workers (Tod and Wheeler 1978: 81).

Owen believed in education and that the "character of man is made FOR him and not BY him" (Tod and Wheeler 1978: 83). Thus, Owen thought that by changing the conditions of people's lives it would be possible to change their character. The final aim of character formation, he believed, should be happiness, for the production of happiness was supposed to be the only religion of man. The desire for the creation of the *New Man* was born. Owen reiterated the vision of a rising generation "educated from birth to become superior, in character and conduct to all past generations" (Folbre 1993b: 97). The proper education should create a new kind of human, one fit to inhabit the *New Moral World*. Women were to be fully equal in this world. Equality should be reached by a communal production style; cooperative labor in agriculture and in manufacturing was believed to be far more efficient than capitalist competition and result in so much superfluous wealth that private property would have to disappear (Harsin, in Rohrlich and Hoffman Baruch 1984: 75). The theory sounded promising, but when the commune solidified, the share of work duties shifted once again. Owen's list of the duties for women in his 1817 plan (for the transitional society) made women responsible for all domestic labor; their first responsibility was "the care of their infants, and keeping their dwelling in the best order" (Harsin, in Rohrlich and Hoffman Baruch 1984: 75). Women were also responsible for all communal domestic work, tending to the kitchen garden, making the clothing, and serving in the communal kitchens, dining rooms, dorms, and classrooms. And additionally they had to spend "'not more than four or five hours in the day' in the 'various manufactures' which would be established" (Harsin, in Rohrlich and Hoffman Baruch 1984: 75). This sounds very similar to the neoliberal plans for the modern working mother. Owen realized that women's domestic responsibilities would cut into the time they could spend in the production of visible products for exchange and into their individual remuneration. In the *New Moral World*, Owen's finished utopia, mechanical inventions unknown in Owen's time reduced domestic duties to such an extent that children and young adults up to the age of 25, when they were to be considered grown up, were thought able to perform that labor with the help of the new technology.

Finally, Owen's utopia was put into practice in four trial communities between the years 1825 and 1845. The position of women was not too good in either one of them. In *Orbiston*, the first community, only the communal labor of women was counted; none of the caring labor provided in the home was rewarded. Also women's official work was remunerated at a lower rate, reflecting the conditions in the outside world, which demanded earning differentials for working women:

> Marshall in his 1881 publication for instance implicitly argues for low wages for women when he calls for women's minimum wage to be set at a different price level from that of men and when he describes as 'injurious' a rise of women's wages relative to men's: such a rise is detrimental not only to men's employment and relative earning capacity but also to the performance of household duties by women.
>
> (Pujol 1984: 65)

This treatment of women's wages and work was consistent in all of Owen's utopian experiments. When economic conditions in *Orbiston* toughened the community turned back to traditional ways and fell apart. In *Ralahine* women's wages were permanently fixed at a rate lower than that of all men, and women were only partially allowed the right to vote in community matters. In *New Harmony* and *Quennwood*, the rights of women were precarious privileges which male members could revoke arbitrarily. The community ended up deciding that "wives of members are not members, and it was finally decided that they should not vote" (Harsin, in Rohrlich and Hoffman Baruch 1984: 78). In short, Owen's utopian communities neglected the few theoretical improvements optional for women, which ended up only functioning partially and for a short time next to men's liberation.

Jill Harsin concludes that "the link between women and housework has maintained itself under capitalism, under communism, and, frequently, in utopia as well, as illustrated by the experience of the Owenite utopian communities in the early nineteenth century" (Harsin, in Rohrlich and Hoffman Baruch 1984: 73). The gendered power struggles of exploitation did not become an issue in most male utopias of that time. Nancy Folbre states that Owen's utopian vision is merely an expansion of the usual family structure, where women always provide and give care for free. Folbre states that in Owen's view "Socialism would be 'as if one family had multiplied as to fill the earth'" (Folbre 1993b: 97). This is in Folbre's view one of the major reasons why Owen's utopia failed, since it left 50 percent of its inhabitants stranded in the same position they were in before:

> Ironically, it was Owen's very confidence in paternal benevolence and familial altruism – which he shared with Smith and Malthus – that undermined his larger vision. While the ideals of family life offered a model for social cooperation, real family life was hardly democratic or egalitarian. Rather it was governed by strict legal rules, economic practices, and cultural norms that gave men the authority over their wives and children and defined their responsibilities to them. . . . Were individual fathers less likely than individual kings to exercise perfect benevolence? The feminists among Owen's adherents answered this question decisively: No.
>
> (Folbre 1993b: 98)

Owen's gender blindness, or rather unwillingness to recognize and reward women's labor for men and children, was not only a gender issue, but thoroughly interwoven with his class background and a somehow naïve belief that "the Rich" would be willing to give up privilege if asked politely. (One is tempted to speculate whether he would have done his own housework, if only he had been asked politely.) Nancy Folbre summarizes as follows:

> Owen addressed his manifestos to a ruling class whose cultivated intelligence he always praised, whose motives he never questioned. In 1833 he published "An Appeal to the Rich." . . . His trust in the "rich and powerful" . . . might be explained partly by his own experience as a successful industrialist. But it was also rooted in a larger view of society as a family in which employers were fathers and workers were children.
>
> (Folbre 1993b: 96)

Pleasurable work and no families

Charles Fourier always rebelled against work, complaining that he had to "participate in the deceitful activities of merchants and brutalizing [him]self in the performance of degrading tasks" (Fourier, in Kreis 1996). Fourier witnessed the silk workers' efforts to unionize and became very critical of the extensive commercial speculation, the cycles of inflation and industrial stagnation that succeeded when the free market economy was re-established. Fourier wanted to better the conditions for workers and break with the tradition of workers' degradation; he did not accept the bourgeois work ethic or the notion that work is unavoidable and has to be toilsome. For Fourier all "manual labor was arduous and irksome – whether in the factory, workshop or field, the plight of the laboring population was intolerably dehumanizing" (Fourier, in Kreis 1996). He believed that all work should be playful, pleasurable, desirable, and satisfying physically as well as mentally. Fourier wanted to make work attractive and to liberate people from the Protestant work ethic and from their lives in hard labor. He thought that the more difficult, uncomfortable, or unrewarding the work was, the higher it should be paid.

Fourier was strongly opposed to *laissez-faire* liberalism and factory production. He predicted that industrialization would not persist as a means of production. Fourier detested the English and economists such as Smith and Ricardo. His line of thought was especially opposed to rational individualism and utilitarianism. Instead, Fourier envisioned a community tied together by emotion rather than competition and profit. In his "theory of passional [*sic*] attraction," Fourier's ideal community was the Phalanx, where people were to live together in a village and work at a wide variety of changing jobs. Each person would only do a minimum amount of work and receive a basic wage. Fourier had little faith in families in the "normal" sense, such as the one in which he had grown up. He replaced the family with a system of free love, with equality between the sexes, and with the Phalanx as a whole taking on the responsibilities for welfare and children. He visualized a situation where marriage and the conventional sexual customs of society were not just abolished, but forgotten, so that their absence would inspire a "host of amorous innovations" (Tod and Wheeler 1978: 91). This is still revolutionary thinking today, when countries like Germany and Northern European countries like Sweden, Denmark, Norway, and the Netherlands are only offering the model of binary, patriarchal family structures also for alternative families. These are then homosexual monogamous partnership rights, but alternative attempts at queer, communal community building still remain marginalized and unsupported by governments.

Fourier is sometimes credited as the one who coined the term "feminism." In 1808 he described the situation of women as follows:

> Is there a shadow of justice to be seen in the fate that has befallen women? Is not a young woman a mere piece of merchandise displayed for sale to the highest bidder as exclusive property? Is not the consent she gives to the conjugal bond derisory and forced on her by the tyranny of the prejudices that obsess her from childhood on? People try to persuade her that her chains are woven only of flowers; but can she really have any doubt about her degradation, even in those regions that are bloated by philosophy such as England, where a man has the right to take his wife to market with a rope around her neck, and sell her like a beast of burden to anyone who will pay his asking price?
>
> (Fourier 1808, online)

Fourier's idea of the Phalanx was put into practice by some of Fourier's U.S. American followers in the form of the North American Phalanx, a utopian enclave established in New Jersey, which lasted from 1841 until 1856. The project was given up after a fire caused much destruction and the costs of rebuilding were exorbitant. A more important reason may have been a split in the commune in 1853 connected with issues of women's rights, abolition, and the idea of adding a religious affiliation to the project.

Next to Fourier, Claude Henri de Rouvroy, Comte de Saint-Simon, was also a utopian thinker who had some importance to the French women's movement, since he postulated that barriers of class and gender could be overcome. His ideas influenced the July Revolution of 1830 and a protest march by women to Versailles and the appearances of women in the National Assembly. This took place in the historical context of 1789 Civil Rights were described in the *Declaration of the Rights of Man*, followed in 1791 by the *Declaration of the Rights of Women* written by Olympe de Gouges. (More on women's status in the context of the French revolution can be found in Chapter 6.)

The benevolence discussion

While Owen was a paternalist prescribing socialism as an extension of the idealized family life, as the utopian social solution, William Thompson and Anna Wheeler, like Charles Fourier, disregarded the patriarchal hierarchy of traditional families. They insisted on individual rights for women and children (Folbre 1993b: 95). Thompson and Wheeler explicitly criticized the arguments recurring in today's *New Home Economics*, namely that men are self-interested in their dealings with other men but altruistic in their dealings with women and children. Where political economists from Smith to Marshall explicitly argued that household work was "unproductive," the Early Socialists addressed issues of productivity and equity in the home, issues that were later explored by Margaret Reid and Hazel Kyrk and other founders of Home Economics. Their practical calls for communalized housework did not lead to building structures with common washing and childcare facilities but overall led to improvements such as municipal facilities, which included among other things schools, nurseries, plumbing, gas, and electricity. Thompson was the first to theorize on surplus value (Folbre 1993b: 98). He believed in equal ownership of production and a reduction in the unequal distribution of wealth. Transcending traditional family structures and values is a key element in utopian thinking, determining many of the envisioned realities: Thompson was among those rejecting patriarchal authority and this element of critique became central to his larger vision of socialism.

The *Appeal of One Half of the Human Race, Women, Against the Pretensions of the Other Half, Men, to Retain them in Political, and Thence in Civil and Domestic Slavery* was written on the inspiration of Anna Wheeler, born in 1785. It was the first book to discuss the discrepancy in economic theory regarding the ambivalent behavior of its agents – their selfishness in the market and their altruism when at home – not only between men and women, but also inherent in men, themselves, who in economic theory are still today thought to change dramatically when returning home from work (Folbre 1993a: 99). Thompson and Wheeler were amongst the first to argue against the inconsistencies between paternal kindness in the home and competitive individualism in the market. Unfortunately, and due to a lack of progress, feminist economists are still caught up in that same discussion: Becker's essentialist "feminism" uses similar arguments of paternal elements. Thompson's critique of patriarchic family structures sounds very radical even for modern times:

> Every family is a centre of absolute despotism, where of course, intelligence and persuasion are quite superfluous to him who has only to command to be obeyed: from these centers, in the midst of which all mankind are now trained, spreads the contagion of selfishness and the love of domination through all human transactions.
>
> (Thompson, in Folbre 1993b: 100)

By stating this, Thompson and Wheeler were radically questioning the core concepts of human "civilized" interaction; they wondered about the reasons postulated for happiness and a society's well-being. Thompson, for instance, argued that the married woman (a model of happiness and feminine achievement) was "'an involuntary breeding machine and household slave' and that patriarchal rather than capitalist authority had distorted the natural instincts of cooperation" (Folbre 1993b: 100). He persisted that women would never gain true equality in a system based on individual competition.

Looking Backward *and* News from Nowhere

Edward Bellamy's most important work is *Looking Backward*, published in 1888. The story is set in Boston, where the book's hero, Julian West, mysteriously wakes up in the year 2000 to find he is living in a socialist utopia where people cooperate rather than compete and where pleasure has replaced competition. The women in *Looking Backward* are not individually working in their homes; housework has been communalized. Women are economically independent of their husbands; equal economic credits are handed out to everyone, including children. Women can choose their professions like men, but a sex-based division of labor remains to avoid competition with men, which he terms "an unusual rivalry" (Rohrlich and Hoffman Baruch 1984: 213). Bellamy solves this problem by creating a separate industrial army which is headed by successful wives and mothers. All women are lead by a female general who is part of the government but may only decide in issues regarding "women's work." Women's occupations and working hours are restricted to preserve the "beauty and grace" of women: "Biological difference is interpreted as feminine weakness in Bellamy, and this provides the justification for male domination, disguised as chivalry" (Rohrlich and Hoffman Baruch 1984: 214). In *Looking Backward*,

> the women of this age are very happy, and those of the nineteenth century, unless contemporary references greatly mislead us, were very miserable. The reason that women nowadays are so much more efficient colaborers with the men, and at the same time are so happy, is that, in regard to their work as well as men's, we follow the principle of providing every one the kind of occupation he or she is best adapted to. Women being inferior in strength to men, and further disqualified industrially in special ways, the kinds of occupation reserved for them, and the conditions under which they pursue them, have reference to these facts. The heavier sorts of work are everywhere reserved for men, the lighter occupations for women. Under no circumstances is a woman permitted to follow any employment not perfectly adapted, both as to kind and degree of labor, to her sex. Moreover, the hours of women's work are considerably shorter than those of men's, more frequent vacations are granted, and the most careful provision is made for rest when needed. The men of this day so well appreciate that they owe to the beauty and grace of women the chief zest of their lives and their main incentive to effort that they permit them to work at all only because it is fully understood that a certain regular requirement of labor, of a sort adapted to their powers, is well for body and mind, during the period of maximum physical vigor. We believe that the magnificent health which distinguishes our women from those of your day, who seem to have been so generally sickly, is owing largely to the fact that all alike are furnished with healthful and inspiriting occupation.
>
> (Bellamy 1888: 25)

Bellamy's gentleman notion of preserving weak women makes one nearly yearn for Campanella, who forbade beauty and punished the role play of weakness in women by death (see Chapter 3). William Morris counters Bellamy with *News from Nowhere* (1891). This work centers around the joy of work, which Morris sees not as the pursuit of productivity, which he claims leads to the manufacture of "rubbish that people have to be duped into buying," but as taking a full interest in the daily necessities of life and elevating them by art. Happiness, he claims, lies in making art out of daily life (Tod and Wheeler 1978: 117). Morris grants women a high status is his world, but although there is increased sexual freedom for women in *Nowhere*, "there is no freedom from housework. While we might be tempted to agree with Morris that housework is undervalued in our world, we are brought up short by the author's assumption that it comes more naturally to women than to men" (Rohrlich and Hoffman Baruch 1984: 214). Bammer summarizes that period:

> From Bellamy's *Looking Backward* in which Edith Leete represents the ideal woman of the future ("feminine softness and delicacy . . . deliciously combined") to William Morris' *News from Nowhere*, a nostalgic fantasy of a pre-industrial world in which women consider it "a great pleasure . . . to manage a house skillfully" and want nothing more than to be "respected as a child-bearer and rearer of children, desired as a woman," the women are portrayed in terms that from the perspective not only of gender, but also of class and race, were conservative even at the time.
>
> (Bammer 1991: 29)

Marxism, utopia, and feminism

Classical Marxism: not utopian

When Karl Marx and Friedrich Engels, in *The Communist Manifesto* of 1848, described the Early Socialists (Saint-Simon, Fourier, and Owen) as *utopian* socialists, they started the conflict between the ideas of the "Early Utopians," as they are referred to in the present day, and their own ideas. With the creation of this conflict, they enhanced the dimensions of the term 'utopian,' which was meant to degrade, and therefore gave a great boost to its further use as a term of abuse, something which would be later applied to their own ideas. Marx and Engels used the term "utopian" to distinguish their own "scientific socialism," which was based on a "correct" understanding of history in which the dominant ideas of an age were seen to derive from its "material" conditions, from the unscientific ideas of their predecessors:[1]

> In 1878, Friedrich Engels distinguished the impractical demands of the early nineteenth-century socialists from the theoretical contributions to which he and Marx laid claim. In his words, socialism could be either "utopian" or "scientific." He argued that the former was idealist, naively confident of the ultimate victory of reason and goodwill, while the latter was materialist, based on scientific principles.
>
> (Folbre 1993a: 94)

According to scientific socialism, the activities of the utopians had to fail because the phenomena of human society inevitably gave rise to their opposites. So history "progressed" by resolving these opposites and creating a completely new situation. An even worse accusation was that the Early Utopians were to be regarded as diversionary to the whole socialist movement. When utopians put their ideas into practice and set up communities or workshops (such as the Owenites did) in the belief that society would be gradually transformed, Marx and Engels believed that they were merely trying to circumvent history, and that they "diverted the proletariat from the important matters of economic and political struggle and political revolution" (Tod and Wheeler 1978: 102):

> Marx dismissed utopianism for the same reason that he criticized Hegelianism: utopianism, like Hegelianism, viewed relations between people and the limitations of those relations merely as the product of consciousness and understood solutions to evolve solely from the human brain in the form of a meta-physical truth that only had to be discovered conceptually to "conquer all the world by virtue of its power."
> (Burwell 1997: 4)

Whether this critique is entirely fair, considering that the Early Utopians did put their concepts into practice, which could have grown and transformed society gradually instead of relying on the sudden explosion of revolution, shall not be evaluated here. Nevertheless Marx's major critique was that utopianism was too theoretical, lacking contact with the real world; he was demanding a macro vision of change. Another critique was even more severe, namely that utopians were circumventing a necessary development of society. If a society were to gradually transform through the formation of utopian enclaves, these would, on the one hand, hinder a process necessary to create a sustainable transformation from capitalism to communism or socialism. On the other hand, Marx did not necessarily see the gradualism of transformation as the major problem, but thought that a premature harmonization attempting to install a utopia before the material conditions allowed for it to be set up in reality could be used by an oppressive government to legitimize its power in a chimera's shape.

Marx claimed to offer a theory of social transformation that was immanent in existing social conditions. He believed that social transformation needed to arise out of the inner contradictions of society, and that these internal contradictions would push society beyond existing conditions. The visionary task should not be the concurrence of an external ideal with existing conditions, through an analysis of existing conditions. It should, however, reveal that what is already contained within itself ought to be brought to the outside in a natural process (Burwell 1997: 5). This means that the utopian would wrongly think ahead of the slower progress taking place in society as a whole and then hinder the process of change by "blabbing out the punch line too soon" (Burwell 1997: 5).

Classical Marxism meets feminist utopia

The dispute between feminist utopias and Classical Marxism evolves around the following conflict: Burwell says that Marxism on the one hand critiques utopia as unscientific, but on the other hand wants to claim completely, for itself, the genre of utopia. A majority of utopia's ideal societies have a socialist leaning to them and Burwell goes so far as to explain that "socialism as the informing vision of utopias has been interrupted on two occasions: once in the late nineteenth century, around the time of the "first wave" of American Feminism, and again in the 1970s, in conjunction with the evolution of contemporary feminism" (Burwell 1997: x). Certainly there are other streams which have also interrupted the socialist tradition of utopias on a large scale, as I described in Chapter 1 and will elaborate on in Chapter 8.

Nancy Folbre, in "Socialism, Feminist and Scientific" (1993a), also describes the dispute between socialism as being either utopian or scientific. While Folbre claims that Engels was wrong in thinking that his and Marx's work was more scientific than the work of William Thompson or the other Early Socialists and that the only difference was their focus on the exploitation of the proletariat and the belief that gender inequality was of subordinated importance, Engels asserted that feminists per se were of the utopian socialist kind. Folbre responds that this view hindered serious consideration of early socialist feminist theorists. Folbre goes on to show that feminist socialism was more present in early utopianists' theories than in Marxism. She lists examples such as Robert Owen's theories, William Thompson's and Anne Wheeler's work, as well as August Bebel's bestseller *Women and Socialism* (1879). She claims that Bebel's views were quite influential and probably shaped some of the family policies implemented by the Bolsheviks. In his vision, housework was soon to be obsolete and replaced by modern household technology. Bebel refused to blame women's oppression simply on the interests of the ruling class; he advanced the feminist tradition of Thompson and Wheeler. Bebel in *Women and Socialism* connects patriarchy and private property holding:

> With the established rule of private property the subjugation of woman by man was accomplished. As a result of this subjugation woman came to be regarded as an inferior being and to be despised. The matriarchate implied communism and equality of all. The rise of the patriarchate implied the rule of private property and the subjugation and enslavement of woman.
>
> (Bebel 1879, online)

Bebel is saying that capitalism also brought patriarchy and he refers to a matriarchy as a utopian place of communist equality. Folbre concludes by saying that gender issues in communist countries might have been different if Bebel's social democratic theories had succeeded over the communist interpretation of scientific socialism.

Classical Marxism meets feminism

At the conjuncture of feminist theory and strategies, and Classical Marxism with its Socialist and Communist practices, are the issues of paid work and caring labor. Those subjects are always a good starting point for a very lengthy discussion among feminists and Marxist feminists and Marxists:

> If feminism, roughly speaking, is the analysis of women's unpaid work and marxism, again speaking very roughly, is the analysis of everyone's paid work, what is the historical relation of the one form of work to the other?
>
> (Russ 1998: 265)

The problem lies with the identification of the Marxist subject: Does the oppressed housewife and factory worker consider herself primarily as exploited for being from the working class or as suffering from patriarchy? Apart from this ranking, the question of subjectivity in Classical Marxism and feminism is a common problem area in both theories. The theoretical roots of radical feminism have similar logical origins to Classical Marxism. A key problem and source of disagreement within the disciplines is the matter of subjectivity as a method. Positivist science demands at least a perceived objectivity and scientific distance from the researched subject. Maria Mies, in her 1978 "Methodological Postulates," argues for solidarity instead of distance between the researcher and the scientific subject. She believes that there should be no hierarchy and that only through experience can mechanisms of gendered oppression be wholly understood and analyzed. The Redstockings formulate this as such:

> We regard our personal experience, and our feelings about that experience, as the basis for an analysis of our common situation. We cannot rely on existing ideologies as they are all products of male supremacist culture. We question every generalization and accept none that are not confirmed by our experience.
>
> (Redstockings, in Burwell 1997: 10)

In Classical Marxism the problem lies with the agency of the researchers. Are they subjects of the oppressed working class, which will need to liberate itself in a dialectic process, or are the social scientists engaged with scientific Marxism removed from the subjects they are researching? Burwell extends this conflict to feminist theory. She claims that radical feminism "retained much of the logic of the left's class analysis, in a sense replacing an understanding of the proletariat with an understanding of women as the oppressed class. But in the last instance, everything comes down to the oppression based on gender instead of economics or race" (Burwell 1997: 11).

Like Marxism, radical feminism initially expressed the belief that there existed some kind of unnatural division or split in the world that needed to be made whole again. This certainly led to the same problems that separate the theory of Classical Marxism from the realities of the proletariat. On the one hand, the suppressed group needs to realize its oppression and bring about a material change on its own. On the other hand, the lack of involvement leads to the theory not reaching those whom it should actually reflect. Burwell describes this conflict thus:

> While Marxism came to understand the proletariat as "contaminated" by dominant ideology, women from the beginning perceived themselves as possessing a dual consciousness that resulted from the tension between their status as women and (in sexist society) their aspiration to full humanness. The fact that they contained within them the contradiction between being "human" and being "female" led feminist women to perceive themselves as "damaged goods" out of whom pieces had been cut.
>
> (Burwell 1997: 12)

The whole problematic issue only arises because the consciousness of the proletariat was seen as simultaneously arising out of an inherent material relation to the means of production and representing the contradiction created in the production process. This means that the larger the proletariat grew, the more contradictory it became. But "to become an active revolutionary subject, the proletariat had to experience itself as contradiction, had to step outside of the illusions fostered by capitalist ideology and realize the truly exploitative nature of its relation to labor: poverty, realizing its causes, would become the lever for revolution" (Bloch, in Burwell 1997: 7). Burwell explains that the main problem lies with the fact that the proletariat was immanent in the existing conditions and that "this immanence caused the 'authentic' consciousness of the proletariat to become at least partly 'contaminated' by dominant ideology" (Burwell 1997: 7). This experience splits the proletariat into two, more or less separate spheres of consciousness; one growing organically out of the proletariat's activity and another that was submerged by dominant ideology. Therefore, this dual consciousness produced the problem of bearing a contradiction in itself and not only existing as a contradiction in society. Marx tried to fix his theory by introducing the "objective observer," who should help to "un-deceive" and free the masses from their inherited dominant ideology and let them step outside of ideology's illusions. However, this led to the problem that the social contradictions were not exposed by the subjects living those contradictions themselves. This criticism is a very important one, since it also plays a role in feminist theory. While feminists are trying to provide a theory of social change for all women, a majority of women might not even feel their repression, since the time for them to realize the contradiction of their existence might not yet have come. (There will always be women who insist that high heels *really* are much more comfortable than regular shoes.) Needless to say, this is also the argument of patriarchal politics, claiming that there is no repression because it is not felt. In Russ the process is described as follows:

> first comes the fact of *exploitation*; then come various kinds of *oppression* to keep the exploited weak, miserable (and busy), and hence exploitable. Then (both logically and chronologically) comes the *ideology* that justifies the oppression and the exploitation in order to pacify the consciences of the exploiters and to muddle the common sense of the exploited, thus *mystifying* the situation of exploitation and oppression so that the exploited will accept it as natural, God-given, nobody's fault, morally correct, and inevitable.
>
> (Delphi, in Russ 1998: 184)

The objective observer thus bears the danger of creating an academic dispute removed from reality; or, even worse, an academic vision probably not wanted or recognized by those whom it seeks to liberate.

Work as a travesty of necessities

But not only is knowledge production at stake for both feminism and Marxism, there are also important similarities concerning the aforementioned methodological question of an emotional science. Audre Lorde, writing on economics and power, says about the issue of work:

> The principal horror of any system which defines the good in terms of profit rather than in terms of human need, or which defines human need to the exclusion of the psychic and emotional components of that need ... reduces the work to a travesty of necessities, a duty by which we earn bread or oblivion for ourselves and those we love. ... [This] is ... profoundly cruel.
>
> (Lorde, in Russ 1998: 358)

Audre Lorde's definition of work as a travesty of necessities is an interesting concept from an economist's point of view. It strongly resembles the concept of the alienation a member of the working class experiences doing factory work. On the topic of alienation, Marx states:

> Let us suppose that we had carried out production as human beings. Each of us would have in two ways affirmed himself and the other person. (1) In my production I would have objectified my individuality, its specific character, and therefore enjoyed not only an individual manifestation of my life during the activity, but also when looking at the object I would have the individual pleasure of knowing my personality to be objective, visible to the senses and hence a power beyond all doubt. (2) In your enjoyment or use of my product I would have the direct enjoyment both of being conscious of having satisfied a human need by my work, that is, of having objectified man's essential nature, and of having thus created an object corresponding to the need of

> another man's essential nature. (3) I would have been for you the mediator between you and the species, and therefore would become recognised and felt by yourself as a completion of your own essential nature and as a necessary part of yourself, and consequently would know myself to be confirmed both in your thought and your love. (4) In the individual expression of my life I would have directly created your expression of your life, and therefore in my individual activity I would have directly confirmed and realised my true nature, my human nature, my communal nature. Our products would be so many mirrors in which we saw reflected our essential nature.
>
> (Marx 1844, online)

Audre Lorde's view of work as a travesty does come very close to Karl Marx's definition of alienated labor. Aside from the utility resulting from the exchange, Marx mentions, in this quotation, the importance of the love felt by the receiver of the product which comes from the producer; an emotion not considered in the neoclassical expression of economic theory. Happiness in economics seemed to result solely from utility and profit, from cleared markets and the beauty of efficiency. Only in the last few years has the "Economics of Happiness" gained some popularity in heterodox economic circles, as was described in the January 2005 edition of the *Economist*, when surprise and wonder accompanied the revelation that people's happiness did not automatically increase with per capita gross domestic product (GDP). I am wondering at this point whether there truly is only rational science, and whether emotion has really been missing in mainstream economic theory from the utilitarian revolution until now. Feminists have for decades been struggling against the labeling of women scientists as emotional and irrational, trying to prove that women are as rational and efficient as men. I have no doubt of this. Maybe the struggle was directed in the wrong way: Maybe women should have tried to argue that men are as emotional as women, but by pretending to be solely rational we were wasting the strength of creative emotion and also establishing a misguided rationale. Hella Hoppe writes that the founding of Cartesian science was situated in a time of great fear and insecurity for mankind. Scientists tried to calm themselves by forbidding themselves their fears, solely concentrating on rationality, facts, destroying all they feared, and conquering those unknown strangers who thankfully turned out weaker than they were themselves. I am claiming that rationality built on suppressed fear cannot be rational; family theory based on the oppression of women cannot be rational or objective either. It seems that modern mankind needs to oppress others to *feel* better, because if it does not do so there are only feelings of being small, unimportant, and afraid. There is emotion in mainstream economics; imagine a great feminist, therapeutical analysis of the discipline: What would we find out about the childhood of economic theory? The therapeutic resolution seems clear: reclaim the emotion, take responsibility for what has been damaged for such a long time, and then sit down together and truly think rationally to solve problems and make amends.

Classical Marxism meets feminist economics

Regarding the "woman's issue," Marx and Engels did condemn "the oppression of women under capitalism, but insisted that their emancipation would follow inevitably from the successful resolution of class struggle" (Folbre 1993a: 101). But this is the key dispute between feminists and Marxists. What seems like a question of "What came first, the chicken or the egg?" is a dispute with more deeply rooted causes. The significance given to the problems is one of the causes of this dispute. Unlike the question of the chicken and the egg, where both are treated as equal entities, the question of whether it is class issues or gender equality that need to be addressed first does involve hierarchical ranking and is conducted within obvious power relations. Nancy Folbre sums up as follows:

> Neither Marx nor Engels disagreed that women were oppressed, but they linked this oppression to the consequences of private property and the interests of capital rather than to men's interests or men's power. . . . What distinguished [Marx and Engels] most clearly from earlier socialist theorists was their focus on the exploitation of the industrial proletariat and their related conviction that gender inequality was of distinctively lesser importance.
>
> (Folbre 1993a: 102, 94)

Not only did Marx and Engels rank the liberation of the proletariat before the liberation of women, they also expected women to give up their priorities in order to support men's class struggle. The same issue was also of importance in parts of the American women's suffrage movement. When women organized to obtain the right to vote, some groups also took on the agenda of the enslaved Black Americans, extending their struggle without necessarily prioritizing their own interests. Marx's suggestion in that regard sounds like this:

> "German women should have begun by driving their men to self-emancipation" rather than "seeking emancipation for themselves directly."
>
> (Marx, in Folbre 1993a: 103)

Where Marx and his contemporaries believed that the transition to socialism would be sufficient to guarantee women's complete liberation, they were simply building upon the arguments of the Early Socialists, who believed that technology would take over domestic labor and that childcare could easily be "industrialized" or at least greatly improved by those technological inventions. Apart from that, the problem was never fully realized, since domestic tasks were never described as aspects of the labor process; "they were relegated to the non economic world of nature and instinct, analogous to a spider weaving a web or a bee building a honeycomb" (Folbre 1993a: 103).

Folbre explains why she looks into the history of early socialism. She believes that thinkers of that time foresaw a lot of the discussions that are being held in contemporary economics:

> The concern for [women's] rights led them to explore at least three issues that classical political economy ignored: the juxtaposition of individual self-interest with paternal benevolence, the organization of household production, and the potential for birth control.
>
> (Folbre 1993b: 106)

Folbre is one of the handful of feminist economists who researches the history of utopian thought and also envisions some of her own alternatives in the course of her work (for more, see pp. 189–191). Others are, for instance, Jane Humphries and Jill Rubery, who aim for a solution of compromise in analyzing connections between the spheres of production and reproduction (Humphries and Rubery, in Regenhard *et al.* 1994). They compare the theoretical conception of those issues within neoclassical theory, approaches of segmentation and Marxist theory; and are developing their own alternative stance. Their paper states that the working class should demand relative autonomy, since what was intended as a defense against the bourgeoisie, namely the organization in groups such as families – where income would be shared and the standard of living for all, also those doing reproductive work, could be raised even with low wages – has ended up as a dividing issue. They suggest that an attempt to reach autonomy for all individuals would mend the gap between men and women of the working class. Wage labor could, for example, be reduced, and wages and jobs for all would increase, whereas reproductive work could be shared more equally. Humphries and Rubery are in this case clearly choosing a utopian approach. They are offering a clear prospect of redesigning gender roles; women should cease to be dependents within the family and they should have individual rights; the collection of rights in the family unit is rejected. On the one hand, this is a truly utopian approach; on the other hand, this line of argumentation leads back to the conflict between Marxists and feminists. The first problem arises with Classical Marxism refusing to be defined as utopian, but rather as a scientific approach, but much more problematic in this regard is the notion of Marxism and feminism having conflicting goals. Not only did Marx and Engels rank the liberation of the proletariat before the liberation of women, they also expected women to give up their priorities in order to support men's class struggle. Humphries and Rubery state that if the proletariat did simply overcome its (in the nineteenth century effective) strategy of bundling up in family clusters to defend itself and ensure its survival, everyone would be better off. By stating that, they disregard the problem that non-feminist Marxists simply do not have the same goal as feminists, which is to improve the economic situation of women per se. In that regard Humphries and Rubery's solution is deemed to be ineffective, since they have failed to incorporate this power struggle in their reasoning. This is an often heatedly debated issue in feminist economics and reminds one of the justifications that women are unconsciously "forgotten" in standard economic theory. The reality that "our Marxist brothers" still want women to wash their socks, even if the revolution has taken place, can oftentimes not be accepted, since it means the realization that one of feminisms largest (potential) allies might not be so much of an ally after all.

Is Classical Marxism color blind?

> If one can claim that marxism is incomplete without a consideration of feminism, it is certainly true that neither is complete without a consideration of racial relations. ... Relations between races have a long and important history which is not reducible to relations between the sexes and classes. An analysis of racism thus should be undertaken prior to, or at least in conjunction with, the discussion of Marxist feminist relations, thus facilitating a better understanding of how to integrate race into a theory of marxism-feminism.
>
> (Joseph, in Russ 1998: 292)

Apart from classical Marxism's approach of giving secondary importance to women's liberation, some thinkers are claiming that the "'Failure' of Marxism to Develop Adequate Tools and a Comprehensive Theory of Ethnicity, Gender and Class Issues is Undisputable" (Belkhir 1994). Others argue that Classical Marxism had indeed considered the problem of class being divided in groups demarcated by other categories such as race, country of origin, etc. An example is a letter dated 9 April 1870 from Marx to Meyer and Vogt, where Marx explains the importance of the Irish struggle for autonomy for the British proletariat:

> Every industrial and commercial center in England possesses a working class *divided* into two hostile camps, English proletarians and Irish proletarians. The ordinary English worker hates the Irish worker as a competitor who lowers his standard of life. In relation to the Irish worker, he feels himself a member of the *ruling* nation and so turns himself into a tool of the aristocrats and capitalists of his country *against Ireland*, thus strengthening their domination *over himself*. He cherishes religious, social, and national prejudices against the Irish worker. His attitude towards him is much the same as that of the 'poor

> whites' to the 'niggers' in the former slave states of the USA. The Irishman pays him back with interest in his own money. He sees in the English worker at once the accomplice and stupid tool of the *English rule in Ireland.* This antagonism is artificially kept alive and intensified by the press, the pulpit, the comic papers, in short by all the means at the disposal of the ruling classes. This *antagonism* is the *secret of the impotence of the English working class*, despite its organization. It is the secret by which the capitalist class maintains its power. And that class is fully aware of it.
>
> (Marx, in San Juan 2003, online; emphasis in original)

E. San Juan, Jr. claims that the paradigm of the intersection of race, class, and gender is wrongly "reducing class, and for that matter race and gender, to nominal aspects of personal identity without any clear historical or materialist grounding" (San Juan 2003), which he sees as a shortcoming when gender, race, and class are considered without the background of a Marxist theory.

Work in feminist utopia

Feminists have reveled at the opportunity to formulate alternative versions of working conditions, surpassing the suggestions by Marx and Engels and imagining something more than the common sex–gender divide between paid work in the marketplace and unpaid work in the home.

Herland

The following example from *Herland* is a good illustration of this point:

> We [the men visiting the women's utopian world] rather spread ourselves, telling of the advantages of competition: how it developed fine qualities; that without it there would be 'no stimulus to industry.' Terry was very strong on that point. 'No stimulus to industry,' [the women] repeated, with that puzzled look we had learned to know so well. 'Stimulus? To industry? But don't you like to work?' 'No man would work unless he had to,' Terry declared. 'Oh, no man. You mean that is one of your sex distinctions?' 'No, indeed!' he said hastily. 'No one, I mean, man or woman, would work without incentive. Competition is the – the motor power, you see.' 'It is not with us,' they explained gently, 'so it is hard for us to understand. Do you mean, for instance that with you no mother would work for her children without the stimulus of competition?' No, he admitted that he did not mean that. Mothers, he supposed, would of course work for their children in the home; but the world's work was different that had to be done by men, and required the competitive element.
>
> (Gilman, in Staveren 2003: 64)

In the section quoted above Gilman does indeed solve the paradox of caring labor, as was suggested in Chapter 1. (It should have become apparent what the paradox is, which cannot be explained when sticking to the rules of mainstream economic thinking.) As Deirdre McCloskey and others are arguing, there is a large segment of economic theory being reported as rhetoric. Gilman's exemplary quotation is nevertheless more than the usual standard rhetorical piece of economic theory. Gilman consciously places a topic under scrutiny in a fictional utopian environment. She creates a dialogue between agents of different opinion and sets them off to toy with the concept of work until it unravels. The paradox could not have been revealed as it was here with the use of the standard tools since the tools themselves, even if used in a narrative, are too blunt to unveil the situation as clearly as with Gilman's approach. Lucy Sargisson explains the process thus:

> Writing from or towards a good place that is no place, glancing over her shoulder at the place whence she came, the utopian feminist escapes the restrictions of patriarchal scholarship. New and inventive languages can best be imagined and employed in a new space, as can different social, sexual and symbolic relations.
>
> (Sargisson 1996: 41)

This is a reason to argue for utopian visions of feminist economics as a technique not only to unveil but also to imagine alternative creations: In *Herland*, there is no individual household production, nor a gender division of labor between housework and market work. The novel not only points out the paradox feminist economics tries to wrap itself around and around: by pointing out empirical data, explaining and comparing gender bias in theory and offering alternative models within the valid framework. Gilman simply leaves the frame of reference and designs a literary model for that very purpose:

> The novel *Herland* seems to solve the paradox found in Gilman's economic texts. The novel shows how non-market production can be efficient when it is carried out outside individual households and without the artificial construct of a gender division of labour between household and market production.
>
> (Staveren 2003: 65)

Unfortunately, this kind of feminist reasoning still has little place in contemporary (feminist) economic theory. Utopian novels are not recognized in (most) standard economic journals and econometrics as an applicative tool will not do the trick described above. This is where Staveren starts to wonder, "How is it that feminist literary imagination contributes to feminist economic analysis? Why can't we find it all just in the economic texts?" (Staveren 2003: 66).

Not only does Staveren ask the questions, but she also explores possible answers at the same time. She finds the first answer given by Martha Nussbaum, who says that first of all "the epistemological value of reading literature [is that] literary imagination reveals actors' emotions and motivations behind courses of action; second, it "also brings in a community's social, cultural and political values, showing how these guide and constrain behaviour;" and, third, it "draws the reader's attention to the vulnerability of human life, showing how uncertainty impacts upon people's behaviour" (Staveren 2003: 66). Nussbaum then concludes that the "added value of fiction to economics, lies in these three characteristics" (Nussbaum, in Staveren 2003: 66). Staveren goes on to apply these findings to feminist economics; she thinks that

> The value of literary imagination seems even more important for *feminist* economic analysis, given the fact that feminist economists challenge the standard notion of economic motivation embodied in the idea of rational economic man, the assumption of the value neutrality of core economic concepts, and the assumption of perfect markets with perfect foresight.
>
> (Staveren 2003: 66; emphasis in original)

Staveren concludes that feminist literary imagination is necessary as an input to feminist economics since it "enables feminist economists to engage with the meaning of economic analysis deriving from the specific context in which a particular economic phenomenon, activity, or concept is situated" (Staveren 2003: 67).

By saying that, Staveren solves what I consider one of the greatest challenges in feminist economics; she uses Gilman's historical work and her strategy of utopian fiction to find a key for utilizing feminist critique in its full scope. Feminist critique on its own might get stuck in a "negative hermeneutic of exposure" where utopia on its own tends to remain too removed to become relevant. By combining both, Gilman bridges the gap between feminism, economics, and utopia in a way no one has ever since.

Staveren argues that feminist critique tends not to fit the given frameworks and needs other tools to fully explore an economic issue with all its implications. The mechanical model of the machine, which needs the economist, the mechanic, to adjust some screws in order to move bolts around and produce a very specific outcome, i.e. a desired interest rate or a growth rate, simply does not account for a whole array of completely different issues. Unfortunately, as Ulla Grapard argues, Gilman's lack of conformity, her lack of academic training, and the gender analysis behind her evolutionary theory could not succeed in influencing the mainstream assumptions of economic theory at the turn of the nineteenth century (Staveren 2003: 57).

Egalia's Daughters

Gerd Brantenberg's *Egalia's Daughters* (Norwegian original published in 1977) is a caricature of powered gender relations which have been completely reversed, with the female sex on the top and the male sex a degraded, oppressed group. The most extreme suggestions from our point of view seem to be the maternity provisions made in Egalia's society and the importance given to childbirth, leaves of absence after childbirth, financial compensation given to mothers, the effects of childbearing on a mother's career path, and the organization of childcare. In Egalia, men are the ones receiving the child, after the women have given birth in public, pompous ceremonies. Due to the hardships associated with pregnancy and birth, Egalia needs to provide stimuli for women to take on that hardship, amongst them long maternity leaves, pregnancy premiums, special diet provisions during the times of breastfeeding, and pay raises to make it attractive for women to have children. After the birth, men are handed the children and they are now the sole nurturers and carers of them. Women may choose to stay at home after birth or return to their workplace just a few days after. If they choose to return to their jobs, men will need to take the babies to the women's workplaces frequently to allow for breastfeeding. Birth itself is a highly valued and important public celebration, which functions as a metaphor for the appreciation of female biology:

> The new Palace of Birth was a huge, red, triangular, stone building with a round bell-tower at each corner, large bow-windows, and a ling marble staircase leading up to the main entrance. . . . The door opened and in came the celebrant in full regalia – with her broad red cape, embroidered in gold – and thumped three times on the floor with her staff. That meant that the childbearer was approaching. Behind her came the choirgirls with their short, red smocks and their pyramid-shaped black hats. They were naked from the navel down. They formed three rows between the head of the bed and the organ, so that their pubic hair formed a long row of dark triangles. They were all the same height. At the end came Ruth Bram, accompanied by two midwifes in their usual white coats. Bram was wearing the black birth-coat. The organ was playing a tranquil prelude as she crossed to the head of the bed in front of the choir. Here, she threw off the black birth-coat and stood before them in her mighty nakedness. And exactly this moment, as she flung away the coat, the organ and the choir burst into the divine prenatal cantata, and Bram swung herself elegantly upon the birth bed.
> (Brantenberg 1985: 129)

The necessary element for practical policies of the kind Brantenberg proposes in her utopian world is a revaluation of reproduction and childcare, as has been suggested by Charlotte Perkins Gilman. Brantenberg takes her suggestions one step further: In her utopia, women benefit extremely from childbirth, both financially and in terms of career. What can be seen as a satirical element here is summarized by Marilyn Waring's feminist critique of the concept of GDP. Waring compares the value of institutionalized military killing, which can be measured in soldiers' remunerations, with the value of childbearing, which cannot be accounted for, is not financially rewarded, and is not measured in GDP. This is becoming more and more of a problem: with policy designations calling for higher women's employment ratios (The EU's Lisbon goal foresees an employment rate of at least 60 percent for women in all EU countries) and no further appreciation of reproduction work, family planning becomes a tough choice. Industrialized countries are currently facing sinking birth ratios, also due to the fact that many women cannot afford to take time off to have a child and because they see no sufficient state-provided aid in that regard.

The Female Man

Joanna Russ has employed a very special style when reflecting on the injustices of gender-based working conditions. This is an example:

> I know that somewhere, just to give me the lie, lives a beautiful (got to be beautiful), intellectual, gracious, cultivated, charming woman who has eight children, bakes her own bread, cakes, and pies, takes care of her own house, does her own cooking, brings up her own children, holds down a demanding nine-to-five job at the top decision-making level in a man's field, and is adored by her equally successful husband because although a hard-driving, aggressive business executive with eye of eagle, heart of lion, tongue of adder, and muscles of gorilla (she looks just like Kirk Douglas), she comes home at night, slips into a filmy negligée and a wig, and turns instantly into a Playboy dimwit, thus laughingly dispelling the canard that you cannot be eight people simultaneously with two different sets of values. She has not lost her femininity.
>
> (Russ 1975: 118)

Russ describes four very different economic systems in *The Female Man* regarding the position of women in her four utopian worlds. They range from women living in the near slavery of the complete housewife to men being kept as love-slaves. Very clearly, she criticizes the status quo of women's unpaid housework and relates it to the backbone of capitalism and militarism:

> Anyway everyboy (sorry) everybody knows that what women have done that is really important is not to constitute a great, cheap labor force that you can zip in when you're at war and zip out again afterwards but

> to Be Mothers, to form the coming generation, to give birth to them, to nurse them, to mop floors for them, to love them, cook for them, clean for them, change their diapers, pick up after them, and mainly sacrifice themselves for them. This is the most important job in the world. That's why they don't pay you for it.
>
> (Russ 1975: 137)

The utopian notion of work takes place on Whileaway. Here Russ plays with the Protestant work ethic: On the one side she stresses the point how everyone has to work and how hard the work is and that the women on Whileaway completely hate it. On the other sides she slips in cues on the length of the work week, which is in total 16 hours maximum and not longer than three hours per day, except in emergencies:

> Whilaway is engaged in the reorganization of industry consequent to the discovery of the induction principle.
>
> The Whilawayan work-week is sixteen hours.
>
> (Russ 1975: 56)

It is also interesting to see that there are no clear boundaries on Whileaway between work and leisure activities, which makes the true amount of working hours rather difficult to count. The women are free to choose where to work, and the older they get, the better the jobs available to them. At the age of five girls start school; at the age of 17 they may embark on educative travels all around their planet. At the age of 22 they are fully integrated into the labor force. Women work with the help of inductive steering helmets, which enhance an efficient telekinetic energy transfer. Older women who have sufficient experience may work with machines carrying actual tools. Computers are operated by even older veterans, who have learned to link themselves to the machines. Only they can take over mental and creative jobs. So only when women are considered to be physically old are they allowed creative and planning skilled work; they have now reached the highest status and never cease to work, until they die – because it is such good fun. The most interesting notion in that respect is that there is no problem of retirement and retirement benefits, since the workload is not divided between genders, but between generations. While the younger women are performing all of the menial and boring work (with the help of technology), the older women are those planning, constructing, and being creative:

> For in old age the Whilawayan woman – no longer as strong and elastic as the young – has learned to join with calculating machines in the state they say can't be described but is most like a sneeze that never comes off. It is the old who are given the sedentary jobs, the old who can spend their days mapping, drawing, thinking, writing, collating,

> composing. In the libraries old hands come out from under the induction helmets and give you the reproduction of the books you want; old feet twinkle below the computer shelves hanging down like Humpty Dumpty's; old ladies chuckle eerily while composing The Blasphemous Cantata (a great favorite of Ysaye's) or mad-moon city scapes which turn out to be do-able after all; old brains use one part in fifty to run a city (with checkups made by two sulky youngsters) while the other forty-nine parts riot in a freedom they haven't had since adolescence.
>
> The young are rather priggish about the old on Whileaway. They don't really approve of them.
>
> (Russ 1975: 53)

Russ' utopia appears rather sketchy and metaphorical. Nevertheless, she does offer some of the more concrete ideas for feminist reform: Starting with her proposals for lifelong learning and employment, which are tremendously advanced from, for instance, the European Union's attempts to avoid the "ageing problem." (The EU is opting for longer working lives encouraged through a reduction in retirement benefits.) The ageing population on Whilaway is the opposite of a burden since old people are the ones who are creating new technologies, who are innovative and are setting impulses for new planning and construction. Should there be an excess of the older population for some reason, the Whilawayan society would simply receive a boost in innovative technology, thereby enhancing the level of productivity in the whole society. Old people are seen as the creators of a better future, not as a burden of forgone productivity. This is all based on a radically different education system and the different organization of the working process, coupled with mentally enhancing technology that seeks to reduce working hours and make work as interesting and as versatile as possible.

Communist anarchism and ecological elements in feminist utopias

Work also becomes relevant when regarding exchange. Pierre-Joseph Proudhon and Mikhail Bakunin suggested a distribution system based on an individual's labor (an idea which is on the practical resurgence in alternative circles these days, where coupons for hours worked can be traded). Starhawk, in her feminist utopia *The Fifth Sacred Thing*, describes a price system more complex than that used in the usual binary supply-and-demand system:

> Our credit functions like money, but they're not backed by gold or silver. They're backed by energy, human or other sorts, and our basic unit of value is the calorie. So a product is valued by how much energy goes into its production, in terms of labor and fuel and materials that

> themselves require energy to produce. And part of that accounting is how much energy it takes to replace a resource that is used. Something that works with solar or wind power becomes very cheap. Anything requiring irreplaceable fossil fuels is generally too expensive to think about.
>
> (Starhawk 1993: 274)

Kropotkin went even further and rejected his own earlier idea of "labor cheques" as just another form of compulsion; he based distribution on need rather than the volume of work. (Some indigenous societies, for instance in Papua New Guinea, still function precisely in that way.) Starhawk has implanted a basic wage in her system: While monetary motivation comes with what is added to a basic stipend, a form of a living wage is provided, which is also connected to sustainability:

> We're each guaranteed a share of the wealth of the past and of the resources, which translates into a basic stipend of credits ... you could live on that, frugally, if you really didn't want to work. But if you do work, you earn work credits, and the more you work the more you earn, so there is incentive for those who want personal achievement. And if you do something really spectacular, achieve something famous, people bring you gifts.
>
> (Starhawk 1993: 274)

Additionally, everyone is obliged to donate a certain amount of gift working hours to the community. Environmental concerns are very often included in feminist utopias, stressing the view of mainstream economics that women's work, just like natural resources, is a natural supply that will never come to an end. In *The Fifth Sacred Thing* this also becomes obvious when very hard and nasty work (like toxic cleanup) is either done by volunteers or else workers are chosen by lotteries out of the contingent of gift hours that need to be provided. Working hours are controlled by the work groups themselves, so no cheating is possible. While there is also a belief in the willingness of people to work, in *Woman on the Edge of Time* a system of punishment for idleness is nevertheless installed. Connie, the time-traveling visitor to utopia, asks:

> "Ever hear of being lazy? Suppose I just don't want to get up in the morning?" Luciente, her guide replies: "Then I must do your work on top of my own if I'm in your base. Or in your family, I must do your defense and your childcare. I'll come to mind that. Who wants to be resented? Such people are asked to leave and they may wander from village to village sourer and more self-pitying as they go. We sadden at it. ... Sometimes a healer ... can help"
>
> (Piercy 1976: 101)

Feminist utopian studies analyze work

This section looks into feminist utopian theories and their stance on work:

> The concept of Utopia draws one normally to the poetic or revolutionary. I begin instead on another tack: the prosaic and mundane. In my vision of a feminist utopia of work and leisure or a utopia of Women's time, I am led to the cleaning of a toilet bowl. An unlikely starting point, to be sure, but I believe that a feminist utopia of work and time must begin with the quotidian, the ordinary, even the trivial. In my utopia, toilet cleaning goes the way of the corset. Of course, every utopia arises in relation to a problem. So what is the problem which has prompted mine? Perhaps most importantly, the time squeeze of modern women.
>
> (Schor, in Lenning *et al.* 1997: 45)

From Thomas More's *Utopia* onwards, many utopian designers assumed that both men and women work for the community and that all caring activities should somehow be carried out collectively. Most utopians were against family egoism, against the idea that someone is responsible for only his/her 'own' husband/wife and children. When the ideas of the utopian movements were put into practice, however, they seemed to be much more difficult than in theory; especially the caring tasks were hardly ever shared by the sexes. (This can be found in examples of Owenite or (other) religious communes, as I have already discussed.) In reality the wives in the utopian revolutions were still doing the care work for the entire family. Some Saint-Simonian men were a notable exception: in 1831, around 40 of them retreated to an estate "to learn what it is to be women;" the men divided the household tasks among themselves and tried to exchange feelings in a kind of "consciousness-raising group" (Poldervaart 1997: 183).

Titia Loenen provides an example of feminist utopian thinking in legal studies: She deconstructs the existing legal tradition regarding work issues from a gender point of view before forming some rather basic ideas she considers utopian, such as typically socialist ideals considering childcare facilities and the like. Loenen points out that the example of the right to work shows that when its universal character is narrowed down it becomes obvious that this right is implicitly designed to a male standard. Loenen claims that androcentrism invades women's rights, since "universality, objectivity and neutrality have been constantly unmasked as hiding male standards and norms" (Loenen 1997: 63). If fundamental rights were to be truly universal a reconstruction to include those previously excluded would need to be made. In regard to work and that reconstruction, the most fundamental issue is the recognition of caring labor as an element of work: "This would mean that the right to work is interpreted as constituting not only an obligation of conduct on the part of the state to promote full employment, but also as obliging conduct to make the combination of paid work and care easier" (Loenen 1997: 63). Loenen offers solutions such as childcare facilities, parental leave, gearing school hours to working hours, etc. She believes that in the long run there needs to be a more fundamental change in the legal conditions in order to guarantee fair recognition and treatment of care and market work (Loenen 1997: 63).

Many utopians linked the right to work for women and men to the right to have leisure time. Because housework was often supposed to be carried out collectively and on a large scale, many utopian communities became famous for their household inventions and their technological applications. This corresponds to Juliet Schor's "profane" introduction in her thoughts on the topic of un-gendering work in utopian models. She uses the example of the cleanliness of toilet bowls to explain that a feminist utopia of the household will not only be achieved by equal sharing, but also by a new structure of prices and incentives associated with household technologies and a new attitude towards evaluating (women's) time spent in the home (Schor, in Lenning *et al.* 1997: 46). Schor suggests some basic principles for a "utopia of time," which are similar to those in Marilyn Waring's *If Women Counted* (1988). Schor demands an (upward) 'revaluation' of women's time. On the one hand, she argues for raising the social value of unpaid labor; on the other hand, for a transformation of the character of that labor. Second, Schor argues for a reduction in paid labor time, hoping that utopia will create much more leisure time due to collective work and technological development (Schor, in Lenning *et al.* 1997: 51). The key element for these reconstructions is the issue of choice, one of the centerpieces of philosophy and central demand in feminist theory. Schor challenges the segmented labor market and envisions a world where men and women can choose how much to work in any segment of jobs, even the best the economy has to offer. She believes that

> short hours would probably become the norm, not through fiat, but because people chose them, once they are given the choice. And choice is a crucial part of my dream. In the nineteenth and twentieth century capitalist economy, there has been almost no free choice in hours for the individual worker. Some collective choice, through unions, has existed, but for the most part, employers have dictated hours, basing time use on profitability, rather than the well-being of people.
>
> (Schor, in Lenning *et al.* 1997: 52)

Schor explains that so far increased productivity has mostly resulted in higher wages rather than more free time. She claims that those added incomes have been spent and therefore helped to produce the "dystopia of time" which is responsible for producing an excessively consumerist culture, in which the lack of time and lack of control over time are a cultural given. The only point of reference is spending money in that precious free time. Interestingly, as Schor points out, it is traditionally the women of the nuclear families who are the traditional consumers of the consumer economy. In Schor's utopia, as work time declines and control over time increases, the importance of consumerism will fade. To some extent this is structural: if we 'consume' economic progress in the form of leisure, there will be less left over for goods. But I believe cultural change will occur as well: the compensatory dimensions of consuming will be less pressing, which Schor describes as the point where the exploitation of the environment and the hunt for raw materials, natural resources, and space will possibly slow down (Schor, in Lenning *et al.* 1997: 52).

Most literary works of feminist utopia are concerned with this "estranged" work, not only in the Marxian sense, but also concerning the gap between reproductive work and, say, work in the arms industry, or in industries which destroy much of the environment, or the pharmaceutical industry, which can be used to control women's minds and bodies (i.e. Piercy, Russ, Waring etc.). But certainly that criticism also relates to the "*Mehrwert*" which goes to (usually male) corporate heads.

> A child free from the guilt of ownership and the burden of economic competition will grow up with the will to do what needs doing and the capacity for joy in doing it. It is useless work that darkens the heart. The delight of the nursing mother, of the scholar, of the successful hunter, of the good cook, of the skilful maker, of anyone doing needed work and doing it well, – this durable joy is perhaps the deepest source of human affection and of sociality as a whole.
>
> (Le Guin 2001 (1974): 205)

Working women/nursing men?

The next section is especially concerned with the reproductive part of the gendered division of labor. Peterson explains the shaping of the current establishment of working relations thus:

> First of all the family, the household and reproduction were associated with the "natural" sphere, second, men's spheres such as private property, wage labor, and free market activity gained esteem, thirdly, labor associated with the household was devalued and received no or low wages. Finally gender identities were reshaped in a bourgeois moral code, placing women as the feminine, soft caretakers and homemakers and man as hard-working, tough and responsible at the same time, needing to compensate the alienation at their work with leisure and a comfortable home.
>
> (Peterson 1992: 43)

Where Peterson claims that the displacement of autonomous kin-communities had large and specifically negative consequences for women in the realms of authority, property, labor, and sexuality, based on the original lack of a distinction between the domestic and the economic sphere, what happens is, to speak in Foucault's terms, the following:

> "[T]he first figure to be invested by the deployment of sexuality, one of the first to be 'sexualized,' was the 'idle' woman" (1978: 121). This was the wife of the bourgeois market-player.
>
> (Foucault, in Cornwall 1998: 76)

In this regard the separation of the economic spheres according to people's sexes was not only a socioeconomic event, but also a matter written on the bodies of men and women. The place where this allegation becomes visible is in the notion of childbearing:

> I consider [utopian ideas on human reproduction] to be the most crucial area in which gender relations are played out. Ideas and ideals about gender relations are often based on the reproductive functions of men and women, and often take the form of ideology. When we read utopian works we notice that for centuries men and women have been struggling with the fact of the biological difference between the sexes – building gender roles on it, trying to construct ideas of superiority and inferiority upon it, trying to understand it, come to terms with it, or even to change it.
>
> (Gupta 1997: 81)

The issue of reproduction has always been a key issue in utopia. While men dreaded losing even more control of the birth process, as in *Brave New World*, either women utopianists wanted control over their bodies and reproduction back for themselves, even if that meant eliminating men from their utopian systems (*Herland*), or they were willing to completely give up control over the birthing process to reach equality (*Woman on the Edge of Time*). The sharing of reproduction in the sense of Shulamith Firestone is seen as the one opportunity to achieve true equality between the sexes: the nuclear (hetero-)family is rejected, conception and pregnancy are mechanized, pregnancies take place in baby factories, and children are the responsibility of the community. The theme of reproduction was already present in Plato's time and continued in eighteenth- and nineteenth-century utopian socialism (Owen, Saint-Simon, Fourier) and the 'scientific socialists' (Marx, Engels, and Bebel). The utopians thought to liberate women by freeing them from marriage and monogamy, by extending responsibility for children to the (female) community; socialists agreed that marriage prevented women's freedom, but believed that emancipation would naturally result from opening the workplace to women (Gupta 1997: 82). Engels, in *The Origin of the Family, Private Property and the State*, claims that the division of labor between man and woman originates from the purposes of child breeding. Therefore biology was the reason for the fundamental division between the sexes. Bebel then added the new dimension of a technological revolution as a solution for women in the socialist revolution. He argued that technological advances would release women from their caring labor (a theme annexed by many (feminist) utopian thinkers). Bebel envisioned cooperative mechanized kitchens where the women (only) would do the cooking in turns in fully electrified kitchens. For childcare Bebel recommended common guardians, such as are introduced in most feminist utopias, for example in *Herland* and also *Woman on the Edge of Time* (Gupta 1997: 82).

In *Herland* the women reproduce parthenogenetically. (Parthenogenesis is a biological process in which a female organism can reproduce without the means of male fertilization.) In *Herland* parthenogenesis symbolizes women's autonomy and ability to be creative and re-creative. It stands for the mother–daughter ties as opposed to the patriarchal father-to-son progression of generations, societies, and wealth. This freedom from male control in the birthing process is carried over into the economic sphere, and Gilman suggests that this creates a species of highly successful, proud, and socially responsible women:

> They have short hair, their manner of dress is based on comfort and function, they are naturally athletic and physically strong, they are all highly educated and have specialized jobs in the community, their self-esteem is not dependent on validation by men, and they are assertive in setting and maintaining boundaries.
>
> (Gilman, in Clemons 2000: 2)

Freed from male oppression and domination, women are able to work creatively in the arts but also in science and agriculture. The women in *Herland* only give birth to one child due to rigid population control (in times of crisis and population decimation that number may rise); childbirth is seen as the highest privilege, as is the work of childcare and education, which is communally undertaken and provided by highly educated specialists.

Vacuuming cyborgs!

Now I want to turn to the role of technology in the relationships of male and female workers: Technology was a key factor for the transformation of the work process in Bebel's ideas to ease women's work in the home. Machines were thought to take over the arduous labor. In feminist utopias, technology plays a more complex and advanced role than a simple vacuum cleaner might for instance play in a traditional household. In the Whilawayan society of *The Female Man*, induction helmets allow the workers to work with their whole muscular apparatus to control the machines in the production process by "induction." (Russ does not go into the details of how this process might function.) It seems as if this technology has given workers the possibility of fusing with machines and becoming much more efficient than regular workers. The mind merges with the machine in order to reduce actual working hours to a minimum. The interesting argument in the background is that Russ sees male aggression as the root problem between the genders, which she regards as the key driving force for technological progress. In a bad world aggression is the drive to build better weapons and thereby enhance technology and induce economic growth. In the case of Jeannine's world, Russ explains the relative lack of progress and a stagnant economy as a result of the ties between progress and aggression in patriarchy. If there is no World War II, as is the case in the Jeannine example, then there is no leap forward in technology and no economic expansion. Russ then juxtaposes this argument and builds the scenario of the ultimate war between the genders, and wonders if this can become the thriving reason for growth, as we consider it, or destruction, as it is being considered from her utopian perspective.

Many feminists believe that "male domination is often linked to the exploitative and destructive uses of science and technology" (Gupta 1997: 84). Therefore sometimes a lot of thought regarding technology in utopia is rather pessimistic and tends to lead to dystopias, such as in Mary Shelley's *Frankenstein* or in Aldous Huxley's *Brave New World*. (The horrors of artificial child breeding in *Brave New World* are the key to liberation with Shulamith Firestone and Marge Piercy, as I explained in Chapter 2. Note the different perspective of men and women in this regard.) Some utopias written by women, such as Dorothy Bryant's and Sally Miller Gearhart's works, have no place for science and technology, as the authors see science and technology as "part of the problem." On the other hand, many utopias see technology as part of the solution, if its employment were to be more decentralized from male use and shifted more towards "women's applications." Examples are Haraway's cyborg concept or Piercy's vision of an environmentally friendly technology.

Donna Haraway has taken a rather unique stance towards the technology-and-feminism problematic: *A Cyborg Manifesto* is an ironical pamphlet describing a powerful technological tool for social change, namely the cyborg. The cyborg becomes a vehicle to travel across existing power relations:

> the cyborg allows us to know different stories about women. The cyborg concept allows us to look at women in ways other than 'child-bearer,' or 'homemaker'. The cyborg concept does not solely apply to women, either. The cyborg also allows us to transcend seemingly permanent mindsets (family organization, work, religion) by scrambling the signal with different ideas and stories. The cyborgs attempt to transcend even the ideas of what "should be" or what is "natural."
>
> (Desantis 1996, online)

The cyborg is a hybrid creature, a warrior. A "modern war is a cyborg orgy" (Haraway 1980, online). The war that is being fought is along the demarcation lines of the "territories of production, reproduction, and imagination" (Haraway 1980, online). Haraway describes modern production as a "dream of cyborg colonialization work, a dream that makes the nightmare of Taylorism seem idyllic" (Haraway 1980, online). Haraway proclaims that the current period of the New Industrial Revolution is once again producing a newly shaped working class with new coding for sexuality and ethnicity. A new "homework economy" (in the sense of Richard Gordon) is established, where men and women are now performing their labor in feminized, precarious working conditions, the vulnerability of the female worker is by the process of deskilling extended to her male counterpart, and the feminization of poverty is spreading quickly across both genders. Haraway then makes the point that with her cyborg vehicle these developments could be observed and countered, and she calls for a cyborgization of feminist strategies.

Feminist economics and work

Roots of feminist economics

The current feminist and feminist economic theory was initiated by women such as Mary Wollstonecraft or Luise Otto Peters, the suffrage movement, and the movements for economic emancipation of the last centuries. The concern with woman's situation related to work in the context of a women's movement was first voiced by thinkers such as Luise Otto Peters (1866) in her writings on women's rights to paid work, or in John Stuart Mill's writings on women, or Helen Taylor's petition on property holding, and before that the radical theories of Mary Wollstonecraft. Rosalind Delmar compares the impact of Mary Wollstonecraft's radical theories in *A Vindication of the Rights of Woman* (1792) to the practical, very conservative work of her contemporary Hannah More, who was providing the feminist "service labor," a non-radical approach, which aimed at soothing the effects of patriarchy felt by women. In my opinion this very difference in radicalism in first-wave feminism is still reflected today in feminism and feminist economics. A radical view of feminism states that a triad of economics, violence, and homophobia is the means of sexism that keeps patriarchy and with it white men's privileges established (Pharr 1988). Women who are actively engaged in radical feminist theory or are involved in radical organizations of the women's movement are trying to re-create the current status quo. This can be seen as a radical approach. Radical in this sense means acting at the root cause of a problem rather than providing "service work for the system." A counter example are the ongoing efforts in the women's movement to nurse the symptoms of patriarchy (such as fighting female poverty and homelessness, staffing battered women's centers, easing the effects of domestic violence, working in counseling centers, etc.), whereas a radical feminist strategy aims to change the system, redefine the structures that cause the symptoms of discrimination, oppression, and battering. Pharr furthermore warns that the degree of radicalism of feminist work will determine the degree of the reaction attempting to squash it (Pharr 1988: 25).

This proved to be true also in the first women's movement: Mary Wollstonecraft's declaration is an example, given that the historical context was very different from today's. Nevertheless, the historical lesson to be learned from my point of view is that there is a possibility of choosing between radicalism in political activity and theory. Wollstonecraft chose an extremely radical stance for her times and succeeded in introducing enormous changes for women. In the *Vindication*, the first great feminist compendium, she argues that intellect will always govern and she seeks "to persuade women to endeavor to acquire strength, both of mind and body, and to convince them that the soft phrases, susceptibility of heart, delicacy of sentiment, and refinement of taste, are almost synonymous with epithets of weakness" (Wollstonecraft 1792, online). Wollstonecraft was an advocate for an egalitarian society; she believed that a philosophy of equal rights and opportunities for men and women would lead towards greater justice and success of all humankind. She argued that all people have a competence of reason as well as "romantic love and physical desirability," rather then the proclaimed dualistic split. She was one of the first to point out the existence of socially imposed suppression used by men to enslave women:

> I have confined my observations to such as universally act upon the morals and manners of the whole sex, and to me it appears clear that they all spring from want of understanding. Whether this arise from a physical or accidental weakness of faculties, time alone can determine; for I shall not lay any great stress on the example of a few women who, from having received a masculine education, have acquired courage and resolution; I only contend that the men who have been placed in similar situations, have acquired a similar character – I speak of bodies of men, and that men of genius and talents have started out of a class, in which women have never yet been placed.
>
> (Wollstonecraft 1792: ch. 4, online)

Wollstonecraft's novel *Maria, or the Wrongs of Woman* develops similar themes in a fictional setting showing that the plight of working women differs little from imprisonment. Wollstonecraft was not only an important role model in regard to feminist demands, analysis, and theory, but also someone who early recognized the social shaping of gender. Her strategy of writing novels to spread her ideas more comfortably was adopted by other feminist writers to come. Another example for the connection of her theories to practice and also to fiction is the application of her work by the utopian Owenite socialist movement and by her daughter Mary Shelley, with *Frankenstein* (1818) starting the newly emerging discourse on the subjectivity of the "cyborg."

Charlotte Perkins Gilman's theoretical work *Women and Economics* (1898) is not as widely known as *Herland*, but is still a pioneering piece as a first comprehensive theoretical approach to economic issues regarding women. It is a good starting point for the history of feminist economics:

> The working power of the mother has always been a prominent factor in human life. She is the worker par excellence, but her work is not such as to affect her economic status. Her living, all that she gets, – food, clothing, ornaments, amusements, luxuries, – these bear no relation to her power to produce wealth, to her services in the house, or to her motherhood. These things bear relation only to the man she marries, the man she depends on, – to how much he has and how much he is willing to give her. The women whose splendid extravagance dazzles the world, whose economic goods are the greatest, are often neither houseworkers nor mothers, but simply the women who hold most power over the men who have the most money. The female of genus homo is economically dependent on the male. He is her food supply.
>
> (Perkins Gilman 1898, online)

Regarding methodology it is interesting to note that Gilman also connects the theoretical approach in *Women and Economics* with the writing of a utopian fiction, *Herland* (Perkins Gilman 1915), which is discussed in great detail by Staveren (2003).

When listing the works of these early feminists side by side it is interesting to point out the deep ideological gulfs which already distanced their beliefs from each other. The socialist stances demanding an end to an unfair distribution of labor and wages are met by the liberal approaches of John Stuart Mill or the capitalist ideals of Helen Taylor. In *The Subjection of Women* (1869), Mill argues that men and women are alike regarding the need for personal and economic freedom; biological differences are just moralist excuses to keep women out of the public sphere:

> If women have different natures, the only way to discover what they are is by experiment, and that requires that women should have access to everything to which men have access. Only after as many centuries of freedom as there have been centuries of oppression will we really know what our natures are.
>
> (Mill 1869, online)

Richard Pankhurst, husband of Emmeline, also pursued the following line of argument in 1867:

> The basis of political freedom is expressed in the great maxim of the equality of all men, of humanity, of all human beings, before the law. The unit of modern society is not the family but the individual. Therefore

> every individual is prima-facie entitled to all the franchises and freedoms of the constitution.
>
> (Delmar 1994: 14)

Helen Taylor, on the other hand, who was the daughter of Harriet Taylor and the stepdaughter of J.S. Mill, links women's rights to the right to hold property. "Property represented by an individual is the true political unit amongst us" (Delmar 1994: 14).

Overall, the toiling for little wages while others are living a comfortable life, and work organization in the family and in the overall society are still central themes in feminist utopia and contemporary feminist economics.

The Paradox of Caring Labor revisited

Feminist economics is deeply concerned with women's exploitation in the home, in the marketplace, and especially in caring labor. This part of my analysis looks into the possibilities feminist economics provides to improve economic givens in the care economy. Most of the few contributions in *Feminist Economics* which I have classified as possessing utopian methodologies (I give a detailed overview of this process in Chapter 6) analyze utopian works in the past and try to apply their findings to contemporary feminist economics strategies. Fewer papers followed a second stream of thought, the creation of current alternative feminist solutions. The most important of such pieces is Nancy Folbre's "'Holding Hands at Midnight': The Paradox of Caring Labor."[2] As was described above, Charlotte Perkins Gilman was one of the first to analyze that paradox in her utopian novel. The solution she offers is one of separatism. Folbre looks into the issue of "care" from a contemporary feminist economics point of view. First, Folbre explores the paradoxical notions arising when one tries to define precisely what "Caring Labor" (Folbre 2005, online) includes. She defines caring labor as

> work that involves connecting to other people, trying to help people meet their needs, things like the work of caring for children, caring for the elderly, caring for sick people or teaching is a form of caring labor. Some kind is paid, some is unpaid.
>
> (Folbre 2005, online)

She continues by exploring reasons for the undervaluing of caring labor. This entails a reflection on the value of caring labor and the connected undervaluing of it in a neoclassical framework:

> What is really distinctive about caring labor is that it is usually intrinsically motivated. People do it for reasons other than just money, even though there is often money involved, like you need to get paid to

> work, or you are exchanging the care of a family member in return for a share of another's family member's wage, still we always think of care work as something which involves a sense of commitment or obligation or passion for the person who is being cared for. That intrinsic motivation is a really important part of what makes caring labor so valuable and what insures it is being provided at a pretty high quality. But it also means that it is very hard to organize caring labor in a market, and that the market wage that you pay for care work is almost always quite low. Historically women have done a very large proportion of our care work, and that is still true today.
>
> (Folbre 2005, online)

In her 1996 article, she summarizes the New Home Economics' view on caring labor. Jacob Mincer and Solomon Polachek conclude that women choose to specialize in lower paying jobs because this is more consistent with their family responsibilities. Folbre also lists Becker's line of argument for women's work being of lesser value, namely that they devote more time to their housework as a specialization. Becker herein also stresses the impact of the supply side only, ignoring demand-side discrimination. Folbre shows some feminist economists' arguments as well, one being Barbara Bergmann's "crowding" hypothesis[3] (Bergmann 1986).

But, most interestingly, her article results in a search for feminist alternatives to unpaid or undervalued caring work. Folbre starts her quest by asking:

> Should we recreate ourselves in a more masculine image? Or should we seek, instead, to eliminate the economic penalty imposed on distinctively feminine norms, values, and preferences?
>
> (Dorman *et al.* 1996: 83)

Should a feminist economics utopia be based on gender equality or difference? Folbre contemplates that question; she explains that "there is a negative rate of return to femininity, and the dilemma, restated is: should those who want to increase their economic welfare try to decrease their femininity, or try to modify the rate of return?" (Dorman *et al.* 1996: 84). Folbre argues that most feminist economists have clearly chosen the first alternative, prioritizing equality with men, while only a few have opted to revalue the ways in which women are different from men. Barbara Bergmann, for example, believes that feminine qualities handicap women in the market, therefore women must shed this femininity to compete with men and better their positions. Myra Strober thinks women should enter traditionally male occupations to receive better pay. This implies a strong belief in the market; if all players act as (are?) equals (equally male?), everyone will be rewarded equally.

Folbre thinks along another line. In her interview with Oliver Ressler, she explains that social utopian thinkers, whether capitalist or socialist, have always "forgotten" the realm of caring labor. Folbre argues that this is a problem that needs to be tackled from various sides, starting with education:

> I think there is a lot of evidence that caring for other people is a little bit like a skill, if you practice it, if you do it, you enjoy it, you take greater pleasure in it. It is also something that grows out of a personal connection with other people. And if you never put into that connection of responsibility for other people then you never become aware of or develop that sense of connection. It should be a central part of our educational process for people to take on responsibilities for other people.
>
> (Folbre 2005, online)

Folbre's own imagination of an alternative society where all labor, including caring labor, has been reorganized is modeled on the metaphor of the family, which clearly displays another of feminist economics' dilemmas:

> The family itself has always been a kind of metaphor for socialism. Socialism is really a family at large, we take care for our brothers and sisters. That's the interesting thing about feminism that feminists always had to challenge the traditional family, the idea of the patriarch, the male-led household, telling all the younger generation what to do and sending the wife to the kitchen to cook the meals and scrub the floors. But at the same time there has always been something about the family, the solidarity, the love and affection for one another that is so central for family life that feminists have tried to lay claim to and to think about how one could take that sense of mutual affection and mutual aid and generalize it to the society as a whole. It doesn't seem that far fetched, if we can do it on the microeconomic level, we should be able to figure out how to generalize it. A society could and should be like a really healthy happy egalitarian family, where people have their own responsibilities, they might go out and earn a living or might specialize in different kinds of work, but they all come home to a set of shared priorities and goals, and they have made a commitment to work together and to respect one another in a really profound way. In a way it is utopian and visionary, but in another way it is very old-fashioned and very traditional.
>
> (Folbre 2005, online)

Arguments along those lines, but with different ideas for a practical approach, come from some feminist economists (e.g. Julie Matthei) who would rather revalue gender differences and are arguing, for instance, for an economy where all labor would be considered just like caring labor; this is described as a socialist feminist economy. Some feminist economists also argue that a market economy cannot function without a caring economy which coordinates the processes of social reproduction without monetary payments. The dispute is about the roles of the market, the state, and the family within the economy. The distribution of care and its status are the specific issue, on which neoclassical feminists and institutionalist feminists have very different views. Marga Bruyn-Hundt offers practical "Scenarios for a Redistribution of Unpaid Work in the Netherlands,"[4] listing possibilities for a redistribution of caring labor. Bruyn-Hundt's favorite scenario is one where men and women share paid and unpaid work equally. She lists eleven practical conditions or prerequisites (legal, tax related, social benefits, etc.) which would enable the Netherlands to reach such a solution.

A feminist economics of time

Nancy Folbre stresses the importance of underlying concepts of value. She continues to ask questions of alternatives for feminist economists. She asks:

> How do we, ourselves, value caring labor? How important do we think it is to the full realization of human capacities?
>
> (Folbre in Dorman *et al.* 1996: 86)

Answers already given are, for instance, the alternative created by Marilyn Waring[5] to evaluate all work equally. Carmen Siriani and Cynthia Negrey, in "Working Time as Gendered Time",[6] Dianne Perrons, in "Care, Paid Work, and Leisure: Rounding the Triangle,"[7] and Susan Donath, in "The Other Economy: A Suggestion for a Distinctively Feminist Economics."[8] also look into a feminist politics of time to solve problems concerning the clash between unpaid care and paid market labor. They promote alternative time arrangements for women and men to foster gender equality in the home and in the market. Sirianni and Negrey offer a feminist critique of contemporary time structures by advocating alternative forms of time organization coupled with pay equity. They believe that this could bring about profound social transformation. In their article they list the asymmetries in working time for men and women in the home and in the market. They argue for a reduction in working time for all workers and also for flexibility without other compensating disadvantages. Perrons lists three contrasting care models as alternatives:

1. The universal worker model: Both genders work equally in the market and care is provided by the state or through the market. This goes with Barbara Bergmann's argument that "anything that romanticizes housework and childcare is bad for women." She believes that all housework should be industrialized so that it can be performed more efficiently in the market, a view which she shares with Deirdre McCloskey.
2. The caregiver-parity model: The remuneration for caring work is increased and therefore the difference between men and women is

removed cost-wise. Some feminists warn that reducing caring labor to some common denominator with market labor might impose a masculine perspective that privileges efficiency over affection, quantity over quality.

3 The universal caregiver model: Perrons quotes Nancy Fraser, who discusses the first two models:

> both of these alternatives are utopian, relative to existing situations, but not "utopian enough."
>
> (Fraser, in Perrons 2000: 107)

That leads Fraser to the third model, an alternative, which "dismantles the gendered opposition between working [for money] and care giving." This model could "overcome both the 'workerism' of the Universal Worker and the domestic privatism of Caregiver-Parity" (Fraser, in Perrons 2000: 107). Perrons claims that this "would also challenge and probably overturn the existing gender order, if not the meaning of gender itself." She sees this as a consequence of making "women's current life-patterns the norm for everyone" so that primary care work would be done additionally to paid work by everyone (Fraser, in Perrons 2000: 107). While this approach might seem a bit too radical to become reality, Perrons points out that the EU's gender mainstreaming initiative indeed calls for the "promotion of long lasting changes in parental roles, family structures, institutional practices and the organization of work and time" (EC, quoted in Perrons 2000: 7). Perrons and also Donath explore practical examples for the two first models. The examples they analyze are the policy effects in France and Great Britain, where the two models were partially introduced. Therefore, both Perrons and Donath argue for the most radical utopian alternative regarding the issue of work and time.

The utopian family in the economic textbook

Finally, since I have been discussing feminist economics' ambivalences regarding the family as a possible option for a utopian setting, it is interesting to look at Diana Strassmann's and Livia Polanyi's take on the family as a difficult metaphor. In "The Economist as Storyteller," they show

> how the situated character of economic texts may be uncovered by careful examination of details in the language and content of the texts. Lying just below the surface of apparently simple illustrative examples of economics writing is a complex of interwoven assumptions about the world.
>
> (Strassmann and Polanyi, in Kuiper and Sap 1995: 129)

What at first sounds slightly paranoid is illustrated very smartly by the use of detailed textual analyses of ordinary and unremarkable accounts which include information on the subjects of economic theory such as race, gender, ethnicity, social status, historical epoch, and geographical location. Their examples are from economic textbooks' descriptions of the microeconomic workings within families: the "enjoyable family" (the perfect nuclear family) and the "other family" (where the one wife manages to work 16-hour days, carry out subsistence farming in the country, and also hold down a full-time job in the city, while at the same time providing for herself and her disabled husband; she doesn't have a car, but apparently teleports herself from her home to her workplace), as they cynically call the two images of families described in economic textbooks. Those are created by "stories evoking pastoral images." This is an interesting notion. Strassmann and Polanyi argue that standard textbooks are using neoclassical utopian visions and concepts of family life to illustrate certain issues in economic theory. The interesting issue in their paper is the unusual formulation of criticism of feminist economics. When they denounce something (in this case the images of textbook families) as utopian, different options for strategies of criticism arise. It would be of a very different effect if, for instance, Strassmann and Polanyi had gone through the trouble of creating an empirical study to work out what percent of the population do live in, or at least close to, the setting as described, and what consequences certain lifestyles might have on mental and physical health, and which costs arise for the health system and so forth.

Tapestry

My excursions into the different levels and times of gendered labor divisions in theory and practice have hopefully helped to illustrate that the current set-up is neither a historical given nor the only option one might imagine. The issue of work is not only closely tied to gender questions, but also incorporates huge potential for a complete restructuring of our society and the economic system as we know it. Connected are concerns of environmental preservation and sustainability which are also chiefly dependent on the technology employed. Technology is said to be the key to economic growth and well-being. For instance, Solow-Swan's neoclassical production function explains economic growth as dependent on technology multiplied by a function of labor and capital. The production factor "labor" is certainly not considered from a gender perspective, even though it might not explode the neoclassical model if one were to add a variant L side by side with a L category, both making up all labor (L), hence adding women and stirring. But, even more important, technology and its effects are usually not researched from a gender perspective. Is there such a thing as "male" technology? And is there such a thing as "female" technology? The cyborg concept might say, "Yes, there is", but it is quite contrary to what one might have expected. (The cyborg is a rather unpleasant vehicle, not a soft, pink, female gadget.) Joanna Russ claims that female technology would rely on "induction." Is there a special ability women might have, which men do not? Another question concerns the production processes: Would women organize production processes differently? Would a woman have installed a model pin factory with labor division enhancing productivity? And regarding environmentalism: Would a female production technology be ecofeminist and/or more concerned with the preservation of natural resources?

Feminist utopian visions give no simple unified answer to all the above questions. But generally, technology depends on creative impulses to design new apparatus. Jules Verne's imaginary space travels to the moon seemed at one stage as unlikely as time traveling. Issues of working conditions for men and women have always been closely connected to the technology used to transform that labor. Worldwide feminization of labor, a revival of industrialization in sweatshops in non-privileged countries, and unsustainable exploitation of the environment are not only horribly wrong, inefficient, and unjust concepts from my point of view; they also lack the creativity of utopian impulses to improve conditions for all.

6 Femeconers and utopia

Paradigm change now?

This chapter looks into the role of utopia in the making of feminist economics and generally into the tools feminist economists work with. Analytically, the discussion in this chapter is a rather difficult one. As an economist, a feminist economist, and an International Association for Feminist Economists (IAFFE) member I am in the position of those who I simultaneously seek to analyze. At the same time, working as a queer theorist and lesbian feminist puts me at the margin of "mainstream" feminist economists. Thus I speak from a marginal perspective and, because of this, I also clearly incorporate certain demands on and criticisms of feminist economics, which represents a marginal category in mainstream economics as such. The question of embracing my standpoint as part of my program, rather than aiming for objectivity and not taking a stand, is related to the pros and cons of this decision. Will I lose credibility by positioning myself further on the margin than others? What am I biased towards? What right do I have to demand more strongly than perhaps heteronormative feminist economists that the "other" be included? Am I a burden on my straight feminist colleagues, because I am not interested, for instance, in changes in the bargaining power in heterosexual households? Perhaps I am a "radical" working toward my own personal goals? Perhaps I thus am endangering my career? . . . In the end, I still chose to come out in my theoretical argument and to call for queering everyone's perspective, because I think this will enhance what I call for in this project: the opportunity to open up thinking space for everyone. This project is also an advantage to straight, married mothers, as considering "alternative" socioeconomic arrangements may provide them with new ideas, some of which their husbands may feel threatened by; however, in the long run, I trust that all genders will profit from the openness and choice which goes beyond merely sticking to the given norms. This also holds true for intercultural exchange.

And this is just the personal level. Yet, the private is not only political, but political choices are backed up with theory, and created knowledge, with what one knows and believes. The choice for openness rather than being closeted and for open-mindedness should be expanded from a private or social concept to a question of epistemology. This is where I think the utopian thought model comes in handy, as it enables both theory and science to develop new spaces for thinking, as I discussed in Chapter 4. Therefore, this chapter looks into the discipline of feminist economics with the goal of seeing to what extent utopian visions are employed to allow new policy implications on the practical side, but also, and more importantly, whether feminist economic epistemology incorporates utopian elements.

I will use Alice Vollmer's pessimistic estimation here as my point of departure:

> Women seem to have a hard time freely creating utopian desires and imaginations. To live in a patriarchic reality obviously binds that imagination, which aims at designing images and existences other than those androcentrically formed. Feelings of emptiness and restriction often arise, when women artists or politicians are trying to create female futures.
>
> (Vollmer 1986: 7, in Shafi 1990: 11)[1]

I agree with Vollmer's observation; however I wonder whether my agreement is based on essentialist biological pre-programming. A female feminist economist who replied to a questionnaire which I had sent out during the process of writing my PhD, stated:

> I can't really think of a feminist utopia. That is, I cannot come up with such a thing in my mind, even when I try to imagine it.

Even so, I doubt that the person could not envision a utopian world because she was born as a woman. As discourse theory has shown, it is more likely that all dominant discourse aims at keeping alternative thought models outside the canon. There are issues of power associated with the fact that people are unable to imagine options they might consider preferable. Foucault has described these inner control mechanisms in his thoughts on discipline and punishment. This control does not remain on a personal level; rather, it becomes embedded into discourses, such as the discourse of feminist economics. Throughout the course of my search for escapes from the dominant discourse in feminist economics I found that concrete recommendations for a new world, or model worlds which are not yet realized but can be seen as alternatives worth working for, are rare. One of the few explicit expressions of a yearning for imagination in feminist economics stems from Drucilla Barker:

> Recognition of the contingent nature of knowledge can free us from dogmatic attachments and thus free us to imagine different possibilities. In the face of the ongoing globalization of capital and celebrations of the inevitably of "free" market capitalism, the freedom and ability to imagine alternatives is sorely needed.
>
> (Barker 2000: 7)

This void and the lack of imagination for the place that can be inhabited by the future's children seem to be key problems in the feminist emancipation movement, not because of a certain lack of creativity, which the great feminist utopias have demonstrated, but rather due to the powerful workings of the dominant discourse that marginalizes any alternatives, for instance by drowning them in sound, as Haraway might say. Whether "good marketing," which I addressed in Chapter 4, can solve that problem is questionable if one agrees with Foucault; however, this still remains to be seen. It is a fact that, at one point, socialist utopias were installed as political reality, or, for example, in the case of the utopian project of Neoliberalism, which I will discuss in Chapter 8.

Change a system from within

One strategy for creating change is to try and change a system from within. This is reflected in the strategy of establishing a critical mass (usually one-third of a certain group). An example would be if one-third of a government consisted of feminist politicians working to enhance feminist goals, or if a large numbers of Marxists worked for the World Bank, thus changing the institution from within. In this sense, feminist economics not only works to change the discipline of economics from within; more radically speaking, feminist economics could be a faction of a feminist movement for changing the sciences from within, for preparing a new paradigm change, for replacing Enlightenment thinking and positivism with other methods of constructing knowledge, which may lead to different power relations and, generally, a shift in priorities worldwide. Thus far, success for feminist economics has not been that prominent and some may claim that this is due to the fact that feminist economics has not yet achieved a strong enough voice and that the critical mass has not been established. My inquiry focuses on the question whether these might not be the only reasons.

Erosion through privilege

On a more pessimistic (realistic?) note, Drucilla Barker reminds us that Foucault has argued that unitary discourse is always willing to recolonize historical knowledge. In the case of feminist economics the connection to mainstream economics and its methodology may allow the mainstream economic discourse to appropriate it (Barker 2007). An example of this appropriation is the justification of the World Bank's engendering development strategy with (liberal) elements borrowed from feminist economics, for instance the demand for increased labor force participation by women (Barker and Kuiper 2006).

Not aiming for a paradigm change?

Another gnawing suggestion that sneaks up on me in this line of thinking is: Maybe feminist economics does not really aim to create a paradigm shift, neither in economics nor in epistemology. An indicator that unfortunately supports this suspicion is illustrated in the following personal experience: In January 2007, the Austrian Feminist Economists organization met for their annual convention. The conference papers presented (in chronological order) were: "Competition and the gender wage gap: a cross-country, time-series analysis" (Martina Zweimüller), "The gender gap in top corporate jobs is still there" (B. Burcin Yurtoglu and Christine Zulehner), "Segregation und gläserne Decke als Stolpersteine weiblicher Erwerbskarrieren"[2] (Birgit Friedl and Margareta Kreimer), "Back to the roots: österreichische Ökonominnen vor 1945"[3] (Christa Schlager and Gabriele Michalitsch), "Bargaining in the family" (Raffaela Hyee), "Gender salience in electronic negotiations" (Sabine Koeszegi), "Gender Budgeting als Beitrag zur Demokratisierung europäischer Wirtschaftspolitik?"[4] (Elisabeth Klatzer and Katharina Mader), "Gender Budgeting in Theorie und Praxis: das Beispiel Oberösterreich"[5] (Margit Schratzenstaller). This adds up to two presentations on wage gaps and careers, two papers on game theory and intra-household bargaining, two on budget policy (changing government spending from within), and one presentation on epistemology, i.e. the annihilation of feminist knowledge production. The audience consisted of Austria's heterodox and feminist economists and interested students. A wide discussion on the methodology and modeling techniques followed each of the six empiricist (add women and stir) presentations; the second stream of discussions was about lamenting over the problems of managing employment and childcare in heterosexual partnerships and how to deal with these difficulties when aiming for a career in economics in academia. Michalitsch's and Schlager's presentation on the history of thought of Austrian women economists (the contents of which are described in Chapter 4) was followed by a very brief discussion and only two questions were raised. (I raised one of the comments and the other came from my dissertation supervisor, who had been asked to elaborate on one of the subjects presented at the meeting.) The unresponsiveness of the rest of the audience made the lack of interest in the topic explicit, with them emitting a wave of boredom and annoyance. On my behalf, I felt uninterested in the economic modeling techniques displayed, alienated by the talk of heterosexual family problems, and disturbed by the elitist stance of the career-networking. I left early feeling that I had lost part of my scientific community of choice.

Regarding the abovementioned experience, I asked myself whether it could really be true that feminist economics is mostly just a career-enhancing network for women economists? Drucilla Barker writes that feminist economists enjoy the prestige of neoclassical economics while at the same time attempting to bend its methodological commitments to anti-sexist, anti-racist, and anti-national ends (Barker 2007). The place this dilemma leads will be described through examining feminist economists' definitions of feminist economics and searching for the goals they set for the discipline.

Feminist economics and utopia: voices from two generations

The collection *Engendering Economics: Conversations with Women Economists in the United States* by Paulette Olson and Zohreh Emami (2002) is a natural piece in which to look for the opinions of the older generation of feminist economists regarding utopia. Olson and Emami put together a study of the sociology of women in the economics profession and the contributions made by women economists. They interviewed eleven female economists who received their doctorates in the U.S. between 1950 and 1975. The questions ranged from family genealogy to their life as students of economics and as professional economists. They were interviewed on their perspectives, major areas of work, gender specific experiences in the discipline, and the like. A few questions were about feminism and economics; some explicitly addressed the respondents' beliefs in the future developments of feminist economics. Here are some of the answers of those much renounced feminist economists, which are related to my research:

Marianne Ferber believes that feminist economics, along with heterodox economic approaches, will be able to broaden and soften economics as a discipline. She argues for opening up feminist economics to people of other disciplines. Her colleague Lois Banfill Shaw also argues for feminist economists to form strong alliances with others who question "the market" in order to change the economics profession. Barbara Bergmann on the other hand argues that feminist economics needs to work much more on practical issues and less on theoretical ones. She believes that neoclassical economics, if adjusted adequately, will be beneficial for everyone. Lourdes Benería thinks that there are many areas in which feminist economists can continue to make theoretical contributions: the care economy, the connection between paid and unpaid work, the establishment of a theory of rights and obligations that can be used to distribute responsibilities, the creation of a welfare economics that is tied to a notion of economic justice, the connections between efficiency and equality, and the nature of markets and capitalism. However, she also believes that feminist economists need to get more involved with the profession, not only on theoretical issues, but also in policy. She says that feminist economics needs to incorporate feminist agendas and methods into specialized areas in addition to general theorizing, and she also warns that the goal of attaining gender equality is insufficient if it is isolated and not contextualized within the wider objectives of human development. In that volume Myra Strober gives the most utopian advice for feminist economics in the future:

> What needs to be done in the next few years is to come up with an alternative paradigm in economics. We will not bury neoclassical economics until we can replace it with something. I am excited about working on that "something." How will we theorize not only how individuals make themselves better off, but also how we as a community,

> indeed a set of communities, make ourselves better off and sustain the planet?
>
> (Strober, in Olson and Emami 2002: 158)

This is a very exciting project indeed, but no further clues on the "something" could be found in the interviews. The voices of the women economists from the older generation as recorded in Olson and Emami's collection are very diverse. Not all women interviewed were feminists; some of those who were feminists still trusted in neoclassical economics. It would be interesting to look into a collection of views of the younger generation of feminist economists, as the voices of our young male colleagues have also been included in Arjo Klamer's projects, but the like is still missing for feminist economics.

Instead, I have looked for some examples of definitions from some younger generation "femeconers" and found that the question of age seems rather irrelevant. For example, Australian scholar Gillian Hewitson relies on Myra Strober's work. When she defines feminist economics, she cites a more recent piece by Strober, titled "Feminist Economics: What's It All About":

> [Feminist economics is] a rethinking of the discipline of economics for the purpose of improving women's economic condition.
>
> (Strober 1995, in Hewitson 1999: 6)

Another example of a definition and also the goals of feminist economics comes from Europe. Dutch authors Edith Kuiper and Jolande Sap define feminist economics in their very prominent collection *Out of the Margin: Feminist Perspectives on Economics* as follows:

> Feminist economists believe that uncovering the gender biases in economics is a necessary prelude to constructing an economics which can encompass the perspectives and embody the realities of both women and men.
>
> (Kuiper and Sap 1995: 4)

U.S. scholar Janet A. Seiz defines the central tasks of feminist economics as:

> (a) To counter "untruths" promulgated by economists (and other) that serve to legitimize the oppression of women (and other groups); and (b) to produce better "truer" accounts of the world that can help us understand the workings of – and eliminate – unjust social relations. ... In our effort to produce better accounts of economic reality, feminists also need to examine the history, the methods, and the "rhetoric" of economic discourse.
>
> (Seitz, in Robeyns 2000: 3)

Hewitson defines feminist economics as follows, which brings feminist economics closer to the political implications of economic theory, where the key issue of the feminist movement is to improve the real-life conditions of women compared to those of men:

> feminist economics can be preliminary defined as an independent research programme (rather than merely an arm of neoclassical labour economics), which has as its primary goal the advancement of understandings of the disadvantaged economic conditions for women. This aim is revealed by most recent definitions of the field, definitions which identify the content and/or the methodology of neoclassical economics as androcentric or masculine and feminist economists as those who wish to eliminate this androcentrism.
>
> (Hewitson 1999: 6)

Given these definitions, it clearly seems as if there was more to feminist economics than careers and women's networks. A core issue of the problem given the wholehearted goals of femeconers seems to be manifested in the issues of what is worked on and which methodology is used. While the workshop I criticized so bitterly earlier on in this chapter may have been set up in "good feminist intent," the actual contents clearly supported mainstream economics either by only "adding women and stirring" or by not challenging the status quo. My next step in this project will lead me to look into utopian moments in feminist economic theory. First of all, I will re-read the above definitions from the perspective of researching utopia and look for alternative thoughts. Second, I will look to the journal *Feminist Economics* for some more answers. More precisely, I will look at the self-proclaimed goals of the journal, employ a quantitative method, and count issues discussed and the methodologies employed. Third, I will use a qualitative approach and analyze the few articles that directly discuss utopian issues. Finally, I will examine indicators of possible ways to go.

I will now direct my focus to the definitions. It is most interesting to see the degrees of utopian potential displayed (or rather not displayed) in those three definitions. Strober's definition is the one most open to the creative potential of feminist economics as a source of non-androcentric future social contracts ("rethinking ... for the purpose of improving"), where rethinking might very well include the re-creation of an alternative. Kuiper and Sap take away some of the creative potential of feminist economics by defining the discipline's purpose as "uncovering gender biases" as a "prelude to construction" of a different gender-neutral economics. Note that feminist economics itself is not seen as the place where this new economics will be constructed, but also that the work of feminist economics will only allow room for such a place and creative force. In contrast, Seitz deems uncovering and reproduction to be equally important concepts, listing them after each other, but not necessarily implying that one needs to come after the other. Hewitson's poststructuralist definition is very interesting. At first reading I thought it placed feminist economics' goal just as the advancement of "understanding the disadvantaged economic conditions for women." And apart from this one goal, which has been identified as the primary aim, she does not list any other goals, but by indicating that there may be other less important goals she implies that there indeed are others. I cannot make out a creative potential in this description of feminist economics per se; not even the necessity for feminist economics to serve as a preliminary tool for a coming change is expressively implied, as was the case with the previously discussed definitions. Poststructuralist approaches are often criticized for being removed from the battlefield of everyday power struggles. But the very last element of Hewitson's quotation is indeed quite powerful. She says that the purpose of feminist economics is to "identify ... feminist economists as those who wish to eliminate this androcentrism" (Hewitson 1999: 6). Now that the clash of interests has been clearly identified, this leads to the question how feminist economists will set out to eliminate androcentric structures. For example, an interesting question is how feminist economics deals with the issue of discrimination as a result of a power struggle. A lot of feminist economics seems to be busy proving that damage is indeed being done or developing ideas to service victims of androcentrism, cleaning up the debris of the power struggle, i.e. earnings inequalities, time distribution for care work, etc. Other feminist economists are busy deconstructing androcentrism in economic theory. Rarely is there a direct approach to the problem of power in feminist economics such as is given in Drucilla Barker's paper "Women, Knowledge and Power: Methodological Challenges in Feminist Economics".

> An explicit consideration of power is necessary in order to understand the disparity between the social, cultural and political authority enjoyed by mainstream economics and its manifest failings as a science.
>
> (Barker 2000: 7)

I regard this approach as a very useful strategy. Neglecting dimensions of power in a Foucauldian sense results in an incomplete analysis. I am interested in how the power dimension is regarded in feminist economics' publications. In the following sections I start with a focus on providing an overview of the strategies and approaches in feminist economics by analyzing the discipline's journal *Feminist Economics.*

The *Feminist Economics* example

Here, I look at a larger sample than the personal experience I have mentioned above in order to analyze the working methods of feminist economics projects. As part of my dissertation I have analyzed the journal *Feminist Economics.* I categorized eight years, i.e. 24 journals with a rough average of 10 articles each (from the founding year 1995 until 2002). In the first place I sought to locate utopian stances, yet the overall picture that emerged here also largely corresponds with my personal experience mentioned earlier. I also agree with Drucilla Barker that distinctions between liberal and socialist feminist economics have indeed become blurred (Barker 2005). Also, the feminist economics that is actually employed in anti-racist and, even more so, in anti-national work is very rare, but let me describe my findings in a more systematic manner.

Previous to the analysis, I found it interesting to look at the self-proclaimed goals of the journal's publishers. In the wonderfully uplifting editorial for the first issue of *Feminist Economics* in spring 1995, Diana Strassmann describes the endeavor of the publication primarily as enhancing the communication process amongst feminist economists. She says:

> In founding Feminist Economics our intent is to enable new and important economic conversations to flourish. … Feminist Economics will welcome contributions from diverse scholars, particularly those who have been previously excluded or underrepresented in economics conversations. These include scholars from countries in the South and persons of color as well as scholars from other disciplines and intellectual traditions.
>
> (Strassmann 1995: 1)

Note that this statement suggests a great openness to issues and contributors and certainly also in communication style, but that my marginal position is not addressed. Does this mean that queer feminist economists are not invited? Or is it simply another intellectual tradition I am coming from? Maybe I should not be so picky; the invitation to converse is extended to all feminists and does not seek to exclude anyone:

> In recognition of the diversity of feminist thought, the journal will claim no one definition of feminism, and will welcome the multiplicity of feminisms currently present in economics as well as those that may emerge when new voices are drawn into this forum.
>
> (Strassmann 1995: 2)

Thus, does queer and lesbian theory count as feminist? Obviously it does, even though it is not explicitly mentioned here. *Feminist Economics* has devoted much space to lesbian and gay research. Overall, aside from my critique, the journal's opening seems to indicate a desire to create new theory, new feminisms, maybe also new paradigms. The goals of the communication process are various and thus entail a utopian undertone, as Strassmann envisions that

> current understandings of what counts as feminist and what counts as economics may change. New theories, some perhaps not even imaginable

> to current participants, may emerge as part of a new and more feminist economics.
>
> (Strassmann 1995: 2)

Strassmann points out the necessity to think the unimaginable, the utopian. Herein Strassmann offers a perfect synthesis in the sense of Burwell, who argued that discourses on social transformation need to follow two strategic approaches: one of them seeking to envision a radical, qualitative break from existing conditions (the utopian), the other based on deconstructing society's claim to unity and legitimacy (the exposure), as was described in the Introduction.

Furthermore, Strassmann stresses the wish to pay attention to power differences between those privileged feminist economists who have the means to publish in a magazine such as *Feminist Economics*, when she states:

> So long as the processes which select and train future economists prevent people with certain experiential and social positions from participating in economic conversations, we must keep in mind that most critical of feminist insights: the relationship between power and knowledge. We who are privileged as current participants in these debates must take care not to abuse our own power.
>
> (Strassmann 1995: 2)

She adds that "many feminists have questioned mainstream economic (and feminist) theoretical edifices predicated on the implicit assumption of the universality of Western lives and perspectives, edifices that neglect the lives and productive contributions of women, men, and children around the world" (Strassmann 1995: 3). This highly ambitious goal to be as inclusive as possible is kept up very well in the journal, as can be seen from the list of published authors' national and cultural backgrounds.

A central issue for *Feminist Economics* is to point out gender bias in the historical construction of disciplinary categories in relation to the composition and other features of communities of economic practice. Another one is to investigate the ways in which important contributions by women, who have been present in economics since its inception, have been lost, disregarded, or pushed into other disciplines:

1 *Feminist Economics* is supposed to question the objectivity of economic methodology and rhetoric by often applying insights from other intellectual traditions (such as philosophy, feminist theory, and cultural studies).
2 Another area of concern is economic education, with its racial and gender bias in disciplinary training and socialization practices, and its biased disciplinary conventions in publication, employment, and promotion practices, all of which serve to reproduce the current disciplinary hierarchy (Strassmann 1995).

Another connection where the utopian impulse can be found to be more pronounced is the aspiration to promote feminist economic policies. Strassmann clarifies that as long as feminist ideas remain neglected by those with disciplinary power, feminist policy recommendations stand a much lower chance of implementation. She lists the topics of relevance for implementation by feminist economics in order to overcome the dominance of the interests of (adult) men. They include: welfare reform, childcare, family planning, economic development, structural adjustment, domestic abuse, sexual harassment, discrimination, affirmative action, pay equity, family leave, and the feminization of poverty. In this regard, Strassmann's conclusion is most important, as she states that *Feminist Economics* will provide an important site for the nurturance and development of more broadly compelling and useful ideas, and that, in doing so, *Feminist Economics* can be a catalyst for change rather than just a career-enhancing medium (Strassmann 1995).

To explore whether the journal was able to keep its promises in its first eight years, I developed a grid based on Diana Strassmann's register to count the issues covered and methodologies used in the articles published in the journal. The issues I have identified are as follows:

1 *Welfare*: This segment comprises issues related to welfare reform, social security provision, unemployment insurance, maternity benefits, pensions, tax-based measures, distribution, etc.
2 *Childcare, housework, and caring labor*: This is mostly concerned with issues surrounding unpaid work in the home.
3 *Family planning*: This covers issues related to population growth and decisions about procreation.
4 *Development*: This segment relates to international inequality, strategies of "Third World countries" to catch up, gendered implications of Structural Adjustment Programs (SAPs) of the International Monetary Fund (IMF), etc.
5 *Education*: This section is concerned with economic effects of education, but also specifically with education in the discipline of economics.
6 *Discrimination and affirmative action*: This points out and theorizes discrimination and affirmative strategies for change.
7 *Pay equity and the (paid) labor market*: This covers inequality of wages for men and women and working conditions.
8 *Poverty*: This covers the feminization of poverty, as well as gender differences in wealth and poverty.
9 *History of economic thought, neoclassical and heterodox economic theory*: This section is concerned with feminist views on current and past economic theories and their implications for women.
10 *Queer economics*: This covers the economic implications of same-sex orientation in all instances of life (family, education, working life, partnership, etc.).

11 *Theory of the family*: This covers concepts of the heterosexual, nuclear family, marriage, and inter-family bargaining.
12 *Race and class*: This covers economic interrogations concerning racial differences and class issues.

The second layer of categorization is based on an expanded version of Gillian Hewitson's categorization, organizing the methodological approaches in *Feminist Economics*:

Epistemology
Quantitative
A – *Empirical*: data collection and interpretation (e.g. wage disparity in migrant women's groups etc.)
M – *Modeling*: creating a (mathematical) model to explain and predict (e.g. gendered effects of financial crisis etc.)
E – *Empiricist*: "add women and stir" and critique of New Home Economics.
FEM – *Feminist practice – Qualitative*
C – *Critical*: general, narrative critique of specific issues (e.g. welfare reforms etc.)
F – *Reflective*: reflection on feminist economic theory
P – *Practical*: offering practical solutions to specific problems
Q – *Questioning Knowledge Production*: *hermeneutic, discourse analysis*
Approaches considering power relations, biases due to standpoints, linguistic turns concealing scientific weaknesses, etc. have been subsumed as "constructivist/deconstructive." Those strategies include at least the following approaches:
c – *Constructive*:
e.g. Feminist Standpoint Theory or, for example, the "gender/value compass" approach
d – *Deconstructive*:
 r – *Rhetoric of economics approach*
 po – *Poststructuralist, postcolonial, and postmodern approaches*
 Considering the tensions between power and knowledge
U – *Utopian*: creatively envisioning radical change

Certainly, it is possible that more than one approach is employed. Hybrid forms and multiple strategies are common. It could be argued that the utopian approach is part of category *d*. For the course of this analysis with its specific focus, however, a singled-out perspective provides clearer outcomes. In previous chapters I have described feminism as utopian per se. Therefore, all approaches of feminism in *Feminist Economics* could be regarded as utopian to some degree. Nevertheless, is it essential to state that a utopian approach envisions a radical alternative to the current status quo. Utopianism may be measured by the degree of radicalism of the envisioned alternative as well as by the creative potential of the vision itself. While deconstruction is an absolutely necessary feminist approach, I have argued in Chapter 1 that it is not fully effective without the utopian envisioning process, and vice versa. The list of approaches employed in Feminist Economics includes one explicit utopian strategy, while all other approaches are tentatively arranged according to their utopian potential, i.e. in the definition above the practical approach is seen as more utopian than the empirical approach.

In this study I analyzed approximately 240 articles, among which are articles that are counted twice or more, since the emphasis here is not on the number of articles but on the (often multiple) approaches within articles of the publication.

Outcomes of classification

Once all the contributions, methods, and issues are counted, the output can be represented in a diagram (Figure 6.1). Looking at Figure 6.1 it is obvious that the dominant issue in *Feminist Economics* is issue number 9 (99 counts), an involvement with neoclassical and heterodox economic theory (from a feminist point of view). The issue with the second highest number is number 7 (63 counts), on the labor market, equal pay, etc., followed by issue number 2 (49 counts), on unpaid labor in the household, care, and childcare. The issues with the fewest occurrences are numbers 3 (6 counts) and 6 (10 counts), on "family planning" and "discrimination and affirmative action." If these issues only appear less relevant, it could also be the case that they have somewhat been subsumed under issues number 2 and 7, respectively. The issue with the third fewest occurrences is "Queer Economics" (number 10, with 14 counts).

Concerning methodology and approaches, the critical approach (C) is the approach most often applied (112 counts), followed by the empirical approach (A, 96 counts) and the reflective feminist approach (F, 53 counts). This outcome is not surprising, as the definition "critical" is highly inclusive to begin with, and, second, it is the most straightforward approach. The "safe," descriptive character most likely accounts for the strong result regarding the empirical approach, as the overall subject itself somewhat demands reflection on feminist economics.

What I had subsumed under category Q (questioning knowledge production) appears most often in the issue of the history of economic thought (15 counts), which is not even half as often as the issues of wages and care (6 counts), but proportionally quite often with the issues race and class (4 counts), which are, as I understand it, surprisingly rare in queer issues. The utopian approach (U) was used less than any other approach (18 counts), followed by the practical approach (P, 19 counts). The utopian approach was most used in discussing economic theory in issue number 9, followed by issue number 2, on unpaid work in the home (see Figure 6.2). Looking

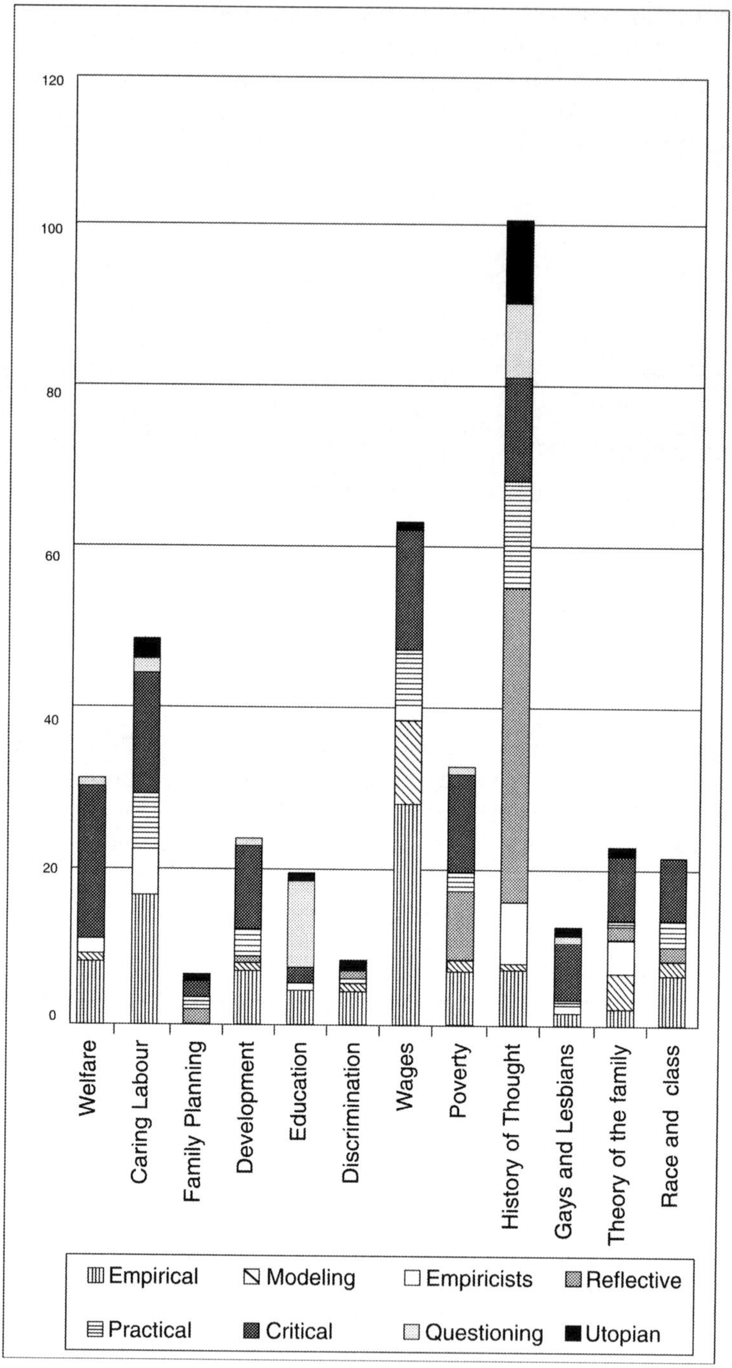

Figure 6.1 Issues and methodology in Feminist Economics.

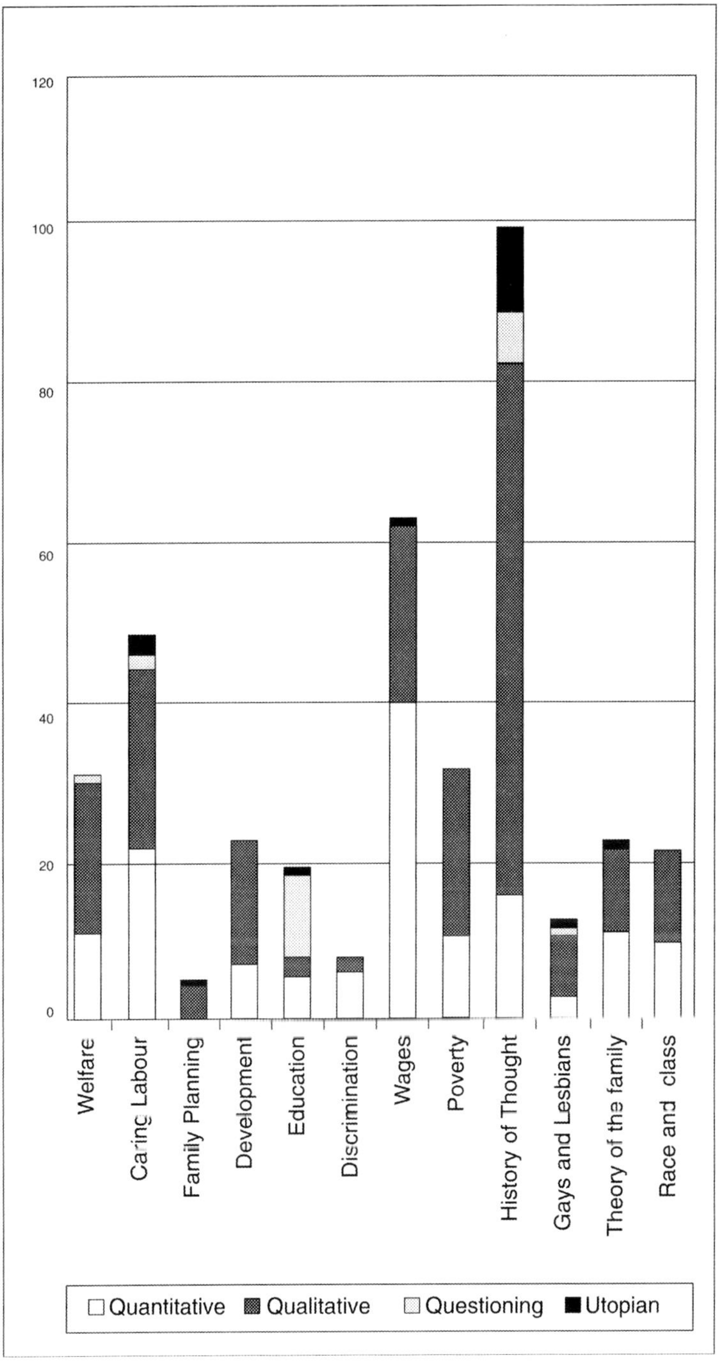

Figure 6.2 Issues and approaches in Feminist Economics.

only at the larger categorizations, it is quite clear that the strictly empirical (positivist) approaches take up most of the content in issues related to wages and caring labor. The largest bar is included in the issue on the history of thought and is a combination of feminist practical approaches, comprising reflection, largely on feminist economics as such, critical issues, and practical recommendations. Epistemological questioning is the second smallest category following the utopian, and it is most frequently mentioned in connection with the history of thought and education. The utopian stance is also most successful in the history of thought and caring labor. It seems as if women in caring labor are most inclined to imagine alternatives to the usual routines of childcare and unpaid reproductive work.

My research on the journal *Feminist Economics* shows that the utopian approach is clearly not a priority in *Feminist Economics*, but an approach that ranked last. Nevertheless, utopian visions or utopian approaches were explicitly mentioned in some journal articles. In the next section I discuss the articles that are concerned with utopian visions and/or approaches in order to find out why a utopian approach might have been employed, how it was used, and to what effect.

Utopian theory reflected in the journal *Feminist Economics*

The following is a qualitative intertextual study of the works in *Feminist Economics* that contain content which directly engages with utopian theory of the past and its implications for current feminist economics. Using five examples I will show how these considerations may be relevant for feminist economics.

Saint-Simonean feminism

The first stream of reasoning with the utopian approach in *Feminist Economics* deals with utopianism in the history of economic thought and its implications for current feminist economics. In "Saint-Simonean Feminism,"[6] Evelyn Forget describes what she calls a preoccupation with the social and economic roles of women by Saint-Simon's followers. Forget's analysis of past utopianism points out some very interesting phenomena with a connection to current feminist thought and strategies. Forget focuses on the events and persons surrounding Enfantin, a leader in the Saint-Simonean movement in the 1830s. Enfantin and his followers believed that women should be barred from the public sphere in order to protect them from the hardships of the evil world surrounding them, which resulted in women being eliminated from the Saint-Simonean hierarchy by 1831. Forget claims that this exclusion was justified by an "increasingly utopian and abstract theory," which claimed that women would only regain their status as distinct but equal to men in the new utopian world once it was established. Forget points out the sexist, discriminating effects these parts of the utopian movement in Saint-Simoneanism had on women, thus providing an example of the restrictions imposed on certain groups within a utopian movement, in this case women. This is very similar to the arguments previously mentioned in discussing Marxism and feminism.

Forget does not stop at this point in her example. She continues by recalling the reactions of the women who were eliminated from the "official part" of the utopian movement. A group of women founded a newspaper, which served as a center for a separate organization that aimed to help create equal political and economic rights for women. The women concentrated on reform of their existing policy, rather than utopian theory for future times. Forget then compares the strategies of the male Saint-Simonean utopians with their theoretical focus, and the practical struggles of their female counterparts with the contemporary disputes in feminist economics.

Forget stresses the point that it is entirely beneficial to study the history of utopianism in order to learn something about current goings-on in feminist economics and the relevance of utopian thought. Nevertheless, Forget argues that all the Saint-Simonean theorists were male, and that they created an analysis that was so abstract it became divorced from any real social issues, while the women of the movement were concerned with pragmatic issues that were focused on the rights and opportunities of individual women. On the other hand, Forget explains that it was difficult for the Saint-Simonean women to keep up their energy, since they lacked a unifying theory and commitment to theoretical development and therefore did not last as an individual movement.

In more detail, the dispute between Enfantin and the women followers of Saint-Simon revolved around arguments for excluding women from the public sphere that were based on religion and utopian theory:

> women were to be protected from the hardening influence of the contemporary world that would corrupt their God-given nature, until universal association was achieved (that is until the new society was fully in place). Women would play an equal political, economic, and social role only when war and slavery were abolished, the conjugal union perfected, the condition of the most numerous and poorest class ameliorated and all human beings associated into a single family.
>
> (Forget 2001: 85)

It does not sound as if that point in time would come along soon, really. Nevertheless, it was planned for women to have active roles in the new society, since together a man and a woman would "constitute an appropriate mix of attributes required to usher in the new age" (Forget 2001: 85). The social system in that new age was to be based on marriage, which was a very different stance than that in the theories of Fourier, a contemporary of Saint-Simon. A fundamental assumption concerned benevolence in the family. (Enfantin later introduced the notion of natural monogamy mainly for the women of the movement and natural non-monogamy mainly for the men in the community. He himself was declared "Father of Humanity" and disciples were sent out to find the "Female Messiah" who would make him complete.) Even though these later developments sound a bit absurd, the case study of the Saint-Simoneans nevertheless serves its purpose, since women's lives were affected by changes in the male leadership, which barred them from being leaders in the hierarchy as they were used to being before. Unable to simply recreate their own movements with their own hierarchies, they founded a newspaper to publish articles only by women, and they reached a consensus that women's condition needed to be improved in the present. Politics replaced Enfantin's mysticism. They argued for education, new marriage laws, and the right to work. They founded an institution to educate women and moved right into practical work. A strong belief in their success rested on working in association with other women, separately from men.

Forget analyses Saint-Simonean feminism in the context of early nineteenth-century economics, in which she relies on the work of Nancy Folbre and Michèle Pujol, which I have quoted in previous chapters. Forget manages to provide a condensed, comprehensive picture of utopianism and feminism, mentioning the role of Owen, the Mills, Thompson and Wheeler, and Say.

Forget describes the Saint-Simonean example as the most important parallel to current economics based on the theoretical grounding of society on the embedding of individuals in social networks. The male/female couple was envisioned as the basic social unit and benevolence was argued to rule the family at home; all society was thought to be reconstructed so that this very benevolence could be extended to the whole of society. The only price to pay while waiting for that transformation was to be paid by women, who would be required to stay in the home until equal rights could be extended to include them. Forget argues that French women thankfully did not comply with these requests.

Forget's paper is a prime example of the workings of power mechanisms that control discourses and prevent the spread of alternative forms of thought. The paper very thoroughly shows the strategies women tried to employ to overcome these restrictions: starting up a paper of their own and providing education. That sounds familiar.

"The Market for Virtue: Jean-Baptiste Say on Women in the Economy and Society"

In an earlier article, "The Market for Virtue: Jean-Baptiste Say on Women in the Economy and Society,"[7] Evelyn Forget argues that certain visions – namely those of J.B. Say concerning women and their roles in society and the economy, which were written during a political revolution and include women demanding their right to emancipation – are still influential in contemporary economics. Forget chooses Say's gender analysis for the purpose of critique, not because it is particularly unique or original, but because it is explicit and

> through Say's economic writing ... this vision of the place of women in society and the economy began to be naturalized into nineteenth century economic analysis. The slowness with which feminist analysis has made inroads into economic theory suggests the power of that vision.
> (Forget 1997: 96)

Forget argues once again that male theorists' utopian visions have not only harmed women but also proven extremely powerful and long lived.

The specific vision she is concerned with here is the one in which women should specialize in their "natural" (and unpaid) careers as wives and mothers. She opens her tale with a description of Claire Lacombe's and Pauline Léon's revolutionary women's club (Société Républicaines-Révolutionnaires), which was founded in 1793. The women supported the Jacobins but later that year women's clubs were outlawed by the deputies of the Convention. The justification given was that it was "unnatural" for women to demand equal rights and abandon their household tasks. Women were easily silenced. Olympe de Gouges had already been guillotined, and Robespierre's terror regime had stopped feminist demands. Then Napoleon came to power and the Napoleonic Code was enacted. Forget nevertheless places Say's vision of women as housewives and mothers in context with the short-lived but powerful women's movement during the time of the revolution. She believes that Say's analysis sacrificed women's independent existence for the greater good of social and political stability.

Say's vision is described in *Olbie*, an explicitly utopian work portraying the ideal republican society in an imaginary nation which has just survived a revolution. In *Olbie* women find their place in marriage and the home, where they are responsible for maintaining the patriarchal family. Women who demand more from life are degraded as an undesirable "third sex." Women are to be kept at home, because they are eternally "gentle" beings who need to be spared the "disgusting occupations men undertake." Since Say recognized that work is essential for women of the poorer classes, he argued that certain professions, such as dressmaking, hairdressing, and cooking, should be reserved for women. Certainly, women's wages were lower than men's, as men's salaries were meant to feed whole families, whereas women's salaries were only needed to feed themselves if they were unlucky enough to not find a husband. Say was the first to adapt the analogy between firms and families, and between captains of industry and fathers. Say explicitly developed the notion that firms and families are the fundamental units of economic analysis. Later economists gladly picked up this notion, which came to be manifested in Becker's New Home Economics (Forget 1997):

> In the family, all the means of subsistence come from the father; it is in his head that all useful thoughts are born; it is he that procures capital; it is he that works and directs the work of his children, who raises them, who sees to their establishment.
>
> (Say, in Forget 1997: 108)

Forget concludes that the analysis of gender Say articulated in *Olbie* functioned as the foundation for nineteenth-century analyses, such as those on the "natural wage" of women being lower than men's, the argument for separate work spheres for men and women, on closing professions to women, and herding women to stay in the home, where they remained to produce (unproductively) all through economic theory up until today. Forget argues that Say's vision made sense in the historical context of revolution, in which he tried to save society as he knew it by sacrificing women, and she continues by arguing that it is essential to uncover the historical context and see that certain realities that were necessary at the time they were established via economic visions and theory may no longer be necessary in current times:

> The analysis survives and develops, even when its social context changes. When we lose sight of the precipitating events and the historical period in which theory developed, we also lose awareness of the implicit assumptions upon which that analysis rests. When we recover the history, it becomes easier to expose the assumptions and to challenge the theory.
>
> (Forget 1997: 109)

Forget deconstructs a pillar of economic theory by pointing out its historical context; further on she identifies the outcome for women caused by this theory and argues that this vision turned out to be extremely powerful and harmful to women's emancipation over the centuries. In addition, she does not stop short, but calls for new powerful visions to replace the old:

> It is not helpful to approach current debates about the social roles of men and women and the place of the family in the political economy as though they were new issues. The concern does have a history, and it is, perhaps, in the context of current political debates that economic analysis might integrate a new vision of the ways in which gender is constructed.
>
> (Forget 1997: 109)

This paper is a key example of the historical processes and the repercussions for those (women) who tried to dissent and turn away from what was expected of them. In essence, degradation practices have not changed much since Enfantin's times.

History of thought and utopian notions

In "On work and Idleness,"[8] Regina Gagnier and John Dupré review a number of important historical and everyday conceptions of work, deciding how domestic work, including caring work, should be seen in relation to other kinds of work. In their discourse they refer to concepts of work, starting with Adam Smith's theories. They then quote the Owenites as a contrasting conception. Where Smith stated that work is clearly the "toil and trouble we expend for goods," the Owenites rejected wage labor and made no theoretical distinction after the initial act of birthing between housework and other work, between work performed by men and work performed by women. What is interesting in this article is that throughout the piece the authors repeatedly return to the example of the Owenites to counter or support the theories and arguments that have become mainstream economic theory as we know it today. Given the historical context, it becomes quite plausible that different basic, now marginalized utopian paradigms might have become mainstream thinking, instead of the ones that are now mainstream.

"Why Feminist, Marxist, and Anti Racist Economics should be Feminist-Marxist-Anti-Racist Economics," by Julie Matthai,[9] is another paper that works with the history of economic thought and utopia. Matthai's piece engages the dispute between Marx and his utopian predecessors. She extends the previously described argument and amends that Marx not only attacked the Owenites, Saint-Simoneans, Fourier's followers, etc., but also attacked socialist feminists as "utopian." Nevertheless, Marx's belief in the "new economic man" who was less selfish and more cooperative does seem somewhat utopian today. I will be talking about this more in Chapter 8.

Other articles in *Feminist Economics* pick up precisely where Forget left off. Therese Jefferson and John King, in "Never Intended to Be a Theory of Everything: Domestic Labor in Neoclassical and Marxian Economics,"[10] provide a comparative study of domestic labor by neoclassical and Marxian economists. They discuss Gary Becker's New Home Economics as well as the findings of Marxian feminists. In the course of their argument, they also quote Charlotte Perkins Gilman. While Pigou defined national income merely as the value of the production of all goods and services measurable with money, Gilman always defied this exclusionary trend. Gilman's argument for accounting for the work in the home and her views on efficiency, as has been discussed before, are mentioned in their paper. The reluctance to regard her work as economics by mainstream or Marxian analysis is stated, but Gilman's striving for the utopian, the alternative, finds no mention in the article.

Resurfacing of Charlotte Perkins Gilman's work

In Frances Woolley's "Getting the Better of Becker"[11] the author points out strategies for reclaiming the economic discourse on the family back from

Becker's New Home Economics. Woolley advises first taking what is useful from Becker's analysis and then utilizing the theory to advocate policies for improving women's condition while discarding the rest; second, she suggests developing alternatives to Becker's analysis; and, third, she claims the features of the economic profession that led to the acceptance of Becker's conclusions must be uncovered and changed. (The third issue here has, for example, been dealt with in Forget's work on Say.) Woolley also returns to Charlotte Perkins Gilman on that account. Like Staveren she states that Gilman's *Women and Economics* (1898) contained some of the ideas that are found in Becker's work. Gilman wrote:

> He is the market, the demand. She is the supply. And with the best intentions the mother serves her child's economic advantage by preparing her for the market. This is an excellent instance.
>
> (Gilman, in Woolley 1996: 116)

This is clearly the same analogy Becker uses. Only where Becker celebrates this as the perfect natural way in which gender relations (in the family) should be run, Gilman concludes:

> It is most common. It is most evil. It is plainly traceable to our sexuo-economic relation.
>
> (Gilman, in Woolley 1996: 117)

Woolley also notes that Gilman's theoretical work is rarely mentioned in mainstream economic theory and, as has been stated before, her utopian novel *Herland* was not even published as a complete work till the 1970s. The slight distortion of Gilman's argument that the family should *not* work like a mirror-image of a firm on the market turned into Becker's New Home Economics, where this analogy is considered desirable and an ongoing phenomenon in the history of the theory of the family. The original creators of home economics, Margaret Reid, Hazel Kyrk, and Elizabeth Hoyt, all emphasized the importance of time in household production starting in the 1920s. All three women argued that market failures need to be met by consumer education and government measures, addressing issues such as income distribution, the status of women, the concept of value in economics, and the measurement of the standard of living only in monetary terms. They placed the household and its economic role in a larger social context, ideas which were lost along the way to Becker's New Home Economics (Woolley 1996):

> If Margaret Reid was right, the current system of national accounting is wrong. While several countries have begun to systematically collect data on time use and household consumption that will help draw a larger and more accurate picture of the economy, progress has been quite limited.
>
> (Folbre and Pujol 1996: 121)

Forget's historical example of Enfantin and the distortion of feminist thought by the Saint-Simoneans seems to be a working analogy for this example. The early women scientists who established the theory of the household started their research to improve the economic situation for women. However, the project ended up in a situation in which it was suddenly perfectly justified and natural for women to stay at home and out of the public sphere – all presumably for the better of society as a whole.

Drucilla Barker's "Economists, Social Reformers, and Prophets: A Feminist Critique of Economic Efficiency"[12] also picks up on the argument concerning economic efficiency. Interestingly, Barker sets off in Gilman's tracks, examining the concept of Pareto optimality once more. She aims to shed more light on the implicit assumptions about the nature of human agency, work, and gender. Barker states that the development of the concept in the 1930s was a response to the methodological tensions between the political nature of economics and the scientific aspirations of economists. She points out that an evaluation of this period will uncover some of the values that became embedded in neoclassical economics which are now hidden behind "the masks of mathematics and abstraction." Note that this line of argument is again the same as Forget's, who claimed that historical context entering economic theory should be filtered out in order to examine whether theory is still useful and valid today. Barker compares the rational economic agent to the citizen in the Aristotelian polis. Citizens made up a relatively small portion of the entire population who could vote and participate in the public sphere. It was assumed that these citizens would act in the best interests of those not represented: women, slaves, and children. She sees a parallel in mainstream economics (and therefore in economic models) that only those who actively participate in the market are considered as agents. Having shown this analogy, Barker continues to state that no matter how elegant the concept of Pareto efficiency (as is argued by Amartya Sen) is, it offers little guidance for making policy decisions, taking responsibility for winners and losers. She concludes by arguing that neoclassical economists have been hiding behind the postulate that the efficiency criterion is objective and universal. She claims that it is also a very well-designed instrument for supporting the status quo and the existing distribution of power and income.

A critique of Rawls's Theory of Mutual Disinterest

Frances Woolley's "Degrees of Connection: A Critique of Rawls's Theory of Mutual Disinterest"[13] demonstrates that an "add women and stir" liberal feminist reworking of Rawls's theory cannot be successful. Woolley stresses that bringing reproduction out of the realm of nature and into the social contract necessitates a radical deconstruction and extension of Rawls's theory. By extending the connections between families in the Rawlsian model it becomes clear that sexual reproduction connects different families within the same generation just as it creates connections inside families. The concern for descendants cannot be divorced from the concern for contemporaries. Altruism spreads from one sphere to the other; concern for one's own child creates concern for others who are concerned with that child; altruism extends to the adults child's parents-in-law and to the wider community. One of the insights of feminist analysis is that connections matter. This insight and the plight of a feminist ethics are found to threaten Rawls's theory, as feminist ethics demands an examination of connections across generations, rendering binary family structures more difficult than they might seem (Woolley 2000). This is an interesting approach that might make feminist economics more open in the sense of a queer theory.

In conclusion, it can be said that the few articles in *Feminist Economics* that are concerned with utopian approaches serve the purpose of retelling the story of dominant discourses and their challenges, which mostly end with the unpleasant notion of failure on a larger scale. The other purpose of discussing utopian elements is to reincorporate lost feminist knowledge and apply space to the feminist economic discourse, i.e. a resurfacing of matter from the archives, as discussed in Chapter 4. Finally, the discussion of present alternatives and how they could be incorporated in practice and epistemology are clearly lacking even in the articles concerned with utopian elements.

Alternative feminist economic theory

From the perspective of the utopian researcher the section on alternative theory creation that was compiled in the approach Q (questioning knowledge production) is also quite interesting. A very compelling piece by Drucilla Barker, questioning methodology in feminist economic theory and also proposing new methodological approaches, for instance the interpretive approach, developed by Spike Peterson and reintroduced by Barker, suggests the following:

> Interpretive approaches call on the insights of poststructuralism, postmodernism, and postcolonialism. These insights facilitate critical evaluations of the dialectic between power and knowledge, examine the ways in which the underlying processes of the economy are discursively constituted, and theorize the conceptual as well as the empirical aspects of gender, race, class, sexuality, and nationality.
>
> (Barker 2005: 2,191)

Based on my findings from the first eight years of *Feminist Economics*, engagement with the ontology and epistemology of economic theory and gender is relatively rare. At the time when I was working on competing this book, the latest issue of *Feminist Economics* was issue 4 of volume 12, 2006. The first two articles employ econometrics for researching development issues. Two articles look into wife–husband relationships and households, one in Germany and one linked to African-American migration. The first of the two articles uses modeling techniques to prove a point; the second article is a critical narrative. The fifth article talks about education in a deconstructive manner. The seventh article is on gender in Eastern Europe. I feel this example proves the point that not many of the priorities concerning the issues of research or the methods employed have changed in *Feminist Economics* since 2002, where my first analysis of the journal articles left off. In this last number, econometric and quantitative methods still dominate over methodologically more daring approaches.

The question of where feminist economics should stand methodologically to improve or change the economic science seems a hard question, if not impossible to solve. Where Barker relies on Sandoval, who says that there is no way to step outside of power, of the network of power relations, and find a neutral vantage point for taking an oppositional stand (Barker 2005), there are some methodological suggestions for avoiding the reuse of feminist realizations by the mainstream to re-establish or justify the criticized status quo or to disempower feminist demands, for example in development theories. Drucilla Barker makes the following claim:

> Interpretive approaches add to feminist economic analyses of work because they are able to bridge the discursive and the material. Moreover, deconstructing the category "women" enables us to speak on behalf of women because doing so forces us to consider explicitly the multiple and conflicting intersections of gender, race, class, sexuality, and nation.
>
> This does not mean that all feminist economists must change their research methodologies. The master's tools may be quite useful in dismantling the master's house, but, if we are to use them, we need to interrogate the problematic epistemological and ontological assumptions in which they are grounded. . . . I am advocating a methodological pluralism that will bridge the chasm between materialist and discursive perspectives. Recognizing the constitutive links between representations and the real and between power and knowledge and using gender as a conceptual rather than an empirical category are both strategies that will further the feminist economics project.
>
> (Barker 2005: 2,204)

Although I find Barker's claim fully justified, it should not be forgotten that, as Sargisson reminds us, it is not enough to fully understand issues of power and concealment and bias in science. Much more, an alternative vision also in methodology is needed to steer out of the chasm into which the stream of science has driven feminist economics. But Barker does mention this need elsewhere (Barker 2007).

Reconsidering the parallel development of feminist utopias and feminist economics in the past will help create a space to explore which visions might still be useful/necessary in order to more broadly apply feminist economics to real-life practices, wherein an impulse from the present should not be lacking, provided it is necessary to resituate old knowledge in new contexts and to incorporate the newest findings.

Some contemporary thoughts

It seems as if the current discourse in *Feminist Economics* does not have much to offer towards truly replacing the current status quo. Its issues are largely concerned with repairing problems of patriarchal economics, and its methodology is mostly removed from being able to transcend old paradigms. Even when put into practice, utopian thoughts from the past do not seem powerful enough to steer away from the mainstream canon. Nevertheless, there are some indicators that point in a direction that may promise more radical results. One thought can be found in Michèle Pujol's groundbreaking piece "Into the Margin!" Pujol first points out five elements that are characteristic of neoclassical economists views on women:

> Assumption 1: all women are married and have children or will do so.
> Assumption 2: all women are or ought to be dependent on a male relative.
> Assumption 3: women are or ought to be housewives.
> Assumption 4: women are unproductive in the workforce.
> Assumption 5: women are irrational and cannot make economic decisions.
>
> (Pujol, in Kuiper and Sap 1995: 18)

Pujol supports her argument using theory and policy recommendations, ranging from Mashall, Pigou, Edgeworth, and Jevons to Becker, Solow, Mincer, and Polachek. She concludes her piece by stating:

> [the] very logic, rhetoric and symbolism of the paradigm [of neoclassical economics] may be inseparable from the five sexist assumptions I have discussed here. Neoclassical economics has a history of stifling feminist approaches. We cannot wait for it to change. We must transcend it.
>
> (Pujol, in Kuiper and Sap 1995: 30)

Looking at the history of economics today, Pujol concludes that an alternative needs to be created and wonders whether the system can, in its current form, be extended to become a place for women in economics.

Another interesting thought comes from Nancy Folbre, describing her view of the role of feminist economists, when she considers alternative societies in an interview for Oliver Ressler's film *Alternative Economies – Alternative Societies*, as follows:

> I am a big fan of science fiction. I like Marge Piercy's science fiction and that of Sherry Tepper, Kim Stanley Robinson that's where the social

> imagination first takes hold. In a way what I am doing is just a sort of coming behind these more imaginative visions and trying to figure out and think about, how we might actually put it together and how we could adapt some of our existing economic institutions to move in that direction. Economists are the kind of engineers of the utopian, our job is to take care of the nuts and bolts of that alternative economic system and I think we depend on artists and writers to help us see where we want to go.
>
> (Folbre 2005, online)

Here, it is a very interesting metaphor: Nancy Folbre (considering her use of utopian methods, she is one of the most creative thinkers in contemporary feminist economics) regards herself as a feminist engineer, a mechanic, who takes care of an economics that still looks somewhat like a machine. Mechanical metaphors have shaped economic theories through all time: the mechanical cog-wheeled clock, which was invented around 1300, was the core concept of a machine that served as a metaphor for a mechanistic worldview; it became the core explanatory element for absolutist regimes, for instance in mercantilism. Physiocratic economics relied on the metaphor of a clock, in which a mechanic ball is inserted into the clock's circular motion by a "god-like" instance (Quesnay's *Tableau Économique*). Classical economic theory relies on the paradigm change that replaces Descartes with Newton. The analogy is now seen with a set of scales, as equilibriums are the core of the new metaphor. With Malthus and Ricardo, Smith's self-steering machine now becomes less of a godly driven device and more of a secular, science-based system with natural laws, functioning in accordance with the laws of balanced forces. Neoclassical economics finally describes economics as a "mechanical theory," as a "physics and mathematics based science" (Oetsch 1993). When artists and writers think up new alternatives, as Folbre suggests, maybe a mechanic is not the right person to set up a new system. It could therefore be an interesting starting point to change the image of the (feminist) economist from a mechanic to something more creative, more holistic, or maybe even more nurturing and less machine-identified.

I have argued for feminist economics to employ utopian tools to transcend neoclassical economics and escape the grip of the mainstream discourse, without failing to be scientific, and ringing in a new paradigm change, which will require a new metaphor. Whether this may be a metaphor of an irreparably broken gadget after the world's climate change has taken its toll, or a cyborg economics in the sense of Donna Haraway, or a new analogy from the realm of physics (most likely from quantum physics) is an interesting question that could be explored in a feminist economics utopia. I think that feminist economists must redefine themselves and their role in the economic discipline, as it is necessary for us to take a proactive stance in creating new metaphors and alternatives, which will shape the discipline of economics more radically than has been done.

7 "Der neue Mensch" and his need to be governed

> "You wanted to see 'Government'. It's working today."
>
> "The town government? Like a mayor? A council?"
>
> Luciente made a face, throwing her slack-clad leg over the bike.
>
> "Look at it and then we'll figure out what it's like, okay?"
>
> (Piercy 1976: 148)

Any introductory economics textbook will include the rudimentary formula that GDP can be measured by adding up private consumption, firms' investments, government expenditure, and trade with the rest of the world. Government as an institution is usually not questioned. Today we are living in a world where the conservative and socialist parties will be united in a call for a liberal form of anarchism, for lean governments that do not interfere with "the economy," and for the establishment of true freedom for all in the world of the new marketplace. Concepts of freedom and anarchism seem closely related, both in neoliberal and also in left-wing anarchist theory. In this chapter and in Chapter 8 I will elaborate on the ideas of doing away with government, either keeping it very small or unobtrusive or fully doing away with the construction. What is of most interest to me is certainly what these considerations may mean to a feminist economics. So this chapter will look at the more leftist views on governance; Chapter 8 is then concerned with the neoliberal ideas of freedom from governments.

So I will start by looking into social arrangements and utopian ideas for different constructions of society from a left-wing and also feminist perspective. I start off with a very brief summary of a feminist critique of the status quo of patriarchy and governance and then turn to some influential historical political programs for feminist utopias. In my case studies I explore the proposals in *Woman on the Edge of Time* (Piercy 1976) and *The Fifth Sacred Thing* (Starhawk 1993). In the course of this chapter I will also discuss some utopian visions of feminist economics that are concerned with changing the role of governance per se. The next section of this chapter is concerned with the concept of the nation-state,[1] its secluded territories, and what these mean for feminist theory and practice, feminist utopian and feminist economic thinking. In the tradition of border studies, I will view the issue of borders from a material and a more symbolical, cognitive aspect. The violence employed to protect borders and political ideas is discussed in this context. I continue by questioning the constitution of the subjects who inhabit the nation-state territory, pointing out that the citizenship of one group is juxtaposed with a situation of an existence in nowhere for others, which holds true not only in a material and symbolical sense, but also in an epistemological sense. Finally, I describe the models presented in *Woman on the Edge of Time* and *The Fifth Sacred Thing* concerning the constituency of those utopian communities as well as the subjectivity of the citizens or their establishment as new and improved subjects. I will underscore the significance of the gaps and breaks in hegemonic systems for feminist economic theory.

Suzanne Bergeron poses the initial question that indicates where this is going:

> The question is to imagine how women's struggles can confront the connected yet "scattered hegemonies" ... of global economic institutions, nation-states, patriarchal households, and other structures that support exploitation, in ways that challenge all of these sites and the connections among them.
>
> (Bergeron 2001: 1,001)

First of all, I will describe the status quo and what feminist theorists – in this case I am relying on Spike Peterson – have to say about the constitution of governance as we know it today.

Feminist critique of the status quo

Today, social organization still rests on the association of rational individuals in family units similar to the concept of the "utopian family" (see Chapter 5) or other entities that may allow a neoliberal consumerist system to function (see Chapter 2). The micro units are all joined together in nation-states. The nation-states' territories are sometimes permitted to merge with other national territories, but more often than not the borders are tightly closed to people seeking to migrate to places outside of their country of birth or nationality. Nation-state governments are nowadays considered harmful when interfering in the forces of the free market; their primary role is not to redistribute, but to provide a legal framework for competition. At the same time, larger institutions are gaining momentum. In 2007 the European Union welcomed two more member states, the population of the 27-nation union is close to 500 million people and common economic rules on financial stability and economic policy are the core of the European connection. To a large extent, nation-states have given up their sovereignty and are competing with each other for companies to choose their territory as production sites. Large international trade agreements promise benefits to its members, while excluding non-members from certain privileges.

Feminist political scientists have been considering the contemporary implications of governments' roles in the economic sphere, especially in the context of globalization and in regard to the patriarchal nation-state, as restrictive to women's issues and exploitative to women and other suppressed groups. Spike Peterson describes the historical formation of nation-states in this context:

> While patriarchal customs precede and enable state formation, it is with early states that systemic masculinist and class domination is *institutionalized*; the exploitation of women as a "sex/gender class" is here backed by the coercive power of the state, and the *reproduction* of gender hierarchy is ensured through a reconfiguration of legitimating ideologies.
>
> (Peterson 1992: 33)

Peterson also points to the economic dimension of that development, describing the basic injustice which is the foundation for a belief in androcentric biases and the need to change this organization:

> Understood in historical context and in relation to what they are formed "against," early states mark a transition form corporate, kin-based communities to the *institutionalization* of centralized authority, gender and class stratification, organized warfare, and justificatory ideologies. The concentration of resources made possible by appropriating the labor of women (and subsequently by war captives and slaves) was crucial for accumulation processes. Moreover, the invention of writing – historically concomitant with state formation and under the control of elite, androcentric power – was crucial for author-izing and reproducing centralized rule.
>
> (Peterson 1992: 34)

Peterson concludes that the state is in a multiple sense "the main organizer of the power relations of gender." Not only does the state express its authority and violence via its executive, legislative, and military branches, but it defines categories (i.e. citizen, security, national interest, moral codes, etc.), shapes cultural institutions and norms, decides who or what to count,[2] and determines the official language as well as the symbols in use. It creates the "acceptable forms and images of social activity and individual and collective identity" (Peterson 1992: 43):

> Of particular significance here is the state's mystification of "its patriarchal base by not only constructing but also manipulating the ideology describing public and private life."
>
> (Peterson 1992: 43)

Following Peterson's categorization and analysis, I will now turn to the alternatives that may be considered when one dislikes the status quo of government and governmentality in the sense of Foucault.

Social organization alternatives

I will start by listing some important historical political approaches that were integral to the formation of thought in *Woman on the Edge of Time* and *The Fifth Sacred Thing*, which I consider examples of the utopias of the radical anarchist-feminism of the second wave; while the later example is also an early 1990s version of spiritual ecofeminism, both bear interesting impulses aside from being pure science fiction. I have chosen these two works because I found that they offer very thorough, insightful ideas of community organizing from a socioeconomic viewpoint. I will now proceed, more or less chronologically, by focusing on how Eurocentric influences, the influence of Native Americans (see also Chapter 2) and other cultural backgrounds are interwoven in the body of the texts. In this analysis I try to consider that the perception of a utopia relies completely on the contextual view of the beholder: what is extremely radical and daring for one person's background may be boring reality or even a backlash for another. Personally, it currently seems very daring and unimaginable to envision a world without nations and governments. Therefore, I aim to explore whether alternatives – such as the anarchist or utopian proposal to forgo nation-states and governments – may offer improvements from the perspective of marginalized groups. Gender relations and social organizing have not always been desired the way they are performed today. Plato's utopian state was, for instance, founded on gender equality, but even more interesting are ideal worlds in which neither governments nor states exist.

Plato's Republic

A first milestone for those considering nation-states with different gender roles is Plato's famous work: In *The Republic*, written around 394 BC, Plato questions the nature of the ideal and actual state. In a feminist analysis of Plato's *Republic*, Elaine Hoffman Baruch describes Plato's historical context. She recalls the defeat of Athens by her neighbor Sparta, which was known for its liberal treatment of women in the Peloponnesian War. She stresses that it was in this atmosphere of commotion – political as well as regarding the discussions of gender roles – that Plato wrote his *Republic*. Hoffman Baruch points out the interesting fact that Plato was one of the first and then also one of the last thinkers, until modern times, who believed that biology is not a satisfactory basis for role differentiation. She summarizes Plato's attitudes as I will be briefly repeating them here: She says that Plato regarded the biological difference between the sexes as insignificant; and that he reduced it to women giving birth and men providing the semen for the children. Therefore she claims that Plato argued that both sexes should be treated equally in a social context and an equal education should train men and women for the same roles. Hoffman Baruch interprets Plato as calling for a total abolition of gender roles and that he stood for the political and sexual equality of women and demanded that women should be allowed to become members of the highest class. Regarding the military, Plato followed the Spartan example and was ready to open it for women, also in the fighting units. Hoffman Baruch claims that Plato thought of realizing a system of childcare, which he regarded as the only option to truly free women and allow them to become full participants of the society: The focus for Plato's liberal attitude was not the individual, but the state. According to Hoffman Baruch, Plato imagined a world of communalized wives, children, and property; a system of eugenics should ensure the best population outcome. This idea is an element of most utopias, or dystopias (e.g. *Brave New World* by Huxley), depending on the perspective. Hoffman Baruch sadly concludes that androcentrism in Plato's liberal utopia still arises when Plato claims that even if women are allowed to do whatever men do, they will still "always be surpassed in excellence by the best of men" (Rohrlich and Hoffman Baruch 1984: 210).

The Golden Age

A more daring utopia concerning even more liberty from governance is described in the first verses of Ovid's *Metamorphoses*, written in the first century AD, which refer to the so-called Golden Age:

> This was the Golden Age that, without coercion, without laws, spontaneously nurtured the good and the true. There was no fear or punishment: there were no threatening words to be read, fixed in bronze, no crowd of suppliants fearing the judge's face: they lived safely without protection.
>
> (Ovid, *Metamorphoses*)[3]

The Golden Age can be seen as an early version of an anarchist constitution, even though it does not imply proposals for gender equality. The original Greek term *anarchia* refers to an absence of authority and government without declaring whether this should be valid for all genders. Generally, the definition of anarchism used in this chapter associates the concept with responsibility and solidarity in the absence of government intervention and greatly diverges from the "TV-news-reporting notion," which usually equates anarchy with civil war, violence, disorder, and chaos; this latter connotation has been interpreted as a strategy used to discredit and criminalize the anarchist movement since its origins (Lohschelder 2000: 17). Having said this, I will now take a historical leap to the anarchism of Pierre-Joseph Proudhon and Mikhail Bakunin, who continued to understand anarchy as the opposite of chaos and whose ideas are incorporated in the feminist visions of Piercy and Starhawk.

Concepts of anarchy

Proudhon and Bakunin saw social harmony as interrupted by the force governments use in the process of governing and only the liberation of society from this force would restore natural harmony (Guérin 1969: 13). The famous male anarchist thinkers of the nineteenth century, such as Proudhon and Bakunin, at best lacked concern for gender issues and women's liberation; Proudhon was a proponent of the misogynist extreme. Tony Cliff summarizes Proudhon's view on women's standing thus:

> According to Proudhon, woman has been chosen by nature merely as an instrument of reproduction; that is, her only use to society is to function as a bearer of children and in herself she does not otherwise have a reason for being. To man, she costs more than he earns and her existence, therefore, is sustained by the perpetual sacrifice he makes.
>
> Only two careers were open to woman, said Proudhon: "housewife or harlot." " ... every woman who dreams of emancipation has lost, *ipso facto*, the health of her soul, the lucidity of her intellect, the virginity of her heart." To guard against such corruption, Proudhon recommended that grounds for wife-killing include "adultery, impudence, treason, drunkenness or debauchery, wastefulness or theft, and persistent insubordination." Why not? Woman was only a "pretty animal". To listen to the "literary eunuchs" who argued for woman's equality was reprehensible: " ... its inevitable consequences are free love, condemnation of marriage, condemnation of womanhood, jealousy and secret hatred of men, and, to crown the system, inextinguishable lechery: such, invariably, is the philosophy of the emancipated woman."
>
> (Cliff 1984, online)

(Proudhon has not only been criticized for his misogyny, but also for his racism and anti-Semitism.)

Although from a feminist perspective some advocates of anarchist thought had unacceptable views, the general anarchist idea of freedom could be expanded to all genders. For instance, Emma Goldman considers both men and women in her theories. She argues for all individuals to take on responsibility without a national authority's guiding or punishing aid. She defines anarchism as follows:

> Anarchism urges man to think, to investigate, to analyze every proposition. [Anarchism is] the philosophy of a new social order based on liberty unrestricted by man-made law; the theory that all forms of government rest on violence, and are therefore wrong and harmful, as well

> as unnecessary. The new social order rests, of course, on the materialistic basis of life; but while all Anarchists agree that the main evil today is an economic one, they maintain that the solution of that evil can be brought about only through the consideration of every phase of life, – individual, as well as the collective; the internal, as well as the external phases.
>
> (Goldman 1917, online)

Hence anarchism rejects authority and governing and stands for educated, aware individuals free to make decisions for themselves to take on responsibility for themselves and others who are considerate of their community and live in the (regained) social harmony without government:

> Government, with its unjust, arbitrary, repressive measures, must be done away with. At best it has but imposed one single mode of life upon all, without regard to individual and social variations and needs. In destroying government and statutory laws, Anarchism proposes to rescue the self-respect and independence of the individual from all restraint and invasion by authority. Only in freedom can man grow to his full stature. Only in freedom will he learn to think and move, and give the very best in him. Only in freedom will he realize the true force of the social bonds which knit men together, and which are the true foundation of a normal social life.
>
> (Goldman 1917, online)

Even though Emma Goldman's writing uses male-oriented speech patterns, she was very concerned with women's issues and had very emancipated viewpoints, such as in her demands for a woman's right to birth control. Today and in its historical evolution, anarchism has never been close to becoming a unified theory or political practice. Aside from the notion of refusing a governing institution, there is no single defining position shared by anarchists that provides a purposeful approach. (In this sense, anarchist theory is kin to queer theory.) Although gender relations in anarchist theory should be egalitarian per definition, most often they are not. Preferred economic arrangements are also a major source of concepts which take the opposing view. Nevertheless, anarchism is often associated with the socialist idea of ending exploitation, yet it always rejects the democratic element: Proudhon argues that the ballot in the hands of those who have been systematically mis-educated only serves as a pious betrayal benefiting the rich and noble. He sees suffrage as a mask hiding the true despotic power of those governing; backed by the banks, the police, and the army (Guérin 1969: 19). From a feminist perspective, the question of women participating in democratic processes was mainly a highly desirable goal. From an anarchist position, democracy mainly serves as an institution that enables capitalism and protects private property holdings.

Anarchism and women's suffrage

Anarchism's critical stance towards democracy and suffrage is, therefore, especially interesting from a feminist perspective. The various issues which the first women's movement involved (such as rights to abortion, rights to divorce, sexual liberation and economic justice and independence for women) were usually most closely tied and sometimes even overshadowed by the one predominant concern: the fight for women's suffrage. While some contemporaries, like Charlotte Perkins Gilman, saw the right to vote as a simple means of achieving other more important goals (i.e. economic issues in the case of Gilman), some groups and individuals regarded *the vote* as the ultimate goal. Emma Goldman[4] expresses the anarchist critique of the democratic element for women in her essay "Woman Suffrage":

> The poor, stupid, free American citizen! Free to starve, free to tramp the highways of this great country, he enjoys universal suffrage, and, by that right, he has forged chains about his limbs. The reward that he receives is stringent labor laws prohibiting the right of boycott, of picketing, in fact, of everything, except the right to be robbed of the fruits of his labor. Yet all these disastrous results of the twentieth-century fetish have taught woman nothing. But, then, woman will purify politics, we are assured. … Needless to say, I am not opposed to woman suffrage on the conventional ground that she is not equal to it. I see neither physical, psychological, nor mental reasons why woman should not have the equal right to vote with man. But that can not possibly blind me to the absurd notion that woman will accomplish that wherein man has failed.
>
> (Goldman 1910, online)

Anarchist attempts to establish societies without governments as we today know them have, with the downfall in the Spanish Civil War, finally failed.

Social organization in the utopian dreaming of feminist economics

Feminist economics is also still concerned with the social and economic arrangements of society. In this section, I look at two examples: one is Barbara Bergmann's thinking on creating a more socially oriented government in the U.S., and the other example is Suzanne Bergeron's concern for subjectivity and resistance.

The U.S. American welfare state

One very common argument of feminist economists, especially U.S. American-based arguments, is not to abolish their government but to demand that (their) government's role changes and becomes more similar to that in active welfare states in Northern Europe. An example is Barbara Bergmann's discussion in "A Swedish-Style Welfare State or Basic Income: Which Should Have Priority?" (Other examples can be found in volume 1 of *Feminist Economics* in 1995, which devotes a section to welfare politics. The notion of more welfare has also been taken up by Julie Nelson, Karen Christopher in *Feminist Economics* (2004), and many more.) Bergmann's work in this regard has been characterized as utopian thinking by feminist economics' contemporaries and herself; therefore it is included in this context, even though I would not classify it as radically utopian from my perspective.

In the last section of the groundbreaking anthology *Out of the Margin: Feminist Perspectives on Economics*, by Edith Kuiper and Jolande Sap, Bergmann argues that a Swedish-style welfare state with state provision of merit goods plus targeted cash payments has a higher priority than large cash payments to all citizens, which are considered, for instance, in the demands for basic-income schemes. She claims that only after the achievement of a well-established welfare state, productivity might rise so much that the state budget could allow universal cash payments. Her paper argues for a two-step program toward better living conditions through welfare.

From a European perspective, universal incomes do seem utopian, although they are currently being discussed at government level and a few examples have already been installed in certain countries. Well-functioning welfare states certainly do not seem utopian from a European viewpoint. Furthermore, Bergmann's suggestions concentrate on budgetary perspectives. She considers which effects specific welfare programs might have and contrasts them to the current status quo in the U.S. Bergmann also remains within the existing preconditions of the economy as it is given in today's USA. This reflects Bergmann's belief in practical solutions and is probably an excellent position from which to achieve fast change for poor women and men currently living in the U.S. – if social politics were to respond to her suggestions.

Subjectivity and resistance in discourse and practice

Bergmann's reliance on a (changed) government for feminist economics issues is an example of a strategy that Suzanne Bergeron describes as reliance on governments. Bergeron states that there are currently only two major positions in political economics literature regarding subjectivity and resistance. She calls one position the global imperative approach, claiming that national governments and national movements cannot efficiently resist in a globalized world, and the other stream claims that governments can remain with some power and have a more management-type function to ensure competitiveness and therefore wealth for its citizens in a globalized world – maybe through forming larger international blocks, such as the European Union or the North America Free Trade Agreement (NAFTA), which to some extent seek to restrict the problematic free movement of capital.

In the line of Bergeron's reasoning, she tries to create more options by asking whether "feminist approaches to the political economy of globalization challenge these accounts and/or contribute to alternative conceptualizations" (Bergeron 2001: 990). She comes to the conclusion that "many feminist accounts of globalization remain partly inscribed within mainstream discourses of economic and political space even as they are reconfiguring them" (Bergeron 2001: 991). She surmises that this means that most solutions in a struggle against globalization see the nation-state as women's primary source of resistance (a reliance which is shared by many critics of globalization, such as Attac)[5], but Bergeron sees that this "limits the range of potential options that can be meaningfully discussed in feminist economics literature" (Bergeron 2001: 993) and that only a few alternatives to this thought exist. In her view, this all depends very much on the way the discourse on globalization is led and which alternatives open up in that discursive context: "These discursive practices create a limited space for imagining agency and practices of resistance within the context of global economic restructuring" (Bergeron 2001: 990). Given that capitalism tends to present itself as an ahistoric given, "there is no alternative," as Margaret Thatcher is fond of saying; it is important to try to cross over that demarcation of permanence. One strategy might be to imagine the solidity of capitalism and also the solidity of the nation-state. I strongly agree with Bergeron's analysis; I even think that the discursive space for alternative strategies is currently becoming smaller and smaller and that the few existing alternatives are constantly being marginalized, suppressed with economic punishments for activists who work within fields of alternative discourse practice – and in extreme cases even physical violence is used to suppress unconventional voices (for example, during anti-globalization events).

In this regard, marginalization can be understood as ignoring or belittling of publications, refusal to publish or quote, more generally exclusion from (academic) discourse by omission. The last issue is very interesting, since not only has exclusion from academic discourses marginalized the voices of political actors, but also the appropriation of grey literature into academic fields has served to transform the knowledge of feminist activist groups and establish it within academia, while at the same time at the price of eliminating a radical edge. At the "Queer Readings" conference in Vienna in 2006, this practice was discussed by Sabine Hark, a renowned German queer theorist and former lesbian studies scholar. Hark reflected on how one could evaluate the process when a young discipline like queer theory, with its characteristic of being fluid and cross-disciplinary, takes realizations of knowledge on board which were developed in the longstanding practice of radical feminist and/or lesbian groups without crediting those groups and their epistemological processes. (This is often the case, because a clear source for the generated knowledge is not visible, since it possibly arises from a lengthy process.) I think this is indeed a very interesting question to raise. Unfortunately, in her talk Hark did not offer strategies for approaching the problem, which I would have liked to report on.

A practical example of how this process works is, for example, when marginalized groups such as migrant cultural/political institutions and their knowledge creation are reported on by white academics who "research" in those fields and then publish the insights they gained; thus writing about those migrant practices often in a career-advancing manner for themselves.

I will now return to the shrinking discursive spaces. In this regard, Bergeron describes the two (only two!) most common resistance strategies in current feminist strategies, which either work toward establishing a global sisterhood to counter globalization and/or to try and transform institutions, such as the World Bank, the UN, etc. from within. In the example of the resistance to structural adjustment, she describes a conflict arising in strategies thus:

> Forms of resistance span and cross multiple social levels, from community organizing, demonstrations, social movements, cross border organizing, and survival strategies to movements at the national level, such as demonstrations to protest budget cuts, pressures on political parties, and feminist movement and non-government organization (NGO) demands on the state.
>
> (Bergeron 2001: 994)

Bergeron notes that this form of organization in activist movements clashes with the organization of individuals as citizens in nation-states, some privileged by their birthrights, others disadvantaged. The alliances across country borders are made more difficult, not just through the categorization of their members by the holding of differently valuable citizenships; rather:

> The privileging of national identities presents a problem for feminist politics because it either renders these other concerns, political collectivities, and forms of resistance invisible or pushes them to the margins of thought.
>
> (Bergeron 2001: 994)

These problems of the "global sisterhood" vision of the second wave of feminism (many feminists then believed that the global struggle for women's rights might render other categories of oppression such as race, class, sexual orientation, nationality, etc. less significant) are repeated when feminist thinkers argue that only a global resistance of a united women's movement can stop capitalism. I agree with Suzanne Bergeron that a more differentiated approach may help overcome those difficulties. Alternatives to the reliance on nation-states as saviors in women's struggles in times of globalization are essential to overcoming the problems that women, as an essentialist group, as well as others on the margin, have generally had with nation-states as their spiritual but also physical homelands.

Feminism and anti-nationism

As I started to argue in the last section, an interesting issue in a feminist discussion on alternative economics is the role of nation-states and how to unite as a feminist movement across national borders. Governments are the official heads of nation-states, geographically located in territory which is populated by the ethnic group(s) of its citizens, thereby excluding foreigners from certain privileges citizens benefit from, such as the legal right to live in that territory, to work there, and to gain access to the social and cultural provisions made for the citizens. This exclusion will be enforced through incarceration and/or deportation of those who seek to cross the borders.

Borders

Borders are an interesting phenomenon. Border studies have questioned the arbitrary lines demarcated by borders and the cultural, historical, geographical, and economic meaning associated with these demarcations. What is remarkable, especially from a utopian perspective, is that border studies, similarly to queer theories, tries to focus on the deconstructive elements of the border concept. The crossing of borders, legally or illegally, and the establishment of subjectivity related to borders and hybrid identities make for a complex analysis and, at the same time, they serve as a source of power. Haraway's cyborg figure may inhabit a borderland, while Gloria Anzaldua's *mestizia* inhabits yet another (Anzaldua 1987).[6] The strength of these constructions is that they forgo the border per se and create new identities and strategic possibilities. The border zone becomes a nowhere land with all kinds of dangers for some (such as the continual murder of women along the Mexican–U.S. American border) and opportunities for others (like *maquiladoras* as production facilities in the border's nowhere land, or borders becoming a passage to new citizenship for unborn children, who may be "smuggled" in their mothers' bellies across the Mexican border to gain the status of U.S. citizenship by being born on the other side of the border, etc.) (Biemann 1999).

Nation-states and their governments will employ armies to guard borders and thereby avoid aliens or other nation-states' armies invading their territory and stealing the nation's wealth, as well as turning their citizens into de-privileged foreigners when conquered. Those governments might choose to take on the invading role and act as the aggressors themselves. Currently, popular reasons for invasion and war are raw materials, such as oil in the Middle East, or minerals in African states, such as in the Congo;

sometimes religious or ethnic justifications are given as a front, while at other times they are reasons for war on their own.

The role of terrorism

Since I am considering violence associated with territorial wars in this chapter, this seems a good opportunity to approach the discussion that links anarchism with terrorism and to discuss terrorism as a critical phenomenon in today's political landscape. Since the Haymarket Days,[7] terrorism has been associated with anarchism. Emma Goldman believed in the "idea of propaganda by deed," i.e. that assassinations were a good way to initiate revolution and social change. In my view, this belief is contrary to the anarchist ideals of respecting each other and consensual decision-making in communities and so on. Apart from the ethical dimension, her judgment proved strategically very wrong even in the course of her lifetime, starting with the attempted murder of the industrialist Henry Clay Finch, which she had planned together with Alexander Berkman in 1892, and followed by the many assassinations of political leaders by anarchists in the next decades (such as the Spanish king or the American president), which were never successful in bringing about social change. After seeing how the Bolshevik leaders operated in Russia, Goldman still accepted that violence was an essential evil in the process of social transformation; however, she did further distinguish it:

> I know that in the past every great political and social change, necessitated violence. . . . Yet it is one thing to employ violence in combat as a means of defense. It is quiet another thing to make a principle of terrorism, to institutionalise it to assign it the most vital place in the social struggle. Such terrorism begets counter-revolution and in turn itself becomes counter-revolutionary.
>
> (Goldman 1925, online)

Goldman believed that circumstances, state oppression, and state terror turned people into assassins and terrorists, justly defending themselves and their causes. When Goldman was released from questioning, she said about Leon Cszolgosz, the man who assassinated President McKinley:

> He [Czolgosz] had committed the act for no personal reasons or gain. He did it for what is his ideal: the good of the people. That is why my sympathies are with him.
>
> (Goldman, online)

Noam Chomsky, the most famous contemporary U.S. anarchist responded to the question "What is terrorism?" in the following way in a speech given at MIT a month after the events on September 11, 2001:

> There is an official definition. You can find it in the US code or in US army manuals. A brief statement of it taken from a US army manual, is fair enough, is that terror is the calculated use of violence or the threat of violence to attain political or religious ideological goals through intimidation, coercion, or instilling fear.
>
> (Chomsky 2001, online)

Throughout the course of the speech, Chomsky explains that this definition makes it impossible to distinguish between private terrorist acts and those of nation-states, for instance the USA's Low Intensity Warfare, which has been employed in a large number of countries in the last decades.

> If you take a look at the definition of Low Intensity Warfare which is official US policy you find that . . . in fact, Low Intensity Conflict is just another name for terrorism.
>
> (Chomsky 2001, online)

Marge Piercy picks up on the question of terrorism at the end of her *Woman on the Edge of Time*. Here, Connie, the main protagonist, poisons the coffee of the doctors of the mental asylum she is confined to against her will and she ends up killing four of the men who had threatened to lobotomize her and an array of other – non-consenting – patients. Piercy describes Connie as the victim of the doctors' decision. Because of their brutal attack on her physical and mental integrity, she finally takes back some of her power and stops the doctors' violence by assassinating them. Connie's justifications for doing so sound very much like Goldman's reasoning:

> "I just killed six people," she said to the mirror, but she washed her hands because she was afraid of the poison, "I murdered them dead. Because they are the violence-prone. Theirs is the money and the power, theirs the poisons that slow the mind and dull the heart. Theirs are the powers of life and death. I killed them. Because it is war."
>
> (Piercy 1976: 375)

Even though I very strongly believe that murder and terrorism are no solution and need to be clearly condemned by all means, as a reader of the novel *Woman on the Edge of Time* I found that I was so glad that Connie had managed to free herself from the oppression and the danger she was in and that the bad guys could do no more harm.

The citizen and the Other

Nevertheless, aside from the dark issue of violence committed by individuals or military regimes, the idea of nation-states headed by governments seems compelling; a world without this order of established countries is simply unimaginable. Very interesting thoughts on the nation-state and the suggested ahistoricity of the concept as such are expressed by Seyla Benhabib. She says:

> Modern liberal democracies owe their stability and relative success to ... the ideal of selfgovernance which defines freedom as the rule of law among a community of equals who are "citizens" of the polis, and who thus have the right to rule and to be ruled. This ideal emerges in 5th century Athens and is revived throughout history in episodes such as the experience of self-governing city-states in the Renaissance; the Paris commune of 1871, the anarchist and socialist communes of the Russian Revolution, and the Spanish civil war.
>
> (Benhabib 2004b: 1)

Here, I read that Benhabib suggests that the success of the democratic nation-state concept relies precisely on those forms of communal organization that refuse to be governed in the structure of a nation-state institutionalization as we know it today, which I find quite remarkable. This notion is further supported when Benhabib says:

> The ideal of the territorially circumscribed nation-state, by contrast, conceives of the citizen first and foremost as the subject of state-administration, or more positively, as the subject of rights and entitlements. ... Since the 17th century democracy and the consolidation of the modern nation-state have marched together ... the ideal of self-governance was increasingly interpreted as the formal equality of the citizens of the demos who now sought to realize the equal value of their liberty in terms of an equivalent schedule of rights and entitlements.
>
> (Benhabib 2004b: 1)

Another issue of interest is the view of the subject Benhabib raises. When she mentions the ideal of "the rule of law among a community of equals who are 'citizens' of the polis," the notion of equality amongst the citizens in that social organization is stressed. One needs to wonder what the repercussions would be for historically disadvantaged groups, such as women or ethnic minorities. Are they truly equals in the Greek ideal of citizenship? What about women or slaves in that society? (As Drucilla Barker has stated, women, amongst others, were not part of the citizenry in ancient Greece.)

Although women have managed to gain citizen status and attain the right to vote in the course of the evolution of the democratic nation-state, in *Three Guineas* Virginia Woolf answers the man who tries to call upon her patriotism and supports his need to fight for his country with the following words:

> Therefore if you insist upon fighting to protect me, or 'our' country, let it be understood, soberly and rationally between us that you are fighting to gratify a sex instinct which I cannot share; to procure benefits which I have not shared and probably will not share; but not to gratify my instincts, or to protect either myself or my country. For, the outsider will say, 'in fact, as a woman, I have no country. As a woman I want no country. As a woman my country is the whole world.'
>
> (Woolf 1938, online)

Her call came from the notion that, in her time and location, it was not possible for women as a group to hold important possessions without the legal patronage of a male relative, and if a woman was married to a foreigner she would become a foreigner herself and lose citizenship of her birth country. Legal frameworks have changed in many countries today; nevertheless, the hindrances that guarantee women the same amounts of wealth as their male counterparts still exist. The UN has stated that women hold only 1 percent of wealth worldwide.[8] So there is not so much *women's* wealth to protect with nation-state armies, or so it seems. Aside from the essentialist "fact" that women "by nature" may be seen as more peaceful and uninterested in military conflict, they do seem less interested in shooting the children other women have borne in the great pains of labor or having their own children shot in that regard; in fact, there has been a plethora of women's peace movements throughout the course of more recent history, for example the women's peace camp at Greenham Common. This kind of resistance was everyday practice in the world of second wave feminist activism. At that time anarchist theories were experiencing a revival in women's movements, particularly through feminist re-readings of anarchist works. Attempts to reconfigure hierarchical thinking, responses to authority, resistance to force and violence suitable for a woman's movement were large topics. Feminist practice at that time involved consciousness-raising groups, organization in anti-hierarchical settings, learning to organize and work with a consensual, communal decision-making body, and so on. These efforts were not always successful; they often ignored real power differences based on race, class, sexual orientation, etc. Nevertheless, organizational structures that were far from the usual were a large issue, a resistance to nation-state practices, including the anti-war and anti-military movements. These practical attempts to organize communally were accompanied and captured by theoretical and utopian writing, such as in Marge Piercy's work, which I discuss further on pp. 175–177.

The Other owns no place

Cixous[9] adds another dimension to Woolf's thoughts on the lack of patriotism women may share when she plays with the stigma of feminism and feminist thinking as hysterical or insane throughout history: She remarks that as "a sorceress and a hysteric – that is, a displaced person – everywoman must inevitably find that she has no home, no where." At one point in her work, Cixous confesses that she "can never say the word 'patrie', 'fatherland', even if it is provided with an 'anti';" she adds that she "revolts, rages, where am I to stand? What is my place, if I am a woman? I look for myself throughout the centuries and don't see myself anywhere" (Cixous, in Meaney 1993: 7–8).

Given the feelings of not belonging, Suzanne Bergeron's description of feminist strategies that reach across national borders to fight the negative effects of globalization becomes very interesting. First, she points out some attempts to overcome those borders in feminist strategies, then she repeats how limiting and narrow these discourses can be, which I will attempt to illustrate with examples from feminist economic thinking on pp. 200–204.

Bergeron states that the "construction of collective subjectivities vis-à-vis economic globalization and sources of resistance might not necessarily coincide with national boundaries. National boundaries have never functioned as 'sealed rooms' ... inhabited by 'insiders' who share an account and interest in national intuitions, values and practices" (Bergeron 2001: 994). Nevertheless, Bergeron continues by stating that the notion of global sisterhood has never really worked when unity regarding certain issues is simply assumed. An example is when she writes that "states that have implemented gender-aware policies have typically been responding to the needs and desires of elite women, which calls into question the ideas that state policy articulates some common national women's interest" (Bergeron 2001: 994). As I have already mentioned, the notion of global sisterhood is already made difficult by the very privilege nationality provides for some.

Bergeron's conclusion is that the discourse is too focused on states and the need to change/improve governments' action in order to counter globalization:

> calls for state intervention to manage the national economy and provide particular kinds of support constrain our ability to imagine many alternatives outside the form of globalization preferred by transnational capital. They are also in part conceived within a "statecentric" discourse, one based on a dichotomous state–market framework that implicitly assumes that the nation-state remains the site of women's political identity and agency in terms of resistance to global capitalism.
> (Bergeron 2001: 994)

I think that the effects of this limitation prove a huge problem in all alternative academic thinking, that the prerequisite of thinking within the given boundaries in order to have a voice in the prevailing discourse becomes the "inner censorship" Foucault is speaking of, which prevents an ultimate shift in the paradigm. The following examples from feminist economics should prove this point.

When feminist economists reach nowhere

Friederike Maier starts the anthology *Ökonomische Theorien und Geschlechterverhältnis: Der männliche Blick der Wirtschaftswissenschaft*[10] with her essay "Das Wirtschaftssubjekt hat (k)ein Geschlecht!"[11] (Maier 1993a). She offers an overview of economics as a male discipline and analyzes male bias in economics. Using this deconstructive approach, she investigates the principles of microeconomics and argues for opening up the conventional assumptions of economic models. One of her major points of critique is the complete gender blindness of macroeconomics. While microeconomic theory incorporates gender to some degree (usually in the tradition of "add women and stir"), macroeconomics – she uses the example of Keynesianism – is completely indifferent to gender. She concludes her piece by quoting Michèle Pujol:

> I had come to economics with a lot of excitement and trepidation: that discipline was going to help me understand what was going on in the world. I soon found out that the neoclassical paradigms, while providing some seductive modeling, did not come close to answering the questions I had. As a woman in the field I started realizing that my own realities were missing, that they were dismissed or trivialized when the issue of women's place in the economy was brought up. What am I doing here if I'm supposed to be at home with my husband and children? How can I be in economics, understand its elaborate theories and models if I am irrational?
>
> (Pujol, in Maier 1993a: 36)

Maier labels and points out the void feminist economists, as non-citizens or "the other" in their discipline (in the sense of Virginia Woolf or Hélène Cixous), are trying to fill; she clearly describes economics as "no place" for women. This leads to a complex discussion on the nowhere issue. Economics as a discipline is not only a field of theory that is void of women's inputs, but also a place in which women are physically not equally represented, neither as university professors, nor as politicians, nor as economic advisors, nor as any other stakeholder. Maier comes to her conclusion using the tool of deconstruction and ends up in the nowhere, a region where being a feminist and being an economist do not merge. This strong realization is nevertheless smothered when Maier concludes that

> feminist economists ... will not put up with the status quo in economic discussion anymore – but for theoretical exploration, inspiration, and stabilization in a male-dominated profession they need more exchange with each other and more critical discussions amongst themselves.
>
> (Maier 1993a: 36; author's translation)[12]

There is a strong dissonance between the realization of being expatriated in a discipline and raising the very weak demands of talking more with other expatriated members of the discipline as a strategy for change. Maier states that there is "no place" but does not demand or suggest a "better place." She demands that "*they*" (the expatriated women economists) talk with each other – probably not to prepare for revolution, but to stabilize their jobs in their male-dominated area of work. She not only puts forward a very insubstantial demand, but by distancing herself from "*them*" she does not position herself in the role of the demanding actors. She argues for solidarity amongst feminist economists and – linguistically – does not offer the same herself. (Seyla Benhabib also raises evocative thoughts related to the notion of being an expatriate of a discipline).[13] Irigaray also describes the argument of finding the gendered void: "I will never be in a man's place, a man will never be in mine. Whatever the possible identifications, one will never exactly occupy the place of the other, they are irreducible the one to the other" (Irigaray, in Barr 1992: 154). After finding it, mapping it out, and keeping that void clear as an open room, Maier still forgoes the creation of a space for creation or taking up space, and therefore a strategy of dissent.

An example of turning the no-place experience of women to a more positive experience in a practical and symbolic manner is described in Bina Agarwal's "Gender, Property, and Land Rights," in Edith Kuiper and Jolande Sap, *Out of the Margin. Feminist Perspectives on Economics* (1995). Agarwal uses the Indian example to illustrate the importance of land rights for women. Women are not legally entitled to hold land in India. For instance, if their husband, the landowner, dies, only male relatives can inherit the land. Agarwal uses the Marxist theory of property and a multitude of practical and empirical examples to illustrate her point: the importance of South Asian women having their own rights to hold land. A utopian interpretation of Agarwal's demand would be that women need to create a space first to be, a good place, a land where women can live, without getting chased off it if the goodwill of male landowners were to change. The establishment of land rights for women in (some parts of) India is a very practical utopian demand. From a Western perspective, it is infuriating to think that women are still not allowed to hold land in the 21st century, but if you think about it women might be legally allowed to hold land, for instance, in Austria, but due to income and wealth disparity they are still most often unable to do so, lest they are lucky enough to inherit. If one were to say something optimistic, when Indian women finally receive the right to hold land they have the advantage of decades of organizing and planning how to proceed with their new rights, which European women did not have to such an extent. Maybe this will lead to unimaginable outcomes, but maybe not. I this will further explore this on pp. 178 ff., and inquire into which political decisions freed suppressed groups might make.

Transformative feminist visions expanding beyond conventional political economy

Now let us get back the very utopian. When Suzanne Bergeron strongly advocates opening up room for alternative thinking and extending discursive space, some of her insights sound like a good starting point for a practical alternative to a feminist anarchist utopia in the sense of Piercy's *Woman on the Edge of Time*. Bergeron's talks of offering

> an alternative feminist discourse of global capitalism, through which contradictory and heterogeneous subjectivities are recognized and produced not only in the processes of global capitalism but also in the gaps and margins of these processes [thus offering] a more transformative feminist vision that expands possible forms of intervention and resistance beyond those offered in conventional political economy discourses.
>
> (Bergeron 2001: 1,002)

Why is this in the sense of Marge Piercy? A possible reading of *Woman on the Edge of Time* and also Piercy's *He, She and It* is to take the design of the anarchist communities, which are also locations of resistance fighters against globalized consumerist worlds, as they are not only literal solutions for alternative community organizations, but also symbolic indicators of a strategy of a counterculture as Bergeron suggests. In the utopias of the anarchist communities Piercy describes, the nation-state is not a given. She claims that it has ceased to exist and has been replaced by a different form of organized society. I will try to illustrate this by the following few examples.

The design of anarchist communities and their governing institutions

> "Look, I don't understand," Connie said. "If workers in a factory, say the kenner factory, want to make more kenners and the planners decide to give them less stuff, who wins?" "We argue," the man said. "How else?" "There is no final authority, Connie," Luciente said. "There's got to be. Who finally says yes or no?" "We argue till we close to agree. We just continue. Oh, it's disgusting sometimes. It bottoms you." "After a big political fight, we guest each other," the man said. "The winners have to feed the losers and give presents. . . . " " . . . political decisions-like whether to raise or lower population-go a different route. We talk locally and then choose a rep to speak our posit in area hookup. Then we all sit in holi simulcast and the rep from each group speaks their village posit. Then we go back into local meeting to fuse our final word. Then the reps argue once more before everybody. Then we vote."
>
> (Piercy 1976: 153)

Underlying changes enabling anarchist utopian visions lie in the alternative organization of communities but also, and even more importantly, in the constitution of the individuals themselves. Regarding communities, Peter Kropotkin's key thought was that society should be organized on the basis of communes, associating in a network of cooperation that would replace the state. This idea is incorporated in Marge Piercy's social networks as described in *Woman on the Edge of Time.* In addition, similarly to Piercy, Starhawk's *Fifth Sacred Thing* incorporates the belief in the limitations of complexity when she argues that systems "attempting too much control over too much complexity" will fail; she thereby argues for smaller entities (Starhawk 1993: 273). Starhawk's utopia is not an island in the middle of nowhere, but a city under siege. It is set as a San Franciscan version of the Paris Commune: it describes a self-governing city, but much more successfully and highly structured than the short-lived 1871 community of her ideological contemporaries. Decisions are made based on direct democracy. However, due to the consensus requirement, discussion processes may be long and time-consuming in the short run, but in the long run conflicts can be avoided, therefore saving time in the long run. Consensus and respect are the backbone of the utopian society:

> "You're threatening the very heart of what we are fighting for! What keeps us together in this city, what allows us to build what we have built, is the respect for this Council, for our mutual consensus. If you violate that, the Stewards [the tyrannical corporations that run the rest of the world] won't have to bother taking over. We will already be destroyed!"
>
> (Starhawk 1993: 465)

The decision-making modes are described in detail by Starhawk and in Marge Piercy's *Woman on the Edge of Time.* Both authors include representation for animals and the environment in their decision-making councils (I have found it remarkable that Al Gore has now named himself "the advocate for the planet"), but in Piercy's work voting finally takes place in a form of basic democracy. "Controversy over the meaning of democracy and feminism is hardly new," as Zillah Eisenstein remarks (Eisenstein 2004: 1). Personally, I think voting is not a functioning process in an anarchist setting, even if the losers may be mollified with food and presents as Marge Piercy recommends. A decision based on consent due to mutual respect and understanding of different positions, with an interest in a common good, could last longer than a decision shortened by a vote, in which case a very large percentage of people who disagree and are not behind the decision might not give their best to work with what has been decided and might possibly try to sabotage the actions taken. If a decision cannot be made, some of the basic prerequisites are in disarray and need to be clarified beforehand (e.g. parties feeling they are treated unjustly, problems that have been overlooked, miscommunications, lack of a common goal, etc.). On the other hand, Piercy seems to look for a democracy that extends the voting process to a political sense of responsibility in the sense of Kathryn Dean, who says:

> Democracy in the sense of entitlement to political voice is an ineliminable dimension of public-spirited citizenship but democracy alone is insufficient since democracy implies nothing about responsibilities. It is associated more with claims on the group, or claims by one group on another, than with responsibilities for the world.
>
> (Dean 2003: 177)

Embedded in this sense of responsibility, a voting process also takes on a different meaning. What is interesting in Piercy's concept is that she adds the component of periodical representation by lot:

> Basically I have always thought that choosing by lot was not a bad way to run things, but I have never been able to persuade other people from that. ... Government is for sale generally, if you have enough money, you can buy yourself a governership or senatorship or whatever. You just simply overload the media. [In *Woman on the Edge of Time's* utopian world] the government is chosen by lot and everybody serves for a year, when they are called upon.
>
> (Piercy 2005b)

Mattapoisett, Piercy's utopian world, is organized into villages populated by approximately 600 inhabitants at the most: "We don't have big cities – they didn't work" (Piercy 1976: 68). The numerical restriction of living together in small villages is similar to the idea of Fourier's ideal community, *The Phalanx*, which was to be inhabited by 1620 people (this number arises through his theory of character traits), who were to live together in a village and work in a wide variety of alternating jobs.

One interesting aspect of Robert Nozick's *Anarchy, State, and Utopia* (which is not a left-wing proposal) deals with the question of alternatively organized communities. Nozick argues that with the absence of a central state, other non-libertarian political ideas and personal beliefs can be accommodated. People who wish to live in a socialist society could get together and buy a piece of land to live on and set up an alternative society there, free from the interference of others. The same is valid for religious groups and people with other beliefs (Nozick 1974: 320). Note that the libertarian society is the given framework and that alternative societies will always be the Other carving out a niche in a surrounding system of competition and free markets. Nozick also posits that it is essential to buy/acquire land before an alternative to the mainstream world can be established.

Der neue Mensch

The new citizen

Instead of picking up the anarchist suggestion of smaller entities and federational decision-making, in *Capitalism and Citizenship: The Impossible Partnership* Kathryn Dean looks for a new citizen concept that proposes a solution to current geopolitical problems and thereby develops a multidisciplinary theory of citizenship. First, Dean seeks to point out how laboring and shopping came to be the defining activities of our world. She draws on analyses of Freud, Marx, Lacan, Habermas, Castells, and Arendt and comes to the conclusion that capitalism impedes the nurturing of abilities that could lead to a post-laboring, post-shopping culture. She looks for "a culture capable of nurturing a public spirited rather than merely formal-legal, mode of citizenship. In doing so [she] is engaging in a form of utopian thinking" which she hopes will "contribute to the revitalization of our political imagination" (Dean 2003: 181). Dean argues for a "strong visionary and extraordinarily knowledgeable leadership supported by either a docile, high tax-paying electorate or an active citizen body which will take on significant responsibility" (Dean 2003: 181) for the resolution of the problems of our times such as global disparities, population ageing, environmental unsustainability and migration flows caused by those problems:

> If there is to be a world government, we must ensure that it is one which is meaningfully accountable to a plurality of communities through the active attentiveness of public-spirited citizens. This will only be the case if those of us who live in the privileged parts of the world direct our thinking attention at the many problems that press in on us now. If we are to think attentively and judge politically, we must regain a sense of reality as the combined activity of a plurality of humans with whom we share a world. ... We can seek to verify our shared reality through the real or imagined presence of others rather than through the pronouncements and activities of politicians and experts. ... We will need to actively cultivate the virtues of a sociability which transcends the networking mode in which we are presently required to function. In doing so, we can begin to resist the pressures toward narcissism coming from capitalism, as well as from a corrupted form of politics, both of which encourage us to mind our own business rather than concern ourselves with the public in a meaningful way. We can begin to expand and transform our rationality. Citizenship is now not only a good in itself but has become the increasingly urgent means of correcting the hubris emerging from the revitalized marriage of capitalism and science.
>
> (Dean 2003: 181)

In my reading, Dean, like most utopian thinkers who call for the New Man, frees herself from the illusions of capitalism and taking on a responsibility for herself, others around her, and for the whole world and its problems which she has become aware of through the networks connecting the global sphere. Interestingly, Dean in her volume manages to completely avoid a gender analysis in describing the formation of the bourgeois family, which she considers an origin of the constitution of the differentiated psyches of relatively autonomous subjects. This is one of the views that feminist economics has repeatedly criticized in economic models: the description of economic man as a Hobbesian mushroom, fully sprung from the earth, without any necessary mention of those who have labored to bear, feed, and raise that agent, thus ignoring women's reproductive work. Disregarding this issue means ignoring a lot of the problems associated with unjust distribution of work and wealth, which will continue to take away the option of attentiveness from those who are busy struggling with their daily caring labor.

The question of the groundedness of the citizen is a second point of critique regarding Dean's very desirable extension of democracy by responsible citizens. Citizenship was originally related to an association with a certain city. Nowadays, it is related to membership of a certain nation and (usually) to exercising some political rights in that nation, and citizenship has become somewhat coterminous for nationality. But isn't the reliance on a nationalism-bound concept to solve the problems of the globe a large contradiction? For a nation, national interests will always be a priority, these being associated with the patriotic propaganda needed to bind people together in a grid of arbitrary geographical borders, people of varying cultures and beliefs in networks too large for an individual to understand or coordinate. Finally, a centrally planned, wise world government controlled by aware citizens might be hard to install, so how would corruption be prevented? How could the citizens prevent those who were trusted with power, in the sense of Hannah Arendt, breaking that trust and abusing the military, the executive, and international relation networks to work for their own interests? Why would a responsible citizen give up responsibility to others who are viewed as wiser? What would make the members of a world government more trustworthy than a member of the general population, given that one of Dean's demands is education that enables everyone to make their own choices? In *The Fifth Sacred Thing*, Starhawk first installs a defense unit for the city under siege, which is based on essentialist characteristics: only very old women are allowed to propose defensive actions, as it is believed that those old women are the most unlikely warmongers, a choice that is changed to less essentialist categories at the end of her book. What about a world government? Who might be the ones most unlikely to lose their integrity?

One of the current strategies in feminist economics for changing the existing system is via knowledge creation and its dissemination in universities as well as in more informal contexts. Education is an option to change individual and collective thought and behavior.

On human nature

> But what about human nature? Can it be changed? And if not, will it endure under Anarchism? Poor human nature, what horrible crimes have been committed in thy name! Every fool, from king to policeman, from the flatheaded parson to the visionless dabbler in science, presumes to speak authoritatively of human nature. The greater the mental charlatan, the more definite his insistence on the wickedness and weaknesses of human nature. Yet, how can any one speak of it today, with every soul in a prison, with every heart fettered, wounded, and maimed?
>
> (Goldman 1917, online)

People working together and for each other are usually a central element in anarchist community design. The belief in people wanting to work and laziness as a sad disease certainly depends on the attractiveness of work. Like Fourier, Piercy, and Starhawk, Kropotkin believed that people are not naturally idle and that if work is useful and freely undertaken in pleasant circumstances it will be satisfying and provide the happiness of working for the common good. The whole logic of functioning anarchist utopias rests on the belief that people will act like responsible, happy, altruistic beings once the force of coercion and repression by governments and other authorities is overcome:

> Anarchism is the only philosophy which brings to man the consciousness of himself; which maintains that God, the State, and society are nonexistent, that their promises are null and void, since they can be fulfilled only through man's subordination. Anarchism is therefore the teacher of the unity of life; not merely in nature, but in man. There is no conflict between the individual and the social instincts, any more than there is between the heart and the lungs: the one the receptacle of a precious life essence, the other the repository of the element that keeps the essence pure and strong. The individual is the heart of society, conserving the essence of social life; society is the lungs which are distributing the element to keep the life essence – that is, the individual – pure and strong.
>
> (Goldman, online)

Opposing views will argue that this New Man is an illusion and that anarchism is nothing but an idle utopia that can never be achieved, since people are unable to live without being governed and cannot socially interact without hierarchical constraint or guidance. *Der neue Mensch*, in the words of Erich Fromm, "finds a new unity through the development of all his human forces, which are produced in three orientations. These can be presented separately or together: biophilia, love for humanity and nature, and independence and freedom" (Fromm 1965, online). The New Man is a child of the Enlightenment age and of modernism, but already the Bible calls for rethinking, for mental renewal, for justice and holiness, e.g. in Ephesians 4:22 ("you were taught, with regard to your former way of life, to put off your old self, which is being corrupted by its deceitful desires"); the plan of the New Man is to create heaven on earth.[14] The concept of the New Man is based on a strong belief in the good nature of man, the idea of happy individuals striving for themselves and for each other as soon as they are free to do so. Personally, I first encountered the utopia of the New Man in historical propaganda movies[15] on the socialist movement in 1920s Vienna. At that time the socialist-ruled city of Vienna had begun to build its community housing palaces, the *Wiener Gemeindebauten*, for its workers and their families. Those huge complexes offered affordable, modern apartments with the luxury of running hot and cold water, indoor plumbing and heating, communal washing rooms and kitchen, childcare centers, and courtyard gardens. The old propaganda clips are enough to make one cry over the beauty of the combined efforts of the happy workers placing the bricks on top of each other, singing of the whereabouts of those very bricks now building their new world, their children being educated to live in goodwill together in this new world – and all this was funded by a special tax applied to citizens in higher income brackets. Unfortunately, this new haven did not last and was never able to prove whether the spirit of the builders' generation could carry over into a "new society." *Das Rote Wien* (Red Vienna) was overrun by the *Reaktion* in February 1934 when the workers lost the battles around the *Gemeindebauten* to the Austrofascists, who sought to establish another kind of "utopia."

Whether the New Man will ever be born is an issue in current debates in feminist political economics. Suzanne Bergeron has wondered whether the marginalized subjects in a globalized world would become followers of the new system or whether they would turn into those striving for a world in which a life, in the anarchist sense of self-responsibility and freedom, could become possible. Bergeron claims that academics and social philosophers have not agreed on whether those economic subjects will "enjoy the benefits of the market once they are included" or whether they will "stand in opposition to global capital" (Bergeron 2001: 987).

Free market visionaries, such as Friedrich von Hayek and Milton Friedman, clearly state that the individual will certainly choose the first option proposed. In that regard, Kathryn Dean questions the proposed concept of choice, since

> the possibility of making 'good' choices, that is, choices which enhance the well-being of individual choosers (however that well-being my be conceived), depends on the intelligibility of the world, on the degree of knowledgeability attained by choosers and on their ability to act in a

> forceful and effective manner in complex, constantly changing circumstances. This is a matter of reality-testing. But, as we have come to understand, reality-testing can only take place when the cultural parenting has ensured the availability of a shared sense of reality. This is not the case in disorganized cultures in which the clear boundedness of subjects and objects which the concept of rational choice entails has been dissolved through . . . de-differentiations.
>
> (Dean 2003: 165)

What Dean stresses in her argument is that the neoliberal organization of our society per se denies individuals the freedom to choose a different set of priorities in their lives; instead of a responsible, caring lifestyle the citizens she talks about must engage in activities that prevent a nurturing attitude towards the world. She calls for

> the kind of citizens the world needs now: citizens who take responsibility for world care. This conception of citizenship is utopian in the sense that contemporary culture provides few of the resources needed for that practice. To the contrary. Our duty to the 'community' involves duties to capitalism (duties to labor and to shop) whose fulfillment renders world care impossible.
>
> (Dean 2003: 178)

Strategies to toy with gaps and margins in the mainstream

Given the difficulties with the idea of a world government of federal nations with responsible citizens, the proposed alternative, an organization of all willing societies in our current world into anarchist communes as described above, is probably impossible, at least in the short run; however, *symbolically* this might be possible. It is hard to imagine that nation-states will cease to exist in the way anarchism demands, but it is conceivable that the nation-state could be simply *ignored*. Ignoring in this sense includes Bergeron's suggestion of seeing the weaknesses of a construction, of "moving away from hegemonic thinking about [for instance the market] as a natural and unstoppable force." In an example she describes how it is possible to deconstruct the seemingly ominous power of global capital by focusing on its weaknesses, seeing global capital as vulnerable rather than unstoppable and thus breaking some of the images created by capitalism about the enormous power of capitalist globalization. (Recall that the Great Depression of the 1920s and 1930s also occurred in a period of globalization.) Relational geography suggests that a relationship exists between subjects and places. In fluid movements marginality seems to be empowered to create geography without center and periphery dualisms. An example of this is the concept of the Black Atlantic, a metaphor created to help understand colonial history and the African Diaspora (Gilroy 1992). In the case of the nation-state and the notion of democratic governments, Sheyla Benhabib describes one of the porosities of the concept through an increasing international migration in a globalizing world:

> Yet one thing is clear: the treatment by states of citizens and residents within their boundaries is no longer an unchecked prerogative. One of the cornerstones of Westphalian sovereignty, namely that states enjoy ultimate authority over all objects and subjects within their circumscribed territory, has been delegitimized through international law [such as the Geneva Convention]. My question then is: how can the project of democracy be sustained in view of the obsolescence of Westphalian models of sovereignty? How can the boundaries of the demos be redefined in an increasingly interdependent world?
>
> (Benhabib 2004b: 8)[16]

Using these changing political hegemonic givens, Bergeron suggests interesting strategies to toy with the gaps and margins and to establish alternative networks and structures replacing those of old importance – also of nation-states:

> There are, however, alternative ways of imagining capital and resistance [than Global Sisterhood and transforming institutions from within] coming out of feminist analysis that might create more space for recognizing these other forms of collective subjectivity.
>
> (Bergeron 2001: 996)

Bergeron resists essentialist strategies that propose revaluing the "feminine" to overturn patriarchy (i.e. replacing the rational in the market with the emotional etc.), since this "has come under heavy fire from women of color, lesbians, and working class women, among others" (Bergeron 2001: 997). Another reason is that this would continue to "represent globalization as a dominant and united force, thus making resistance seem utopian and/or destined for defeat" (Bergeron 2001: 998). She also rejects strategies employed by the UN women's Forum in Beijing, a form of transnational feminism where "local interpretations are collapsed into a homogenous identity of 'women's interests'" (Bergeron 2001: 1,000). Rather than that, Bergeron calls for what Bina Agarwal and Gayatry Spivak have established as "strategic sisterhood":

> This notion of strategic sisterhood recognizes a whole range of different possible feminist identities, alliances, and forms of resistance to globalization.
>
> (Bergeron 2001: 1,000)

Strategic essentialism, like strategic sisterhood, is a strategy that ethnic or minority groups or women can temporarily use to present themselves by bringing forward their group identity in a simplified way to achieve certain goals. When this strategy is considered from a position out of Marge Piercy's *Woman on the Edge of Time* the essentialist notion becomes even more playful. Piercy describes the villages in her utopian world as populated by ethnic groups, such as Native American tribes or Harlem Blacks or Ashkenazi, the interesting twist being that no tribe or group member has to be a genetic or physiological successor of such a tribe or ethnic group. In fact:

> grand-council-decisions were made forty years back to breed a high proportion of darker-skinned people and to mix the genes well through the population. At the same time, we decided to hold on to separate cultural identities. But we broke the bond between genes and culture, broke it forever. We want there to be no chance of racism again.
>
> (Piercy 1976: 103)

The members of individual communities adopt the culture and beliefs of their chosen ideals and are thus creating another level of de-essentialized being. The cultural and genetic plurality is in stark contrast to Ursula Le Guin's dystopia *The Lathe of Heaven* (1971), where, in an attempt to end racism, everybody ends up equally grey and colorless without any individual identity.

The Viennese Dyke March is an example of strategic essentialism and unconventional cooperation in a lesbian feminist way. In the Austrian lesbian feminist tradition organizing was often taken on in an essentialist, separatist way. These forms of organization have served their purpose and in many contexts they still do so. In other contexts there have been recent experiments with new forms of solidarity. In 2004 the first European Dyke March took place in Vienna, organized by Lila Tipp in cooperation with the first Austrian Ladyfest. The dyke march was themed "Lesbolove: anti-commercial utopias in motion." The idea of a dyke march is to open a new political non-commercial space, opposing the commodification of GLBT culture in the traditional gay pride parades, which has been a practice in many cities since 1993. Lila Tipp thought of opening the march to individual non-lesbian groups who wanted to be supportive of their issues, but without the loss of lesbian visibility and voice, which often tends to be the case in mixed contexts. The solution was to invite "lesbians and everyone who feels included in the (political) concept." Since it was set in Vienna, the march toyed with Freud's pathologizing of lesbian women, the gruesome history of persecution of sexual and other minorities in the Third Reich, and aimed to generate positive, supportive surroundings for happy interactions between lesbian women and other supporters, celebrating difference from the mainstream concepts of private organization. Here is an extract from the March's opening statement:

> Welcome all perverse people, would-be perverse people . . . to the first ever European Dyke March. We are very very pleased that we are staging

> this fantastic event in Vienna and with all of you. ... The motto for this first ever Dyke March is "Lesbolove:[17] anti-commercial utopias in motion." This wonderful country was and is the home of inquisitors, Nazi spies, informants, patriarchal sexual researchers, Christian Socialists, exploitative and sexualizing sexists, the precursors of the campaign to monotonize and assimilate lesbians and gays and many more. But because we overcome the hurdles of internationalized homophobia anew every day and have to argue about our existence with more or less stupid/ignorant people; today, for a change, we don't want to talk about it at all! Instead we are going to celebrate the space we have created for ourselves and make ourselves right at home.
>
> And how? Namely with Lesbolove! Lesbolove praises non-traditional female and bodily/physical forms; Lesbolove celebrates lesbians and everyone included in this idea; Lesbolove is an antidote to homophobia. Lesbolove can be found in each one of us; its symbolic manifestation is distributed by market stall holders. You can share it with your sweetheart or you can keep it all for yourself. Welcome to the Dyke March! Have fun and plenty of Lesbolove! Feminism will save the world!
>
> (Goutrié and Schoenpflug 2004)

This example of practical humorous strategic essentialism is an illustration employing Piercy's (and communist anarchists', such as Kropotkin's) idea of the anarchist community in a symbolic manner. A very strong network of "resistance towns" helping, interacting, and trading with each other may finally become of more importance to certain individuals than a nation-state one may be a citizen of. This is where the idea of ignoring or replacing the nation-state takes hold – for instance if political oppression forces people to seek refuge in another country, joining the masses migrating into Europe and other Western nations, thus destabilizing a nation-state in the way Benhabib has posited. These refugees might at least temporarily be forced to live in a legal void *sans papiers* in their new host countries, therefore relying on social constructions other than the nation-state to provide them with the opportunity to work or go to school, the right to settle, chances to be politically active, obtain health insurance, a bank account, etc. Feminists should seek to help establish such networks also for people living legally who are faced with other oppressions, be these economic, cultural, or otherwise.

In Chapter 8 I will examine a utopian project with a different goal than (feminist) anarchist utopias have proposed. I will recount the success story of a utopia that has become a global reality and a top-notch hegemonic concept, namely Hayek's utopia of Neoliberalism.

8 The vision of the free market

"Free to choose?"

The purpose of this chapter is to give an example of the rise of a utopian idea that has unexpectedly become part of mainstream thinking. (This all takes place within an existing epistemological paradigm, whereas in Chapter 3 I analyzed a paradigm change and the role of utopia in such revolutionary times.) So this chapter looks into the rise of Neoliberalism, or "the neoliberal turn" (Oetsch 2007b), which has become the most prominent economic doctrine since the 1970s and which currently presents itself as an ahistoric, God-given and natural state. I believe that it is not common knowledge that Neoliberalism started as a purely utopian concept, which once had huge problems finding a place in economic institutions and mainstream economic discourse. This success story is connected to an interesting process of linguistic recodification, as key terms associated with Neoliberalism are, for example, "freedom" and the "free market," in which one set of meanings was replaced or distorted to fit new metaphors, underlying new narratives in economic and political theory. I retell the story of the rise of Neoliberalism not purely because it is an amazing example of the marketing of ideas, but because I believe it is a useful example for encouraging new thinking from marginal spaces that then might move to become common knowledge and be put into political practice.

However, I will also include critiques of neoliberal policy and its effects. An interesting discourse that demonstrates the diversity of views in the community of femeconers is the discussion on the benefits or problems of the *free market*, which was reproduced in *Feminist Economics* in 1996. Subsequently, I will present a view on a different kind of feminism and its relationship to Neoliberalism, which I discuss towards the end of this chapter. The very last sections are concerned with options for alternative strategies, which have not yet become part of the ideological mainstream. But, first of all, I will investigate the policy implications of neoliberal theory.

Libertarianism at work: neoliberal experiments and critical opinions

"Libertarianism" is the political philosophy which has been the core of the so-called "New Right" and influenced Thatcher and Reagan administrations in the 1980s, then became the dominant doctrine of neoliberal political philosophy in the past 20–30 years. This thinking follows the thoughts on classical liberalism, highlighting liberty as the most important value that is often used synonymously with *freedom*, which needs to be protected by strong private property rights. It also demands that a *free market* unfold its potential and the smallest possible government is installed (Hammerton 2003, online). Classical liberalism can be regarded as a unity of political and economic liberalism, whereas in Neoliberalism the economic aspect of the theory has distanced itself from the political aspect. This is connected to the reconceptualization of moral instances; Smith's concept of moral sentiments has been renounced and replaced with the purely formal concept of the *homo oeconomicus*, the calculating machine-person (Oetsch, personal communication).

In political implication, Neoliberalism is mainly concerned with the wish for a "small" government, which is very different from the wish for a state of being wholly without a government, as anarchist theories suggest, and there may also be a great difference in concepts regarding the meaning of "small" itself:

> the Right favors a strong role for the state when it comes to enforcing order at home or abroad, be that through the means of the military, the police or religiously inspired codes of conduct. At the same time the Right wants the state to refrain from distributing wealth, power and legal rights more equitably throughout society. In the policy realm, the Right opposes the government when it taxes the rich, provides for the poor, regulates business, or intervenes against racially or gender-based discrimination.
>
> (Diamond 1996: 11)

From my point of view, the concept of a small government strongly resembles "big" governments in all respects, minus "interfering" in the market and without taking on the responsibilities of a welfare state. The ideal neoliberal government should be based on "conscious social control" but let individuals decide whether a particular occupation is sufficient to compensate for the disadvantages connected to it. It also involves a trust that competition is, for instance, compatible with limited working hours, requires certain sanitary arrangements, and provides an extensive system of social services. Required state activity should be minimized to striving to ensure competition, since the belief that competition will overcome most problems (maybe apart from externalities such as pollution) is the key argument. Peters describes Neoliberalism as a utopian vision, imagining a world of corporate freedom uninhibited by a state, which Neoliberalism seems to generally associate with a dystopian regime as depicted in the movie *Brazil*: bureaucratic, totalitarian, highly inefficient, and chaotic:

> The issues of neo liberalism have all sprung from a simple utopian metaphor and have spread and seeped into a huge variety of economic issues in national and international economics. Economic liberalization or rationalization is characterized by the "abolition of subsidies and tariffs, floating of the exchange rate, the freeing up of controls on foreign investment; the restructuring of the state sector, including corporatization and privatization of state trading departments and other assets, 'downsizing', 'contracting out', the attack on unions and abolition of wage bargaining in favor of employment contracts; and, finally, the dismantling of the welfare state through commercialization, 'contracting out', 'targeting' of services, and individual 'responsibilization' for health, welfare and education."
>
> (Peters 1999, online)

A lot of the non-feminist critical discourse on Neoliberalism is between "left" and "right" notions of government involvement, neglecting many more complex power dynamics, such as the ones postcolonial theory questions. In neoliberal theory and practice the notion of government is highly ambivalent and conflict-laden. Michael Roesch explains:

> There is no possibility to justify any activity of the state ... in neoliberal theory. This means a guarantee of totally equal opportunities, protection of the individual, prevention of discrimination and assurance of the necessary frame conditions of free markets. In Friedman's theory ... the only justified intervention of the state in the economy is the prevention of monopolies since monopolies harm the free markets. In this respect there is the biggest discrepancy between theory and practice. Contrary to the theory, the "Chicago Boys" accepted the authoritarian regime of Pinochet and the military junta. But this policy is not as contradictory as it seems. A powerful state is a necessity to carry out unavoidable, but usually unpopular measures involved when the economy is to be changed radically. ... The function of the state in neoliberal thinking is very close to Robert Nozick's theory of the minimal state – but just in theory. In practice, the government is only important for the enforcement of the reforms.
>
> (Roesch 1999, online)

In the presidential race of 2001, Buchanan simultaneously argued for a smaller government and an increase in military spending, disregarding the fact that the military is a part of the government. Noam Chomsky describes this phenomenon of this U.S. American move towards a "smaller state" as "Pentagon Keynesianism."

Feminist economics' critique of Neoliberalism

The application of the *free market* vision to the real world, which is subsumed under the term Neoliberalism, and the effects on women, the poor, and the environment have been of deep concern in feminist economics. Prue Hyman (1996) has worked on the issue regarding the situation in New Zealand and the so-called neoliberal "New Zealand Experiment;" Elson and Nilufer (1999) have analyzed the effects of globalization, World Bank and International Monetary Fund (IMF) policies on developing countries from a gender point of view; Suzanne Bergeron's thoughts are discussed in this piece; in her "Short History of Neo-liberalism" Susan George (1999) explains the historical transformation of Hayek's utopia into the dominant worldwide economical and political program; and there are many others who cannot be mentioned here. I will now turn to an example of feminist economics' critique:

In "Invisible Hearts – Care and the Global Economy," Nancy Folbre (1999) uses a utopian approach to criticize the issue of unlimited competition and unrestrained *free markets*. Her paper emphasizes the contributions that feminist theory makes to this larger critique. Folbre starts her work with a comparative "*utopian fairytale*" of societies competing in the race of the global economic system. By doing this, she applies a radical overall view to the workings of different economic systems. She then points out one area in caring labor that is hardest to measure, namely the emotional skills that this job requires. Research on this issue shows that the emotional skill of the caregiver has an enormous effect, for instance, on attaining educational, cognitive test scores, and many socio-demographic variables. She also points out that "care" does not just concentrate on the young, the old, and the sick, but is also essential to keep the workers going in the competitive global system. Her analysis lists three changes in caring work caused by globalization:

1 Less care is provided in the home, more is bought in the market.
2 Markets become less embedded in local communities.
3 Care might become scarcer, since the market penalizes altruism and care. Also, both institutions and individuals are tempted to free ride on the care provided most often by women.

Folbre then links these findings with mainstream economic theory and explains how caring labor fits into the paid labor market. She then proceeds to connect caring labor to gender differences and quotes (astonishing) findings, such as that

> cross cultural research shows that when men take an active role in the details of running a home and raising children, they develop emotional sensitivities, avoid boastful and threatening behavior, and include women in community decision making. Increasing men's involvement in family work thus has the potential to increase women's public status and decrease men's propensity for violence.
>
> (Coltrane, in Folbre 1999: 27)

Men's participation in childcare is said to be good for them and for the society as well. Folbre argues, though, that men know their decision to be involved in the home is nevertheless a costly one and they might therefore choose to remain in the public arena.

Further on, Folbre describes the relationship between caring labor and public goods and fiscal externalities, pointing out that children always cost mothers more than others who profit from them. An example is the remuneration through public pension schemes. Another interesting example in the larger picture of globalization is as follows:

> Consider a mother who devotes much time and energy to enhancing her children's capabilities and a country that devotes much of its national budget to family welfare. In the short run both are at a competitive disadvantage: they devote fewer resources to directly productive activities. But in the long run their position depends on their ability to claim some share of the economic benefits produced by the next generation.
>
> (Folbre 1999: 80)

Folbre concludes her piece by describing the process of the "commodification of care," which is caused by globalization that demands privatization and more participation in the *free market*. Privatization usually cuts costs, but loss in quality is the downside of the trade-off for everyone. (Folbre uses nursing as an example.) Losers in the second aspect are mostly children; women only benefit if they do not have kids. If they do, the changing system will not be beneficial for them. As an alternative, Folbre points to the Scandinavian countries, just as Barbara Bergmann does, where family commitment is rewarded without reinforcing traditional gender roles. Folbre also suggests that the project of caring labor should not be restricted to the family; however, it might be organized, but it should rather increase community service, such as mandatory work times in the field of care for young people in exchange for free education and the like.

Folbre's work shows how a utopian approach is more than a practical adoption of already existing alternatives. A utopian approach envisions new alternatives and takes the value of envisioning into account. Folbre has not only pointed out alternatives to the *free market*, she has also made references to the developments of globalization as a utopian experiment itself:

> Consider the words of Dow Chemical executive Carl E. Gerstaker: I have long dreamed of buying an island owned by no nation and of establishing the World Headquarters of the Dow Company on the truly neutral ground of such an island, beholden to no nation or society.
>
> (Gerstaker 1974, in Folbre 1998: 37)

His dream has not come true completely, but considering the *maquilladores* in the no-man's-land on the Mexican border or the islands off the coast of industrial countries, it seems as if reality is rapidly approaching his dream scenario since the 1970s.[1]

In her piece Folbre works with utopian elements, she names the visions currently being established in the globalization process and points to the status quo for realizing feminist visions. She offers radical alternatives considering issues of work, reproduction, and technology, and also gender relations. Finally, she describes the conflicting issues between Neoliberalism and feminist economics, for instance in her examination of competition versus care. Nancy Folbre succeeds in opening up space for thinking in terms of alternatives; in this example, for a changing system instead of competing in the free market.

Even though there are more examples of very precise and sharp critique, and fewer that offer alternatives, but a lot of the analysis of feminist economics on Neoliberalism is still very fragmented.

The utopian vision of Neoliberalism[2]

In this section I will explore the historical backgrounds and theoretical foundations of neoliberal thinking that have initiated economic policy, as discussed above. Some of the important origins of Neoliberalism and its economic, theoretical, and philosophical background can be found in Austria during the early twentieth century. At the same time and in the same place as utopian "Red Vienna" was unfolding, Friedrich von Hayek received his doctorates in law and political science from the University of Vienna in 1921 and 1923. He is one of the most famous thinkers in the Austrian School of Economics and he is probably the single most influential individual economist and political philosopher to shape what is now understood as Neoliberalism. He was a scholar of Carl Menger, Eugen Boehm-Bawerk, and Ludwig von Mises. He was particularly influenced by Mises's ideas of antisocialism, which formatively shaped his work on business cycles. After having lost the famous wartime debate with Keynes over government interventionism in the 1940s, Hayek and his ideas of a liberal world were dismissed. However, Hayek started to gather around him a number of thinkers committed to the free market, some American scholars such as Milton Friedman, James Buchanan, Gordon Tullock, and Gary Becker of the Chicago School (Peters 1999). Meanwhile, the New Deal had politically reorganized society in the USA, and Europe had been reconstructed with the help of the Marshall Plan. Hayek's ideas of liberalism became highly unpopular in those postwar days:

> In 1945 or 1950, if you had seriously proposed any of the ideas and policies in today's standard neo-liberal toolkit, you would have been laughed off the stage or sent off to the insane asylum. At least in the Western countries, at that time, everyone was a Keynesian, a social democrat or a social-Christian democrat or some shade of Marxist. The

> idea that the market should be allowed to make major social and political decisions; the idea that the State should voluntarily reduce its role in the economy, or that corporations should be given total freedom, that trade unions should be curbed and citizens given much less rather than more social protection – such ideas were utterly foreign to the spirit of the time. Even if someone actually agreed with these ideas, he or she would have hesitated to take such a position in public and would have had a hard time finding an audience.
>
> (George 1999, online)

In 1944, Karl Polanyi proclaimed: "To allow the market mechanism to be sole director of the fate of human beings and their natural environment . . . would result in the demolition of society" (Polanyi in George 1999, online.) Susan George (1999) argues that Hayek's idea of liberalism only became popular when Keynesianism could no longer sufficiently explain the happenings in the economy, which was the case with cost-push inflation, initiated by the oil crises. She claims that only then could Hayek and the Chicago School promote the application of their economic utopia to form a new economic world order. Walter Oetsch, who is not only an economist but also an neurolinguistic programming (NLP) expert, has put together a more thorough observation of the rise of the neoliberal project (Oetsch 2007a). Oetsch researches communication networks, institution formation, and, most importantly, the use of metaphors, folktales, and images that the propaganda project of Neoliberalism employs. His analysis is quite interesting, as he builds on the metaphors economics has always used and expands them to produce more psychological theories that explain the effectiveness of concepts which might otherwise seem absurd, as spin master Walter Lippmann, an important thinker in Neoliberalism, describes in his *Public Opinion* (Lippmann 1997 [1921]). Lippmann believes that a person's actions are not dependent on her knowledge and experience, but rather depend on inner mental images, those images form a "world" of their own not influenced by actual experience. Examples of this process are the "life" of stereotypes, which are not easily changed via direct incidents but still unconsciously form our social understanding. "This meant that men formed their picture of the world outside from the unchallenged pictures in their heads," as Lippmann puts it (Lippmann, in Oetsch 2007a: 11). Propaganda aims at directly changing inner images about social givens, i.e. replacing unconscious images with another set of pictures, for instance with slogans and slick metaphors, thereby not only changing the perception but also the actions of individuals and collectives[3] (Oetsch 2007a).

As Geoffrey Hodgson points out, the neoliberal thought project is closely tied to a utopian vision, which is exemplary for the fact that utopian thinking is not exclusive to the political "left," but is rather a phenomenon that is woven through all political ideologies:

> Utopian thinking is typically associated with socialism and communism. However, the contrasting politico-economic schemes of pro-market libertarians can equally be described as utopian. Karl Polanyi (1944: 3) referred to the free-market ideal of many in the nineteenth century as 'a stark utopia'. Robert Boguslaw (1965: 136–42) cited similarly 'the utopia of laissez faire'. The utopia of the free market has had prominent exponents in both the nineteenth and twentieth centuries. For example, Krishan Kumar (1987: 49) noted that the utopian element in "free trade" was especially clear in the writings and pronouncements of John Bright and Richard Cobden'. Vincent Geoghegan (1987: 3) pointed out that 'Thatcherite conservatism is a glaring example of right-wing utopianism, with its summoning up of the supposed glories of Victorian Britain'. Friedrich Hayek, the Nobel Laureate and intellectual champion of free-market individualism, was candid about his own utopian agenda.
>
> (Hodgson 1999: 3)

Hodgson's statement is very interesting. On the one hand he claims that utopia is not necessarily a "left-wing" phenomenon, and on the other hand he points out that economists such as Hayek and Friedman have clearly considered parts of their work as purely utopian. Hayek lays out his strategy of promoting the liberal utopia in this most astonishing and fiery appeal:

> We must make the building of a free society once more an intellectual adventure, a deed of courage. What we lack is a liberal Utopia, a programme which seems neither a mere defence of things as they are nor a diluted kind of socialism, but a truly liberal radicalism which does spare the susceptibilities of the mighty (including the trade unions), which is not too severely practical and which does not confine itself to what appears today as politically possible. We need intellectual leaders who are prepared to resist the blandishments of power and influence and who are willing to work for an ideal, however small may be the prospects of its early realization. They must be men who are willing to stick to principles and to fight for their full realization, however remote. The practical compromises they must leave to politicians. Free trade and freedom of opportunity are ideals which still may rouse the imaginations of large numbers, but a mere 'reasonable freedom of trade' or a mere 'relaxation of controls' is neither intellectually respectable nor likely to inspire any enthusiasm . . . if we can regain that belief in power of ideas which was the mark of liberalism at its best, the battle is not lost.
>
> (Hayek 1949: 26)

Robert Nozick then made libertarian political philosophy respectable within mainstream academia, which he did just in time to strengthen the re-emergence of Hayek's theory during the abovementioned economic crisis in the

1970s. In his 1974 *Anarchy, State and Utopia*,[4] Nozick argues for liberty that entails considerations regarding the just distribution of goods. A distribution is seen as "value-free" or just, as long as it has been created by voluntary exchange, which is very similar to the concept of Pareto efficiency, both disregarding inequalities. Nozick questions the primacy of one of Rawls's two basic principles of justice, namely his arguments in *A Theory of Justice*, which conclude that inequalities are only morally justified if they at least improve the fate of the worst off. (This is how Rawls's contractarian system defends libertarianism in economic theory.)

Nozick's libertarianism holds that everyone has the rights to "life, liberty and property," given that these are rights of non-interference and entitlements to resources. For example, the right to life means that others are not allowed to kill you and the right to property compels others not to use any of your possessions without your permission. The only rightful functions of the state are to guarantee those rights and to defend the country from enemy invasion. Nozick wants to ban taxation on the grounds that it violates the right to property; laws and regulations should only be there to enforce rights. Libertarianism advocates a minimal state that does not interfere with the free market economy but protects people's rights:

> Regulations protecting the health and safety of workers, for example, would be repealed on the grounds that they are a violation of the freedom of contract. The welfare state would be dismantled and nationalised industries privatised by libertarians. Some libertarians hold that even a minimal state is inimical to natural rights and would abolish the state, and have private competing law agencies for the protection of people's rights.
>
> (Hammerton 2003, online)

The libertarianism Hayek proposes is slightly less radical than Nozick's. Hayek subsumes his ideas as "the liberal argument." This should not be mistaken for *laissez-faire*, meaning to leave things just as they are; instead, liberalism favors making the best possible application of competition in order to coordinate human efforts. The effective creation of competition is the best way of guiding individual efforts. To help insure that competition works, Hayek declares that a functioning legal network is essential. On the one hand, the government should not interfere in the economic activity to curb distortion, and on the other hand Hayek regards competition as superior, because it is the only method that does not require the intervention of authority.

The free market

On *freedom*: between anarchist interpretations, such as those put forth by Emma Goldman, and neoliberal interpretations, a phenomenon of seemingly amazing parallels between anarchist and (neo)liberal ideals seems to appear. Where freedom from suppression combined with open-minded education will help the anarchist individual to become more like the *New Man*, liberal thinkers like Friedrich von Hayek and Milton Friedman argue that only the competition on the market or the *Invisible Hand* will guide people to their true freedom. (This is in stark contrast to Goldman's thinking. She believes that the production process and consumerism, such as created by a free market, only function as a prison preventing people from being self-sufficient, free, responsible and socially mature. Finally, she sees the government as an institution that is only set up by those who prosper from the exploitation of the laborers in the market.) A very thorough analysis of the concepts of freedom and competition in the neoliberal discourse can be found in Holger Furtmayr's master thesis *Freiheit und Wettbewerb: Eine Kritik des (neo)liberalen Verstaendnisses zweier grundlegender Begriffe*[5] (2005).

The confusing linguistic parallels tied to the discussion of *freedom* or even *true freedom* in anarchist or liberal concepts are an example of differences between signifier and signified in a poststructuralist sense. Both anarchists and libertarians seem to agree somehow on the fact that governing inhibits people in their desire to live in freedom and that without government responsible caring people will enhance well-being for all, but the implications behind this consensus on the term "freedom" are ultimately divergent. Speaking with Hayek's concepts, the word "freedom" has become a "weasel word," a terminus that is absolutely hollow and can be used to fully distort the meanings of other words it is attached to, such as that the concept of the market changes when it is coupled with *free*, which is the case with the *free market*, a key issue in neoliberal theory.

Metaphorically speaking, the free market is the purest location of freedom per se. Hayek, of course, did not think that the free market concept is a weasel concept (or perhaps he did), but he certainly claimed that only the market has proven to work over time. Hayek thought that the most successful societies in history were market based in some way. Hayek characterized the free market as it is nowadays described in most economic textbooks:

> The market is superior to other economic systems since it handles human ignorance by passing information in coded form through the price mechanism, which indicates areas where profits could be made and resources efficiently used. It does all this and allocates resources, without being predicated on any specific goals or assuming what the goals of people were. It also facilitates freedom, in that for it to work there need to be rules demarcating 'protected domains' for each person, where no other has the right to interfere. This of course is referring to private property rights. Hayek viewed strong property rights and the free market as the best way of protecting liberty, although this did not lead to as strong an anti-state stance as with Nozick and other libertarians.

> Indeed Hayek did not argue for the total abolishment of tax, or even that it should be restricted to law enforcement and defence, he thought taxes could be used for welfare, or to provide certain goods which the market might fail to adequately supply. However, in practice Hayek believed it would hardly ever be necessary to use taxes in this way.
>
> (Hammerton 2003, online)

A more thorough discussion on Hayek's and liberal market conceptions can be found in Oetsch (2007b).

Battlefield free market

The utopian thinkers of the right not only created their own model worlds, but also spent a great deal of their time on dismissing the utopian models and ideals of the political "left." This is because, as Hayek points out in his *Road to Serfdom*, "socialism was early recognized by many thinkers as the gravest threat to freedom" (Hayek 1945). Hayek explains his resistance to centrally planned economies as opposed to free markets and focuses on state authority as the key component of his critique of socialist thought. He describes socialism, which is the only kind of utopia he considers, and communism as being authoritarian, as he sees them as a reaction against the new liberalism of the French Revolution. This interesting twist in history is argued in such a manner that the thinkers who founded the basis for the French Revolution believed their ideas could only be realized by a strong despotic government. He shows this by quoting Saint-Simon, who in his view predicted that those who would not comply with his anticipated planning boards would be "treated as cattle" (Hayek 1945). Hayek's criticism concentrates purely on the form of government, which is assumed to function as an authoritarian regime, using similar arguments to the Anarchist thinkers that government is repressive, but when arguing for democracy they are simultaneously arguing for government. Why should a democratically elected government in a free market system operate differently from a democratically elected government in a socialist system? Hayek answers this by saying that the socialist system of central planning will concentrate power more than a conglomerate of free individuals. But Hayek picks up the socialist quest for a demand for freedom and compares it with the search for freedom of "the Right." Without going into detail when claiming to possess the "true" freedom, Hayek argues:

> [With socialism] the word "freedom" was subjected to a subtle change in meaning. The word had formerly meant freedom from coercion, from the arbitrary power of other men. Now it was made to mean freedom from necessity, release from the compulsion of the circumstances which inevitably limit the range of choice of all of us. Freedom in this sense is, of course, merely another name for power or wealth.

> The demand for the new freedom was thus only another name for the old demand for a redistribution of wealth.
>
> (Hayek 1945, online)

Property is theft?

Apart from the fact that the anti-state notion of "the right" seems to be mostly a front, anarchism and the libertarian idea of freedom clash over the principle of capitalism. Marge Piercy says about feminist utopian fiction:

> Usually there is pretty much classlessness. Usually the problems of having enough have been dealt with. Nobody seems to be terribly interested in being filthy rich, but there is also no poverty. Things are pretty well spread around. That is characteristic of all utopias that women have created.
>
> (Piercy 2005, online)

Proudhon considered "property as theft" and called for a complete reorganization of modern society that would do away with most of its "traps," such as money and the state itself. He advocated communitarianism as a form of reorganization of society and believed that "goodwill" would emerge naturally if those traps were abolished. Left-wing anarchism rejects the accumulation of personal wealth, but this accumulation is (Neo)liberalism's core goal and is thought to be carried out in the competition of the free market. Critics such as Diamond cynically call competition a "dog-eat-dog-game;" they do not believe that an individual's well-being can be ensured through the accumulation of commodities, which would, in a second step, guarantee a kind of social spirit of voluntary donations for the needy. In contrast, the neoliberal view believes that this is the only way to achieve social justice:

> David Friedman, in his book The Machinery of Freedom, notes that there are only three ways to get something: (1) by trading, (2) by receiving a gift (from love or friendship), or (3) by force ("do what I want or I'll shoot you"). Honest, peaceful people operate in the first two ways. Criminals and the state operate by force, aggression, coercion. Dog-eat-dog is defined as "ruthless or savage competition." This is an absurd description of the free market. And besides, it's unfair to dogs. In truth, the marketplace has a civilizing, humanizing effect. If honesty didn't exist, the marketplace would invent it, because it's the most successful way to do business. In the free market we see, not a survival of the fittest, but a survival of the kindest. Survival of the most cooperative. Survival of the friendliest. A gentle Darwinism, if you will. In a free society, the most considerate prosper. As Thomas Sowell says,

> "Politeness and consideration for others is like investing pennies and getting dollars back." A smile has currency.
>
> (Harris 1998, online)

The above quotation from Sharon Harris goes right to the core of dissimilarities between the apparently similar but actually quite opposite beliefs in individual freedom by anarchists and libertarians. It is interesting also how Harris supports the free market idea and all the options it creates for men and women of all backgrounds alike: "Yes, there are rude people in the marketplace. But it's easy to quit doing business with them" (Harris 1998). This is along the lines of Becker's theory of disappearing discrimination. In 1971, Becker argued that in the free market it does not pay for firms to display discriminating behavior, and so this behavior will eventually die out. Becker's prediction has not yet been empirically proven.

Whereas socialists and anarchists see a part of personal freedom as relying on the independence of economic oppression and exploitation, neoliberal reasoning does not honor this argument. For instance, Nozick explains in his Wilt Chamberlain example[6] that a theory of just distribution is not sound: any distribution that results from free exchange between agents and their rightful belongings must be just. He sees that free exchanges will always disturb any favored pattern of allocation. The allocation is then based on free trading, where some will profit and others will not, and this will be carried on to the next generations. Those results may be displeasing, but they are not considered unfair. For instance, one of the things "the right" tackles as unjust is the abuse of power in communism. It is taken as an example of Marxism's inability to create the "True Freedom." It is important here to bear in mind Hayek's historical context:

> To those who have watched the transition from socialism to fascism at close quarters, the connection between the two systems is obvious. The realization of the socialist program means the destruction of freedom. Democratic socialism, the great utopia of the last few generations, is simply not achievable.
>
> (Hayek 1976, online)

The key element of a utopia for "the right" which can bring true freedom (to those who deserve it) is the free market and its system of healthy competition.

Even those who work on employing strategies of free market economics sometimes criticize that system. In a world-famous outcry, the former World Bank chief economist Joseph Stiglitz condemned the World Bank's free market recommendations for structural adjustment as exploitative and neocolonial. He called the World Bank's approach to privatization "Bribarization" and elaborates on this in his 2002 book on the unfairness of redistribution between rich and poor countries under the cover of "free trade." Another example is John Gray, a former advisor to Margaret Thatcher. He now teaches "European Thinking" at the London School of Economics. In his 2001 book he comes out as a critic of the dogma of globalization with right-wing arguments, blaming multiculturalism for the failure of globalization. In a newspaper interview[7] he states:

> I have called the project of a global free market strictly utopian – similar to global communism, because both have tried to force a single form of political and economical institutions on enormously different cultures, religions. I foresaw, that this attempt would rapidly lead to a break down, and – without foreseeing September 11th – I said that the most important opponents would not be the anti-globalization movement but ethical nationalism and religious fundamentalist movements, which would have become strengthened by the dogmatic realization of a market economy of American style, the "Washington Consensus."
>
> (author's translation)[8]

Anarchists also described a need to distance themselves from communism, also on the grounds of issues associated with freedom as they saw it: historically, anarchists and communists shared common goals, such as ending workers exploitation and, at some stages such as during the preparation for the Russian Revolution, they also operated in common groups. Other anarchists nevertheless already left the First International in 1872. Bakunin summarized the ideological differences thus:

> I hate Communism because it is the negation of liberty and because for me humanity is unthinkable without liberty. I am not a Communist, because Communism concentrates and swallows up in itself for the benefit of the State all the forces of society, because it inevitably leads to the concentration of property in the hands of the State.
>
> (Bakunin, in Thomas 1980: 303)

The ultimate failure of communism in Russia seemed to prove Bakunin right in that regard. Emma Goldman at first had higher hopes than him for the functioning of communism in Russia. After she was expelled from the USA, where she had agitated against U.S. participation in World War I, she returned to St. Petersburg full of hopes that the old Russia she had left would now have been replaced with something much closer to her vision. Her happy expectations turned to horror at the 1921 Kronstadt uprising of Soviet sailors. The sailors turned against communist rule, demanding, amongst other issues, freedom of speech and of the press for workers and peasants, for the anarchists and for the left Socialist parties. After brief negotiations with Lenin, Leo Trotsky, who was then minister of war, sent in the Red Army, killing around 1,000 of the sailors, wounding thousands and driving around 8,000 people to flee to Finland. Goldman then left Russia for good, and describes her disappointment in *My Disillusionment in Russia*:

> Kronstadt broke the last thread that held me to the Bolsheviki. The wanton slaughter they had instigated spoke more eloquently against them than aught else. Whatever their pretences in the past, the Bolsheviki now proved themselves the most pernicious enemies of the Revolution. I could have nothing further to do with them.
>
> (Goldman 1925, online)

Emma Goldman hence followed Bakunin's critique of communism as authoritarian and violent, at least after the Kronstadt example, far from the freedom she had believed in.

Feminist economics and the free market

Feminist economics and especially the more traditionally socialist branches of the discipline are employed in a critique of neoliberal economics. Still, the next part of this exploration will look into the discussions of feminist economics on exchange and the market question. It is a good example of the diversity within the discipline, of what happens in narrow discursive spaces, how spaces can be narrowed by discussants, why discourses may be so narrow in the first place, i.e. whose interest is it in to keep a discourse so tight? Finally, it shows how utopian quests will be smothered and how they will disappear from a discourse.

One of the most interesting discussions in feminist economics concerning utopian visions was what has colloquially been called "The Market Debate." "Debating Markets," by Dorman *et al.*, was published in *Feminist Economics* 2(1), 1996, and reflected on a debate that had taken place on the email list Femecon-l in the spring of 1994. The debate involved most of the list participants and IAFFE members. Weisskopf and Folbre edited the debate by quoting from contributions of four participants, three men and one woman. That article was followed by Lynn Duggan and Jennifer Olmsted asking "Where Has All the Gender Gone?"[9] Richard Wilks's "Taking Gender to Market;"[10] Susan Feiner's "A Paradigm of Our Own;"[11] Linda R. Robertson's "'Debating Markets': A Rhetorical Analysis of Economic Discourse;"[12] Roxanne Harvey Gudeman and Stephen Gudeman's "Gender, Market and Community on Femecon in May and June 1994;"[13] Barbara Hopkins's "Argument and Community in the Markets Debate;"[14] Douglas Orr's "Not Only Gender: More on Debating Markets;"[15] Lisa Saunders's "If You Can't Stand the Heat;"[16] and, finally, Roxanne Harvey Gudeman and Stephen Gudeman's "Competition/Cooperation: Revisiting the May 1994 Femecon Debates."[17] This adds up to ten journal publications discussing the debate that began on the mailing list. The question that had started the discussion, and was also the first line in the first journal article, was posed by Nancy Folbre. She asked:

> What is the role of markets in a feminist vision of a fair and efficient economy?
>
> (Dorman *et al.* 1996: 70)

This is clearly a question concerned with utopian visions of feminist economics, an invitation to create, discuss, and build theory and practice. Interestingly, what happened in the first publication of the Markets Debate was that Deirdre McCloskey fiercely argued for the free market, namely that the free markets would, "if they are not interfered with, in time create a culture of moral sentiments. . . . The market is a school for courtesy, honesty, and imagination" (Dorman *et al.* 1996: 84),[18] while others had more socialist arguments:

> I think there should be limits to the scope of markets, even those based on trust and persuasion. Because I think that commitments based on affection and obligation should not be replaced by those based on self-interested (even if not purely selfish) exchange.
>
> (Dorman *et al.* 1996: 84)

Bridal bazaars, prostitution, the USSR, whether love could be marketed, and the like then became issues in the discussion.

The next article, by Lynn Duggan, comments on the gender ratio in the edited version of the debate, which is far from representative of the list. Duggan states that the "original debate centered on whether women benefit from free markets, yet gender is eclipsed in this distillation" (Duggan and Olmsted 1996: 86). She (correctly) points out that the issue of gender was not an issue in the discussion anymore, which stayed at the level of a pro or contra free markets debate. She also reminds us that simply including discussions of women's experiences does not make a discourse feminist, as Sandra Harding pointed out in the very first article in *Feminist Economics*. She further remarks that individualism and the nuclear family were seemingly implicit in the debate as it was represented. She adds some other arguments she recalls from the original debate with more feminist content, i.e. Prue Hyman's retelling of the New Zealand Experiment; cultural expectations versus market shaping; tools of economics and their fitness for measuring events in marriage and caring markets; growth in non-market work; etc.

Richard Wilk then comments on ethnocentric assumptions made in the debate. He offers examples from other cultures to support his argument and also gives his opinion on the free market, stating that it is "a superstition and a self-validating essay in logic" (Wilk 1996: 92).

Susan Feiner states that this discourse is about utopia, and this is not just the utopian vision Nancy Folbre has asked for, but the neoliberal utopia of the free market. Feiner says that feminist economics will create its own vision, once it has a room, a place where women can sit down to think up their vision. She also says that feminist economists are yet not ready to voice their own visions. She claims there is no appropriate room and that women have not had time to gather and speak to one another.

Feiner uses Virginia Woolf's analogy of a *Room of One's Own* and calls for a "paradigm of one's own." She claims that McCloskey, like so many economists, fell for the vision (scorned by Napoleon) of a "nation of shopkeepers." She claims that these economists, "transfixed by their reflection in this vision of markets, can't see woman-subjectivity erased, rendered invisible – and don't notice that production, conflict, exploitation, warmth, and affective connection disappear too" (Feiner 1996: 95). She does not stop there with the deconstructive critique; moreover, she is the one who asks for a utopian space as a possibility for creating alternatives:

> But an economics written in a room of our own could resist this negation. From a room of our own we could give voice to a paradigm which articulates a theory of desired social relation (not things) secured and reproduced by economic arrangements. ... Within these walls the siren song of free markets can be heard for what it is – fantasy, illusion, dimly remembered security as one drifts into dream, nestled in the bosom of domestic bliss. From the margins this dream is a nightmare, so from the margins we will build a paradigm of our own.
>
> (Feiner 1996: 95–96)

The Gudemans analyze the discourse on markets by using empirical tools. They count words and contributions of men and women and arguments concerned (Gudeman and Gudeman 1996: 25).

Barbara Hopkins uses personal experience from this debate to illustrate how relationships of power were used to silence opposing arguments and dominate debates. She urges feminists to work together and to reject power games. Lisa Saunders states that how we treat each other says a lot about us and that it will most likely determine the future of IAFFE. She hopes that Femecon-l might remain a safe haven for women scholars in a male-dominated field and that IAFFE will not further support scholars who cannot make convincing arguments in a positive, respectful manner.

The article by Linda Robertson analyses the Market Debate using a rhetorical approach and states, first, that Folbre's question was not answered but replaced by other discussants' off-topic agendas. She points out that male-identified discourse rules were put into place, which "reproduced an intolerable level of intrusion and exclusion" (Robertson 1996: 100), and that any attempt to question these rules was interpreted as censorship. The introduction of the "God-term" "the Market" (which Robertson describes as a metaphor that limits discussion) is furthermore not questioned by any of the participants; all agree to play according to set rules and terminology. Robertson further explains that it becomes extremely difficult, if not impossible. to "formulate a vision of feminist economics … given the restrictions on the terms of the debate" (Robertson 1996: 107), since the terms have been dichotomized. The only alternatives left for feminist economics are either to be pro market or contra market; pro state or contra state – Liberty and Freedom versus Constraint and Restriction. She uses the analogy by Aristotle, which Barker also used; McCloskey uses the term "the Market" for issues described by Aristotle as the public domain. Having limited the rhetoric in the discussion so far, it is not surprising that the creation process for alternative visions also becomes rather limited:

> The utility of rhetorical analysis as a critical tool should be obvious for its capacity to clarify how false dichotomies inhibit the production of economic knowledge because they narrow the terms of the debate.
>
> (Robertson 1996: 110)

Robertson picks up McCloskey's argument that markets are about persuasion, simply because they are not about coercion. In contrast, she concludes that the consumer becomes a commodity in the market herself and that the market

> is not about persuasion, it is about propaganda and the creation of desire. It is not about citizens, it is about consumers. It is not about freedom of thought or creativity or expression; it is about wanting what everyone else wants, but feeling as if that desire distinguishes you as an individual, when in fact it simply makes you part of a very large crowd.
>
> (Robertson 1996: 110)

Within all the turmoil, Folbre's invitation to actively create a feminist utopian vision has been pushed aside; "the substance of the transcription does not address the original question, in an odd and undoubtedly unexpected way" (Robertson 1996: 101). It is replaced by another agenda and another already dominant vision (the neoliberal vision of the free market). The quest for finally creating feminist alternatives together has been forgotten; list participants who might have liked to discuss and create visions together have not had the chance to do so, since all energy quickly went into the discourse on the market. Issues of domination, abuse, and modes of discussing were widely analyzed in the articles following the edited version of the debate, yet no one except Robertson and Feiner pointed out that Nancy Folbre's original question was never answered and that the very rare chance for creating *more* than a room of one's own was completely trampled on. On that account, an interesting question might be: Why was the question so threatening that attention needed to be taken away from it so badly? Why did the discussants fail to notice that the original question was lost? Duggan stated that the "original debate centered on whether women benefit from free markets" (Duggan and Olmsted 1996: 86), which is not fully true. The original question and the resulting debate would have been to address new ideas on how feminists envision markets in a fair and efficient economy. Robertson wonders whether it is not part of the economic academic discourse to develop a "feminist vision of economics." She concludes that this should be the case and that there needs to be a political discourse about the aims of feminists' desire.

There seem to be a multitude of feminist theorists waiting and hoping for the creation of alternatives – for example Feiner, Barker, Bergeron, Folbre, and doubtlessly many others – but a coherent feminist alternative has not been founded; nor has the paradigm shifted. Let me conclude this section with an example of a very market-oriented feminist utopia by Kelley Ross of the Friesian School.

Neoliberal feminism

As a contrast to the very differentiated debates in feminist economics (as one usually knows it), this section attempts to illustrate how right-wing theory combines Neoliberalism and feminist agendas, thus shifting toward a new utopia of its own. One of the most fascinating links between the divergent agenda of the "free individual" of anarchism, Neoliberalism, and feminism can be traced by following the chart developed within the somewhat obscure Friesian School, a project carried out by the Valley College and the California State Universities of Los Angeles. The Friesian School directly links eighteenth-century philosopher Jakob Fries (1773–1843), on the one hand, to Karl Popper, Friedrich Hayek, and Milton Friedman, and, on the other hand, to Rudolf Otto, C.G. Jung, and Camille Paglia, self-declared feminist anti-feminist. Kelley Ross from the Department of Philosophy at Los Angeles Valley College and founder of the Friesian School project also works in the field of a particular kind of feminism, which he connects to the Friesian School. (This is another example of what Walter Oetsch (2002) in his book on demagogy explained as the strategy of claiming certain words or concepts, filling them with new or distorted meanings, and reintroducing them to the public.) Ross, a proponent of the school, claims that, according to the definitions given in the first chapter of this work, feminists clearly operate in an anti-feminist manner. In *Backlash: The Undeclared War against American Women*, (1991) Susan Faludi extensively describes this phenomenon. In Ross's analysis, he establishes and deems exemplary a system of so-called feminism that tries to dismantle the achievements of feminism, in the sense defined above, by using a theory that is closely connected to the beliefs of the neoliberal agenda. Ross offers a whole array of arguments; for this reason, I will provide more detailed quotations here. He starts out by declaring that feminism ("Feminism is all about creating choice" is usually one of the most uncontested definitions of feminism) is totalitarian:

> The charm that totalitarianism had for feminism was real enough, even though the desire to control human nature wasn't just confined to radical theory. It has crept up on us from all directions. F.A. Hayek says there are basically two views on how society should be organized, tribalism and the free market. Karl Popper more crisply contrasts the Closed Society with the Open Society. Ayn Rand says that the paradigm of humanity in the Open Society of the marketplace is that of the trader. Feminist theory mostly still hates capitalism – "patriarchy" is often simply equated with war, racism, and capitalism; feminism with pacifism, socialism, environmentalism, multiculturalism, and even vegetarianism – in short, any case that might be regarded as "progressive" from a leftist point of view.
>
> (Ross 1997, online)

If one compares this section, for instance, to Mary Mellor's utopia of eco-feminism, it becomes obvious that Ross is right. Feminism usually declares itself leftist not only because it strives for women's liberation, but also because it supports the goals of the peace movement and environmental organizations and includes an anti-racist and anti-homophobic agenda, as gender and race are both considered socially constructed. Ross's feminism stands for other issues as well. Ross confuses the sex of a political proponent with a gendered agenda. Feminism is usually not a concept based on one's biological sex; rather, it is measured by actual improvements in women's concerns, such as wages, work hours, and the like. Because of this confusion he states:

> Hence the ironic move of doctrinaire feminists dismissing with contempt Margaret Thatcher, one of the most successful, powerful, and historically important women, and the longest serving British Prime Minister, of the 20th century.
>
> (Ross 1997, online)

It is amazing, yet somewhat predictable, that this icon of the neoliberal agenda who made economic conditions significantly worse for British women while in power became Ross's model for feminist achievement. Ross argues that feminism is somehow primitive and tribal and still aims to destroy family ties. (If one is feminist and therefore "tribal," how can one be anti-family at the same time?) His argument continues thus:

> Hayek is clear that the marketplace is "unnatural" in a way and that people, yearning for the old tribalism, can simply hate it. The difference is that the old tribal societies were personal. Capitalism is impersonal. Tribalism involved mutual positive obligations. Capitalism involves voluntary trade and contract. Tribalism provided a secure place for everyone. Capitalism denies that absolute security is possible or that we have a right that strangers provide it for us. Tribalism left no doubts.

> Capitalism tells us nothing. Tribalism always provided for needs, to the extent that the group could provide. Capitalism doesn't care what we need, but will provide what we want . . . if we will work for it. Tribalism valued people. Capitalism, indeed, values what people do and want, which is reflected in prices. Thus Marx accused capitalism of reducing even the family to a cash relationship. The choice, indeed, is between security and insecurity, but also between slavery and freedom and, in fact, between poverty of secure socialism and wealth of insecure capitalism. It is hard to choose between security and freedom, and it is easy to hope that they could be had together, that tribalism (or socialism) could be combined with capitalism. With that hope, "freedom" can be pursued in a way that surprisingly leads to tribal slavery. That is what happened with both Marxism and feminism.
>
> (Ross 1997, online)

Bearing in mind the diversity of the utopian struggles of Marxism and feminism, Ross's findings seem even more superficial. Nevertheless, Ross offers a utopian vision, which he calls feminist in the tradition of Hayek's and Friedman's struggle for utopia; therefore he deserves a (small) place here, although contemporary feminist economics clearly does not follow arguments in such a mode.

Some alternatives proposed

In their introduction to a compilation called *Exchange and Deception: A Feminist Perspective*, Caroline Gerschlager and Monika Mokre state that the

> conviction that societies are based on principles of exchange is deeply rooted in modern thinking. The outstanding importance those societies attribute to the market is perhaps the most obvious demonstration of that assertion. However, exchange cannot be reduced to the economic sphere, but must be regarded as fundamental to the modern understanding of social relations in general.
>
> (Gerschlager and Mokre 2002: 3)

Exchange in communist anarchist systems

From my point of view, what Gerschlager and Mokre are referring to becomes very clear in Marge Piercy's *Woman on the Edge of Time*, where she explains how goods are acquired in the absence of a free market in that utopian society:

> "You make a lot of things that fall apart quickly. They did that in my time also. Called it planned obsolescence." "Playthings, flimsies, some

> pretty things we make for a moment. They're called butterflies. But objects we make for daily use, we make to last. It would be a pity to use up scarce copper or steel on a machine that worked poorly." ... "Luxuries fall into two categories: circulating and once-only ... "Circulating luxuries pass through the libraries of each village – beautiful new objects get added and some things wear out or get damaged. Costumes, jewels, vases, paintings, sculpture – some is always on loan to our village. And always passing on. Some are for personal wearing, at feasts and rituals. Some are for enjoyment in the children's house, the meetinghouse, the fooder, the labs the diving gear factory. Outside as we walk around." "But you have to give them back! You don't get to keep anything for yourself! It all belongs to your government?" "We pass along the pleasure ... Imagine for my birthday last year I wore a sable cloak like the Queen of the Night. I have worn emeralds and for a month a Michelangelo hung where I could see it every day. All the pleasure I can suck from such things I've had and pass on to pleasure others."
>
> (Piercy 1976: 176)

Pierre-Joseph Proudhon and Mikhail Bakunin suggest a distribution system based on an individual's labor as an alternative to the free market regarding exchange. (This idea, which is experiencing a resurgence in the practice of alternative circles these days, is one in which coupons for hours worked can be traded.) In feminist economics discourse Frances Hutchinson, in "A Heretical View of Economic Growth and Income Distribution" (1995), describes the Douglasian New Age Social Credit System, which was popular in the English-speaking world during the interwar period. She claims that this system explicitly considered the needs of women within both formal and informal economies. The system dismisses the *homo oeconomicus*, the actor of neoclassical economics, as well as the *worker* who needs to feed a family, as the actor of Marxian economics. At the same time, he establishes the *citizen* as the economic actor whose motives are influenced by roles and learned behavior derived from non-economic influences. Douglas and his predecessor Veblen saw the competitive motivation behind capitalist decision-making as predatory and parasitic. Veblen believed that the endurance of employment arose through "the acceptance of the ruling class ideology of patriotism, militarism and imperialism and from the treadmill of emulative consumption" (Hutchinson 1995: 37). Veblen and Douglas thought that technical means existed to "adapt the world's natural resources to highest requirements of humanity using a very small fraction of the (labor) hours available" (Hutchinson 1995: 42), offering an alternative to constant growth in production. (This theory is revived in the more recent *Factor Four: Doubling Wealth, Halving Resource Use* (Weizsaecker and Amory 1998).)

Hutchinson explores the different versions of social arrangements for women in social credit systems and also explores James Mead's *Agathotopia.*

The Douglasian social credit movement offered "every woman a birthright income i.e. the National Dividend on the productive capacity of the community to ensure economic independence and freedom" (Hutchinson 1995: 38). Feminist approaches to economic theory and policy will be enhanced through closer scrutiny of the communal regulation of finance, which is a core issue in the Douglasian system. Hutchinson shares the belief that the "veil of money" needs to be lifted and that the "capitalist financial system facilitates production and distribution only incidentally" (Hutchinson 1995: 52)

The New Age Social Credit system sounds revolutionary in our days. In the interwar period it was not clear at all that a neoclassical economic theory with a belief in the free market would become mainstream at some point in time. Indeed, first Keynesianism made the race before the neoclassical paradigm became dominant. Yet before all that a Douglasian system might have looked just as probable as a neoclassical system, which is an interesting thought. Hutchinson concludes her paper by saying:

> The range of effects of such heretical[19] policies upon the national and international socio-economic environments should keep economists, feminists and others, fully employed for the foreseeable future.
>
> (Hutchinson 1995: 47)

Feminist spiritual writer Starhawk is also concerned with issues of limited resources; she describes a price system more complex than the usual supply and demand binary in *The Fifth Element*:

> Our credit functions like money, but they're not backed by gold or silver. They're backed by energy, human or other sorts, and our basic unit of value is the calorie. So a product is valued by how much energy goes into its production, in terms of labor and fuel and materials that themselves require energy to produce. And part of that accounting is how much energy it takes to replace a resource that is used. Something that works with solar or wind power becomes very cheap. Anything requiring irreplaceable fossil fuels is generally too expensive to think about.
>
> (Starhawk 1993: 274)

Kropotkin goes even further and rejects his own earlier idea of labor checks as just another form of compulsion; he bases distribution on need rather than on the volume of work. (Some indigenous societies, for instance in Papua New Guinea, still function precisely in that way.) The idea that prices in their current form do not reflect full information regarding supply and demand is an issue often raised by environmental economists and others who do not believe in unlimited growth.

> Our principal constraints are cultural. During the last two centuries we have known nothing but exponential growth and in parallel we have

> evolved what amounts to an exponential-growth culture, a culture so heavily dependent upon the continuance of exponential growth for its stability that it is incapable of reckoning with problems of nongrowth.
>
> (Hubbert 1975, online)

Some economists, such as Herman Daly, have summed up the problem using the concept of "uneconomic growth" (Daly forthcoming). On the political right, Fred Ikle has warned about "conservatives addicted to the Utopia of Perpetual Growth" (Ikle 1994). To incorporate a notion of limited resources before their near depletion is not a given in today's prevalent price mechanism. This problem will be interesting to observe over the next decades in regard to the depletion of raw oil. According to pessimistic calculations, we have reached Hubbert's peak.[20] When will prices start to react, when should we have realized that it might not be a good idea to simply use up the entire planet's resources of fossil fuels, which had accumulated over millions of years, in just one or two centuries?

The gift economy

An interesting example of ecofeminist theory on exchange comes from matriarchy researcher Genevieve Vaughan. Vaughan believes that capitalism and the focus on the market and market economy lastly does not aim at fulfilling actual needs, but at winning and losing in an economic system of often artificially created scarcity. She claims that this finally creates useless waste, poverty, and war, which harms the majority of people and benefits a small elite. Vaughan deduces this currently prevalent economic system from the establishment of a gendered world in a system of patriarchy: she claims that men must refuse to give gifts to others, like their mothers did for them when they were children, in order to establish their masculinity (by being unlike their mothers):

> Exchange creates and requires scarcity. If everyone were giving to everyone else, there would be no need to exchange. The market needs scarcity to maintain the level of prices. In fact when there is an abundance of products scarcity is often created on purpose. . . . On a larger scale scarcity is created 1. by the channeling of wealth into the hands of the few who then have power over the many; 2. by spending on armaments and monuments which have no nurturing value but only serve for destruction and display of power; and 3. by privatizing or depleting the environment so that the gifts of nature are unavailable to the many. The exchange paradigm is a belief system which validates this kind of behavior. Individuals who espouse it are functional to the economic system of which they are a part. Exchange is adversarial, each person tries to give less and get more, an attitude which creates antagonism and distance among the players. Gift giving creates and requires abundance.

> In fact, in scarcity gift giving is difficult and even self sacrificial while in abundance it is satisfying and even delightful.
>
> (Vaughan 1997, online)

The establishment of a gift economy sounds practically impossible in the current state of affairs. The luxury of utopian thinking is nevertheless to allow one to simply consider what would change if this system were to replace our current tradition of exchange. In doing so, we could try to decide whether this might truly solve all problems associated with the current system of Neoliberalism and globalization or even with past and current systems of socialist welfare states and other alternatives.

Vaughan also reflects on the feminist economics of IAFFE, which I find interesting as this is only ever rarely done, even though her comments are not all flattering as she dismisses the work of feminist economists of IAFFE collectively as unfit for truly changing economic paradigms:

> Now some women economists, who like other women have been socialized towards mothering and the practices of giftgiving, are applying gift values to the study of exchange and to their profession and are experiencing a great deal of healthy cognitive dissonance. However, they have not yet begun to question the validity of the exchange paradigm itself as a world view, perhaps because they are still more or less successfully operating within it. [Here a footnote says: "The International Association for Feminist Economics (IAFFE)."] It is easier for those who are at least partly outside the exchange logic to identify and promote giftgiving as a socially relevant paradigm – indeed as the solution to the problems being caused by exchange.
>
> (Vaughan 1997: 54)

It is debatable whether Vaughan is right; it seems to be true that no IAFFE member has thus far argued for something as radical as forsaking exchange and replacing it with a gift economy. This is indeed a radical utopian proposal. In an oral interview, Marge Piercy also refers to the idea of gift-giving as an alternative economic system:

> I was very struck a few years before I wrote *Woman on the Edge of Time* by a book about the Pony Indians, called *The Last World*, written by an anthropologist, who interviewed all the remaining members after they had been uprooted. And one of the things I learned from that book was that, while they were what we would call primitive technologically, socially they were far more sophisticated than we are. ... If somebody stole something from me, I would have to give him another present, because you would only steal if you felt that you didn't have enough, and so you should be made to feel that you have enough. So they were sophisticated in social ways, their constant aim was to keep

> resocializing people, to be good to each other. And that struck me as an extremely sophisticated society in that sense, and I was very impressed by that and thought a lot about that before I wrote *Woman on the Edge of Time.*
> (Piercy 2005, online)

Issues of gift giving, instead of practicing exchange in some kind of market with the intent of reciprocity, seem largely uncommon in Western societies. For instance, Rauna Kuokkanen provides anthropological examples of societies that solely rely on gift giving in her *The Gift As a Worldview in Indigenous Thought*. The article not only lists various motivations for giving gifts in indigenous societies, in this case the Sami of Finland, but also discusses the Western inability to receive gifts if reciprocity is not guaranteed or at least expected. Kuokkanen quotes, for instance, Helene Cixous's *The Laugh of the Medusa*, in which she reflects on the fact that "the masculine economy" reacts with uneasiness when confronted with generosity. For alternative feminist economies Cixous suggests not to imply a form of exchange, but to affirm generosity and the establishment of relationships. This is also Starhawk's solution to curb the invasion and destruction of the utopian enclave in *The Fifth Element*. Whereas Cixous's suggestion seems rather theoretical in a utopian sense, it is a good point that "it is interesting to find that ideas basic to market economy, i.e. the necessity of competition and the freedom of the market, to my knowledge, for some reason have not been deconstructed, but are constantly gaining new ground," as Hildur Ve notes in *Gracias a la Vida: On the Paradigm of a Gift Economy.*

Participatory economics

Generally speaking, compared to the early twentieth century, anarchism today has little influence. A focal point of American anarchist thought is Noam Chomsky, Howard Zinn, and Michael Albert's *www.zmag.org*. Much of *zmag* deals with economic and political issues, teachings on racism, sexism, political activism. The website also contains a questionnaire on utopia, in which users are invited to vote on approaches for utopian action. Possible choices include anarchism, socialism, communism, feminism, etc. Michael Albert[21] offers an Internet course on economic alternatives, which he introduces with a question on visions:

> For some people the question "why vision?" may appear silly. It is like taking a trip, they might reason. We need vision to know where we are going. How else can we organize our journey so it points in the right direction and so nothing about it diverts us from our destination? Vision tells us where we want to arrive and reveals how our present locale falls short of our desires. Vision raises hope and desire. It motivates and secures our efforts against temporary setbacks.
> (Albert and Hahnel 1991: 1)

Zmag further on engages in a synthesis of left-wing politics with views from non-European non-U.S. areas, offering an anarchist economic vision sensitive to gender issues. A 1970 staff paper put together by a collective publishing on *zmag*, relying on a "Bread and Roses"[22] publication, states:

> Women must be enabled to participate in the economy on a basis of equality with men. We believe that the nature of work in our system is demeaning to human beings, and we do not want merely to upgrade women into the alienated jobs that men now hold. However, we refuse to do the low-grade, low-paid, and service work any more. Such jobs must be shared by men and women, as must housework be shared, and be recognized as legitimate work that deserves pay.
>
> (Bread and Roses, 1970, gray literature)

This statement brings together the anarchist and Marxist views on demeaning work within general production processes and women's work in particular, also in the household. Where early utopians and Marxists assumed women would swipe the stage for the revolution, *zmag*'s anarchist vision clearly states that this cannot be the case. *Zmag* pleads for an economic system that embodies anarchist means regarding decision-making. A tremendous amount of power should not be allotted to a few people; rather, it should be shared amongst many people. Generally, people are thought to have an input into decisions regarding how much they are affected by the decision. They create models for an economy in which interaction is based on empathy and cooperation and solidarity vs. anti-social competitiveness and egos. Regarding income, Albert believes that value, which is reflected in how well people are paid, needs to be reconsidered. The system in which "a lot is given to a few and the rest is taking orders" needs to be redesigned. Albert states that currently people are rewarded for the power they can gain, but instead one should be rewarded equally for one's contribution to society. Effort and sacrifice should be rewarded, not power. On their website, Albert and Howard Zinn sketch out Albert and Hahnel's specific models and means for their employment called the "parecon" project:

> Participatory Economics (parecon for short) is a type of economy proposed as an alternative to contemporary capitalism. The underlying values parecon seeks to implement are equity, solidarity, diversity, and participatory self management. The main institutions to attain these ends are council democracy, balanced job complexes, remuneration according to effort and sacrifice, and participatory planning.
>
> (Albert and Hahnel 1991: 2)

I will now close this very brief exploration into a few more current proposals for alternatives. These examples are by no means exhaustive, nor do I mean to install any kind of ranking of the different proposals. Moreover, these examples have been chosen to demonstrate different takes on specific and interesting issues, such as sustainability, exchange, and methods of inclusion.

All in all, this volume has compiled ideas on utopian possibilities for gender relations, working conditions, social arrangements, use of technology and reproduction, and called for a new paradigm change, led by feminist economics. Drucilla Barker reminds us that it

> could be the case that no amount of "better" science and analysis will ever replace the pseudoscientism that characterizes neoclassical economics – because neoclassical economics does one thing very, very well: it articulates the ideology of contemporary capitalism in a manner that makes it seem natural, inevitable, and beneficent. It does not "speak truth to power" but, on the contrary, accommodates and naturalizes power.
> (Barker 2005: 2,195)

If this is the case, feminist economics is truly free to envision completely different ways to go. Rather than having to strain ourselves in thinking up increasingly smart arguments to replace and overcome neoclassical economics and Neoliberalism, wasting energy on a solution that might not be feasible, it might be time to set up our own utopia to set out and replace Hayek's ideal design. This might then be exemplary for an even greater project, the end of Enlightenment. But this is enough envisioning for this instance. "Go, little book," as Joanna Russ says in the last pages of *The Female Man*. "Rejoice, little book! For on that day, we will be free" (Russ 1975: 214).

Notes

Preface

1 I have chosen an open gender concept in this project, allowing the category gender to also include other categories of oppression such as race, class, sexual orientation, place of origin, etc. aside from the core gender categories male and female. I also regard gender as a fluid, non-binary category rather than a static concept.

2 Femecon List. Online. Available HTTP: http://www.listproc.bucknell.edu/archives/femecon-l/200202/msg00036.html (accessed 30 April 2007).

1 Introduction

1 This line has been rewritten to read "A utopian vision can be seen as a thought experiment for philosophers, social scientists, economists, and other theoreticians, no matter whether they are feminists or not" in the definition used in this work.

3 The Cartesian Turn in utopia

1 "Die passive Benevolenz der organischen Naturkonzeption lädt geradezu zu einer Ausbeutung der Ressourcen ein; das chaotisch-unheilbringende Element wiederum legitimiert Unterwerfung und ordnende Intervention. Beiden Vorgangsweisen liegen koloniale Diskurse im Allgemeinen zugrunde und sie beeinflussen besonders die großen Renaissanceutopien, deren Rahmenbedingungen meist Entdeckungsreisen bilden. Es lassen sich daher organische wie mechanistische Ausrichtung den Utopien der frühen Neuzeit als gegensätzliche Weltanschauungen ausmachen. Im Folgenden wird auf diese fiktiven, utopischen Texte eingegangen und gezeigt, wie sehr auch hier dieser ambivalenten Geschlechtlichkeit eine Schlüsselfunktion zur Verwirklichung der jeweiligen utopischen Vision zukommt" (Klarer 1993: 32).

2 An interesting thought in that regard is that the creation of modern science was a process that took place simultaneously with the unfolding of colonialism and the ultimate establishment of nation-states as they are constituted today. This parallel development will be further explored in the chapters on feminist innocence in science (Chapter 4) and feminist anarchism (Chapter 7).

4 Nuts and bolts: methodology

1 Most of my ideas on the *archaeology of knowledge*, especially in queer contexts, were inspired by Hanna Hacker's lecture series in 2007.
2 The title is a pun on issues not relevant for discussion. It roughly translates to: No need to mention women.
3 In the German language a lack of gender sensitivity can lead to absurd sentences like "Why should every lesbian have *his* coming out?" etc.
4 In contrast to the reference term "Black," I will write "white" with a small "w," given that I consider whiteness not a political category.
5 Online. Available HTTP: http://www.uscab.org/biography.htm (accessed 11 June 2007).
6 Hermsen comes to this conclusion by analyzing the literary works of the writers Ingeborg Bachman, Robert Musil, and Samuel Becket.
7 Online. Available HTTP: http://www.eche.eu.com/conf2005.htm (accessed 30 April 2007).
8 Flax 1990.
9 In this section I am relying mostly on U.S. thinkers to explore the issue of "color" in science. I am aware of the fact that I am probably lacking a thorough Austrian or European perspective by concentrating on those U.S.-based thinkers. Given that their roots are also in feminist, lesbian backgrounds, their argumentation is what I can relate to most.
10 Gender and economic sciences.
11 Deirdre and Donald McCloskey are the same person. McCloskey is quoted as Donald before 1995 and as Deirdre after 1995.
12 The first thing that comes to my mind is the practice of many Australian aboriginal cultures of storing highly sophisticated knowledge in long and complicated songs. Without written history, knowledge certainly dies with the last educated member of the tribe.

5 Work

1 The significance of critical-utopian socialism and communism bears an inverse relation to historical development. In proportion, as the modern class struggle develops and takes definite shape, this fantastic standing apart from the contest, these fantastic attacks on it, loses all practical value and all theoretical justification. Therefore, although the originators of these systems were, in many respects, revolutionary, their disciples have, in every case, formed mere reactionary sects. They hold fast to the original views of their masters, in opposition to the progressive historical development of the proletariat. They therefore endeavor, consistently, to deaden the class struggle and to reconcile class antagonisms. They still dream of the experimental realization of their social utopias, of founding isolated phalansteres, of establishing "Home Colonies," or setting up a "Little Icaria" – pocket editions of the New Jerusalem – and of realizing all these castles in the air. They are compelled to appeal to the feelings and purses of the bourgeois. By degrees, they sink into the category of the reactionary conservative socialists [...], differing from these only by more systematic pedantry, and by their fanatical and superstitious belief in the miraculous effects of their social science. They therefore violently oppose all political action on the part of the working class. Such action, according to them, can only result from blind unbelief in the new gospel. The Owenites in England and the Fourierists in France, respectively, oppose the Chartists and the Reformistes (Manifesto of the Communist Party. Online. Available HTTP: http://www.marxists.org/archive/marx/works/1848/communist-manifesto/ch01.htm) (accessed 30 April 2007).

2 *Feminist Economics*, 1(1), 1995, 73–92.
3 Women are crowded from well paying jobs into less well paying jobs by men's collusive behavior. The wages in those jobs then further decline due to increased labor supply.
4 *Feminist Economics*, 2(3), 1996, 129–133.
5 Feminist political economist Marilyn Waring became a Member of New Zealand's parliament in 1975 at the age of 22. She was highly influential in her position and managed to incorporate some issues of a highly radical feminist utopian economics. One core issue of her work is about incorporating time surveys to measure the real extent of the economy. She believes the United Nations System of National Accounts (UNSNA) system of GDP measurement is wrong and highly biased:

> When international reports and writers refer to women as statistically or economically invisible, it is the UNSNA that has made it so. When it dawns on you that militarism and the destruction of the environment are recorded as growth, it is the UNSNA that has made it so. When you are seeking out the most vicious tools of colonisation, those that can obliterate a culture and a nation, a tribe or a people's value system, then rank the UNSNA among those tools. When you yearn for a breath of nature's fresh air or a glass of radioactive-free water, remember that the UNSNA says that both are worthless.
>
> (Waring 1988)

Even though Waring became very popular, feminist economics has not adopted her ideas and strategies of implementation to a large extent. She presents a highly creative utopian approach, which has actually led to some changes in women's and men's real-life experiences – at least in New Zealand, which is still nuclear free. Her strategies include the unconventional strategy of seemingly naïve public questions of mainstream economic "natural laws." By questioning those entities, she manages to deconstruct them, for instance the concept of economic growth. But, most important, she also creates room for feminist utopian strategies: One of her 1999 papers arguing for her approach is called *Looking Forward* (rather than *Looking Backward*).
6 *Feminist Economics*, 6(1), 2000, 59–76.
7 *Feminist Economics*, 6(1), 2000, 105–114.
8 *Feminist Economics*, 6(1), 2000, 115–124.

6 Femeconers and utopia: paradigm change now?

1 Frauen scheint das freie utopische Wünschen und Phantasieren schwer zu fallen. Die Lebenspraxis in der patriarchalischen Ordnung fesselt offenbar jene Imagination, die versucht, Bilder und Existenzen jenseits männlich beherrschter Denkmuster zu entwerfen. Oft stellen sich Empfindungen der Leere und Begrenzung ein, wenn Künstlerinnen oder auch Politikerinnen sich bemühen, eine eigene, weibliche Zukunft zu schaffen (author's translation).
2 Segregation and glass ceilings as hindrances for female working careers (author's translation).
3 Back to the roots: Austrian female economists before 1945 (author's translation).
4 Gender budgeting as a means to enhance democratisation of European economic policies (author's translation).
5 Gender budgeting in theory and practice: the example of Upper Austria (author's translation).
6 *Feminist Economics*, 7(1), 2001, 79–96.

7 *Feminist Economics*, 3(1), 1997, 95–111.
8 *Feminist Economics*, 1(3), 1995, 96–109.
9 *Feminist Economics*, 2(1), 1996, 22–42.
10 *Feminist Economics*, 7(3), 2001, 71–101.
11 *Feminist Economics*, 2(1), 1996, 114–120.
12 *Feminist Economics*, 1(3), 1995, 26–39.
13 *Feminist Economics*, 6(2), 2000, 1–21.

7 "Der neue Mensch" and his need to be governed

1 Antonio Gramsci defines the state is as "the entire set of agencies, office-holders and even extra-governmental institutions responsible for preserving the structure of power and wealth in a society. The state involves coercive bureaucracies such as police and military agencies. But it also involves consent winning institutions, such as schools, churches and the mass media" (Diamond 1996: 11).
2 Nancy Folbre describes the historical development of discounting women from the GDP in her article "The Unproductive Housewife: Her Evolution in Nineteenth Century Economic Thought" (Folbre 1991). This practice was then questioned in Marilyn Waring's "Who Is Counting?"
3 "Aurea prima sata est aetas, quae vindice nullo, sponte sua, sine lege fidem rectumque colebat. poena metusque aberant, nec verba minantia fixo aere legebantur, nec supplex turba timebat iudicis ora sui, sed erant sine vindice tuti." Translation from http://www.latein-pagina.de/ovid/ovid_m1.htm (accessed 12 January 2007).
4 Emma Goldman most prominently represents the feminine side of historical anarchism. Although she was born in 1869, her ideas are still influential and are regarded as dangerously progressive. During her lifetime, Goldman was publicly an anarchist, argued for free speech, the right to birth control, women's equality and independence, for union organization, and an eight-hour workday. Because of her criticism of compulsory drafting of young men into the military during World War I, she was imprisoned for two years. In 1919 she was deported from the USA and today (post mortem) she is still censored for political reasons related to current events in the contemporary USA. The *New York Times* of 14 January 2003 reported that in a struggle over freedom of expression, university officials at Berkeley refused to allow a fundraising appeal for the Emma Goldman Papers Project to be mailed, because it quoted Goldman on the subjects of suppression of free speech and her opposition to war. In one of the quotations from 1915, Goldman appealed to people "not yet overcome by war madness to raise their voice of protest, to call the attention of the people to the crime and outrage which are about to be perpetrated on them." In the other censored quotation, starting in 1902, she warned that free-speech advocates "shall soon be obliged to meet in cellars, or in darkened rooms with closed doors, and speak in whispers lest our next-door neighbors should hear that free-born citizens dare not speak in the open." Absurdly, Berkeley officials said, "the quotations could be construed as a political statement by the university in opposition to United States policy toward Iraq," and censored the mailing.
5 Online. Available HTTP: http://www.attac.org/?lang = en (accessed 12 January 2007).
6 The *mestizia* refers to the hybrid consciousness of those living in a borderland with multiple backgrounds.
7 Haymarket Square is a historic site in Chicago, Illinois, which was the site of a bombing during a labor demonstration in 1886.
8 *Auf*, September 1995: 19.

9 French philosopher Hélène Cixous plays with the concepts of women's past, present, and future possibilities, utopian ones as well as probable ones.
10 Economic Theories and Gender Relations: The Male View in Economic Science (author's translation).
11 The economic subject is of (no) gender! (author's translation).
12 Feministische Ökonominnen ... wollen den gegenwärtigen Status Quo in der ökonomischen Diskussion nicht länger hinnehmen – für theoretische Weiterarbeit, gegenseitige Inspiration und Stabilisierung im Männerberuf brauchen sie mehr Austausch und kritische Diskussionen untereinander.
13 "Thinking of the utopian space as the other 'country' protects political theory from addressing the ideological contradictions involved in the polarity of home and elsewhere, city and outside. 'Country' is neither home nor city, but countryside, khora, the undifferentiated, uncultivated, unmapped and wild space that can be re-inscribed with familiar utopian visions of either home or city, domesticity or statehood. Benhabib's feminist utopian politics reclaims the retreat to utopia only to re-inscribe it within the familiar ideal of empathetic care. To the critique that such a vision remains essentializing and exclusionary, Benhabib replies that at this historical moment there is no better alternative vision: 'Yet what are we ready to offer in their place?'" (Shafi 1990: 51).
14 "Wir wollen hier auf Erden schon das Himmelreich errichten," Heinrich Heine 1844.
15 The film was *Die vom 17er Haus*, by Artur Berger, from 1932, 68 minutes. It was the last promotion movie of the Socialist Party before it was declared illegal.
16 Online. See also Benhabib 2004a.
17 "Lesbolove" is a concept inspired by the Boston Dyke March 2002, where affirmative slogans were distributed on colorful stickers for all participants to wear.

8 The vision of the free market: "Free to choose?"

1 See, for instance, Ursula Biemann's documentary *Performing the Border* (2001), on the Free Trade Area bordering the USA and Mexico.
2 A cynical definition of (neoliberalism) is derived from Marcos at the Zapatista-sponsored "Inter-continental Encounter for Humanity and against Neo-liberalism" of August 1996 in Chiapas, where he said: "what the Right offers, is to turn the world into one big mall where they can buy Indians here, women there" – and, he might have added, children, immigrants, workers, or even a whole country like Mexico (Martinez and Garcia 2000).
3 For instance, Lippmann helped to install the term "Cold War" in 1947[0].
4 An interesting book title, using anarchy not in the more common communist-anarchist context, but referring to the capitalist stream of anarchist thought.
5 Freedom and Competition: A Critique of the (Neo)liberal Understanding of Two Rudimentary Concepts (author's translation).
6 The example nowadays would question whether it is just that so many people pay enormous amounts of money to see a certain sports talent like Michael Jordan.
7 *Der Standard*, 9 December 2002.
8 In meinem Buch ("*Die falsche Verheißung. Der globale Kapitalismus und seine Folgen*" – Alexander Fest Verlag) habe ich das Projekt eines globalen freien Marktes als strikt utopisch bezeichnet – ähnlich dem globalen Kommunismus, weil beide versucht haben, eine einzige Form der politischen und wirtschaftlichen Institutionen auf enorm verschiedene Kulturen, Regionen aufzuzwingen. Ich prophezeite, dass dieser Versuch rasch zusammenbrechen würde und – ohne dass ich den 11. September vorhersagte – dass die wichtigste Gegenbewegung nicht die Globalisierungsgegner sein würden, sondern ethnischer Nationalismus und religiöse fundamentalistische

Bewegungen, die durch die dogmatische Umsetzung der Marktwirtschaft amerikanischer Prägung, dem 'Washington Konsens', gestärkt werden würde.

9 *Feminist Economics*, 2(1), 1996, 86–89.
10 *Feminist Economics*, 2(1), 1996, 90–93.
11 *Feminist Economics*, 2(1), 1996, 94–97.
12 *Feminist Economics*, 2(1), 1996, 98–113.
13 *Feminist Economics*, 2(2), 1996, 1–39.
14 *Feminist Economics*, 3(1), 1997, 113–120.
15 *Feminist Economics*, 3(1), 1997, 121–126.
16 *Feminist Economics*, 3(1), 1997, 127–129.
17 *Feminist Economics*, 3(1), 1997, 131–142.
18 This statement reminds me of Harris'sperception of the market as a place from which "rude people" will be excluded.
19 Heretics: "They ask embarrassing questions, investigate problems which are not generally accepted as legitimate, and provide answers which rely on unusual concepts, unfamiliar reasoning and inadmissible evidence" (Hutchinson 1995: 47).
20 "Peak Oil" or "Hubbert's peak" refers to a singular event in history: the peak of the entire planet's oil production as can be depicted in a Bell curve. Following Peak Oil the rate of oil production on Earth will terminally decline, since production will become profoundly more difficult and therefore expensive.
21 Howard Zinn comments on Albert's vision thus: "I can't count the number of times when serious critics of our social system would say to me: 'Why can't we come up with a vision of what a good society would be like?'"
22 Nowhere was [the feminist utopian] vision more clearly expressed than in the call for "bread and roses" that was reiterated with such frequency by feminist activists in the Western European and American women's movements, particularly those on the political Left, that it became one of the defining mottos of this period. Taken from the famous strike of women millworkers in Lawrence, Massachusetts, in 1912, this motto functioned as a symbolic reminder of the fact that in the emotional and political dynamics of a movement for change, struggle ("bread") and dreams ("roses") are equally important (Bammer 1991: 54).

Bibliography

Aerni, L. *et al.* (1999) "Toward a Feminist Pedagogy in Economics," *Feminist Economics*, 5(1), 29–44.

Albert, M. and Hahnel, R. (1991) *Participatory Economics*, Princeton: Princeton University Press.

Andreae, V. (1619, 1999) *Christianopolis*, ed. and trans. by Thompson, E., Archives internationales d'histoire des idées, Dordrecht: Kluwer Academic Publishers.

Anzaldua, G. (1987) *Borderlands/La Frontera*, San Francisco: Spinsters/aunt lute.

Arizona State University (2007) Tempe, Arizona, February 8–10. Online. Available HTTP: http://myweb.dal.ca/lt531391/findex.html (accessed 12 July 2007).

Bacon, Francis (1601) *On Marriage and Single Life*. Online. Available HTTP: http://ourworld.compuserve.com/homepages/mike_donnelly/lottwo.htm#marriage (accessed 21 June 2007).

—— (1627, 1999) "New Atlantis," in *Three Renaissance Utopias: Utopia, New Atlantis, The Isle of Pines*, ed. by Susan Bruce, Oxford: World's Classics. Online. Available HTTP: http://onlinebooks.library.upenn.edu/webbin/gutbook/lookup?num = 2434 (accessed 30 April 2007).

Bacon, F. (1964) "The Masculine Birth of Time," in Farrington, B. *The Philosophy of Francis Bacon: An Essay on Its Development from 1603 to 1609, with New Translations of Fundamental Texts*, Liverpool: Liverpool University Press.

Badgett, L. and Jefferson, F. (2007) *Sexual Orientation Discrimination. An International Perspective*, London: Routledge.

Bammer, A. (1991) *Partial Visions. Feminism and Utopianism in the 1970s*, London: Routledge.

Barker, D. (1995) "Economists, Social Reformers, and Prophets: A Feminist Critique of Economic Efficiency," *Feminist Economics*, 1(3), 26–39.

—— (2000) *Women, Knowledge and Power: Methodological Challenges in Feminist Economics*, paper presented at the 9th annual Conference on Feminist Economics, Bogazici University, Istanbul, Turkey, 15–17 August.

—— (2005) "Beyond Women and Economics: Rereading Women's Work," *Signs: Journal of Women in Culture and Society*, 30(4): 2189–2209.

—— (2007) "Beyond Women and Economics: An Interpretive Reading of Caring Labor," paper presented at the Association of Feminist Epistemologies, Methodologies, Metaphysics, and Science Studies Organization, second conference, Arizona State University, Tempe, Arizona.

Barker, D. and Kuiper, E. (eds.) (2003) *Toward a Feminist Philosophy of Economics*, London: Routledge.

—— (eds.) (2006) *Feminist Economics and the World Bank: History, Theory and Policy*, London: Routledge.

Barr, M. (1992) *Feminist Fabulation. Space/Postmodern Fiction*, Iowa City: University of Iowa Press.

Bebel, A. (1879) *Women and Socialism*, New York: Socialist Literature Co. Online. Available HTTP: http://www.marxists.org/archive/bebel/1879/woman-socialism/ch02.htm#s1 (accessed 30 April 2007).

Beechner, J. and Bienvenue, R. (1971) *The Utopian Vision of Charles Fourier*, Boston: Beacon Press.

Behringer, W. (1999) *Climatic Change and Witch-Hunting: The Impact of the Little Ice Age on Mentalities*. Online. Available HTTP: http://ff.org/centers/csspp/library/co2weekly/20061031/20061031_10.html (accessed 30 April 2007).

Belkhir, J. (1994) "'Failure' of Marxism to Develop Adequate Tools and a Comprehensive Theory of Ethnicity, Gender and Class Issues Is Undisputable," in *Race, Gender & Class*, 2(1): 79–107.

Bellamy, E. (1888, 1960) *Looking Backward*, New York: Penguin.

Benhabib, S. (2004a) *The Rights of Others. Aliens, Citizens and Residents*, Cambridge, UK: Cambridge University Press.

—— (2004b) "The Rights of Others. Aliens, Residents and Citizens," paper presented at Yale University conference on Migrants, Nations and Citizenship. Online. Available HTTP: http://www.crassh.cam.ac.uk/events/2003–4/BenhabibPaper.pdf (accessed 12 January 2007).

Bergeron, S. (2001) "Political Economy Discourses of Globalization and Feminist Politics," *Signs: Journal of Women in Culture and Society*, 26(4): 983–1006.

—— (2007) "Performativity, Economic Science, and Social Reproduction," paper presented at the Association of Feminist Epistemologies, Methodologies, Metaphysics, and Science Studies Organization, second conference, Arizona State University, Tempe, Arizona.

Bergmann, B. (1986) *The Economic Emergence of Women*, New York: Basic Books.

—— (2001) "A Swedish-Style Welfare State or Basic Income: Which Should Have Priority?," draft of 20 November 2001. Online. Available HTTP: http://www.ssc.wisc.edu/havenscenter/VSP/readings2sort/pdf/bergmann.PDF (accessed 31 October 2007).

Berneri, M. (1950) *Journey through Utopia*. New York: Schocken Books.

Biemann, U. (1999) "Performing the Border," video essay. Online. Available HTTP: http://www.geobodies.org/ (accessed 1 October 2007).

Brantenberg, G. (1985) *Egalia's Daughters. A Satire of the Sexes*, Oslo: The Seal Press.

Brown, L. (1994) "'Gender' und die Wirtschaftswissenschaften. Eine feministische Perspektive," in Regenhard, U., Maier, F., and Carl, A. (eds.) *Ökonomische Theorien und Geschlechterverhältnis – Der männliche Blick der Wirtschaftswissenschaft, fhw-forschung 23/24*, Berlin: edition sigma.

Burwell, J. (1997) *Notes on Nowhere. Feminism, Utopian Logic, and Social Transformation*, Minneapolis: University of Minnesota Press.

Butler, O. (1987) *Dawn*, New York: Popular Library.

Campanella, T. (1602, 1981) *La città del sole: dialogo poetico/The City of the Sun: A Poetical Dialogue*, ed. and trans. by Daniel J. Donno, Berkeley: University of California Press. Online. Available HTTP: http://www.levity.com/alchemy/citysun.html (accessed 30 April 2007).

Cavendish, M. (1666, 2000) "The Description of a New World, Called the Blazing World," in. S. Bowerbank and S. Mendelson (eds.) *Paper Bodies: A Margaret Cavendish Reader*, Peterborough: Broadview Press. Online. Available HTTP: http://math.cofc.edu/kasman/MATHFICT/mfview.php?callnumber = mf148 (accessed 18 July 2007).

Chomsky, N. (2001) *The New War against Terror. An Evening with Noam Chomsky*, Boston: MIT. Online. Available HTTP: http://www.zmag.org/GlobalWatch/chomskymit.htm (accessed 12 January 2007).

Cixous, H. (1982) *Limonade tout était si infini*, Paris: Editions des Femmes.

Clemons, T. (2000) "Feminism in Herland: A Utopian Vision of Charlotte Perkins Gilman." Online. Available HTTP: http://www.womenwriters.net/domesticgoddess/pdf/clemons.pdf (accessed 1 November 2007).

Cliff, T. (1984) *Class Struggle and Women's Liberation*, London: Bookmarks.

Cornwall, R. (1998) "A Primer on Queer Theory for Economists Interested in Social Identities," *Feminist Economics*, 4(2): 73–82.

Daly, H. (forthcoming) *Ecological Economics and Sustainable Development, Selected Essays of Herman Daly*, Cheltenham, UK: Edward Elgar.

DasGupta, Sayantani (1999) "Reinventing the Feminist Wheel. Feminist Report," in *Literature and Medicine*, Columbia: Columbia University Press.

Davis, A. (1982) *Women, Race and Class*, London: The Women's Press.

Dean, K. (2003) *Capitalism and Citizenship. The Impossible Partnership*, London and New York: Routledge.

Delany, S. (1976) *Triton*, New York: Bantam.

Delmar, R. (1994) "What Is Feminism?," in Hermann, A. and Stewarts, A. (eds.) *Theorizing Feminism*, San Diego: Worldview Press.

Desantis, M. (1996) "A Cyborg Manifesto. A World out of Balance," Working Paper. Carnegie Mellon University.

Diamond, S. (1996) *Facing the Wrath*, Maine: Common Courage Press.

Donath, S. (2000) "The Other Economy: A Suggestion for a Distinctively Feminist Economics," *Feminist Economics*, 6(1), 115–24.

Donawerth, J. and Kolmerten, C. (1994) *Utopian and Science Fiction by Women. Worlds of Difference*, Syracuse, NY: Syracuse University Press.

Dorman, P., Folbre, N., McCloskey, D., and Weisskopf, T. (1996) "Debating Markets," *Feminist Economics*, 2(1): 69–85.

Dreher, S. (1997) *A Captive in Time*, Victoria Publishers.

Duggan, L. and Olmsted, J. (1996) "Where Has All the Gender Gone?," *Feminist Economics*, 2(1), 86–89.

Eisenstein, Z. (2004) *Against Empire. Feminisms, Racism, and the West*, London and New York: Zed Books.

Eiseley, L. (1973) *The Man Who Saw through Time*, London: Macmillan.

Elam, D. (1994) *Feminism and Deconstruction*, London and New York: Routledge.

Elgin, S. (1970) *The Communipaths* (Coyote Jones Series), New York: Ace Books.

Elson, D. and Nilufer, C. (1999) "Engendering Macroeconomic Policy and Budgets for Sustainable Development," paper presented at the First Global Forum on Human Development, United Nations, New York.

Engel, A. (2006) "Gefeierte Vielfalt. Umstrittene Heterogenität. Unbenannte Provokation. Sexuelle Lebensformen in spätmodernen, pluralistischen Gesellschaften," paper presented at the conference "Heteronormativität und Homosexualitäten," at the University of Linz, Austria.

England, P. (1993) "The Seperative Self: Androcentric Bias in Neoclassical Assumptions," in Ferber, M. and Nelson, J. (eds.) *Beyond Economic Man: Feminist Theory and Economics*, Chicago: University of Chicago Press.

Faludi, S. (1991) *Backlash: The Undeclared War against American Women*, New York: Powell.

Feiner, S. (1995) "Reading Neoclassical Economics. Toward an Erotic Economy of Sharing," in Kuiper, E. and Sap, J. (eds.) *Out of the Margin: Feminist Perspectives on Economics*, London: Routledge.

—— (1996) "A Paradigm of Our Own," *Feminist Economics*, 2(1), 94–97.

Ferber, M. and Nelson, J. (1993) "The Social Construction of Economics and the Social Construction of Gender," in Ferber, M. and Nelson, J. (eds.) *Beyond Economic Man: Feminist Theory and Economics*, Chicago: University of Chicago Press.

Firestone, S. (1970) *The Dialectic of Sex*. New York: William Morrow and Company.

—— (1975) *Frauenbefreiung und sexuelle Revolution*, Frankfurt am Main: Fischer.

Flax, J. (1990) *Thinking Fragments: Psychoanalysis, Feminism, & Postmodernism in the Contemporary West*, Berkeley: University of California Press.

— (1992) "The End of Innocence," in Butler, J. and Scott, J. (eds.) *Feminists Theorize the Political*, New York: Routledge.

Florida, Richard (2002) *The Rise of the Creative Class. And How It's Transforming Work, Leisure and Everyday Life*, New York: Basic Books.

Folbre, N. (1991) "The Unproductive Housewife: Her Evolution in Nineteenth Century Economic Thought," *Signs: Journal of Women in Culture and Society*, 16 (3), 463–484.

—— (1993a) "Socialism, Feminist and Scientific," in Ferber, M. and Nelson, J. (eds.) *Beyond Economic Man: Feminist Theory and Economics*, Chicago: University of Chicago Press.

—— (1993b) *The Economics of the Family*, Cheltenham, UK: Edward Elgar.

—— (1996) "Hearts and Spades: Paradigms of Household Economics," in *Care and the Global Economy*, Working Paper.

—— (1998) "Care and the Global Economy," unpublished draft of Folbre, N. (1999) "Invisible Hearts – Care and the Global Economy," United Nations Human Development Report. Online. Available HTTP http://hdr.undp.org/en/media/hdr_1999_ch3.pdf (accessed 10 November 2007).

—— (1999) "Invisible Hearts - Care and the Global Economy," United Nations Human Development Report. Online. Available HTTP: http://hdr.undp.org/en/media/hdr_1999_ch3.pdf (accessed 10 November 2007).

—— (2005) "*Caring Labor*," in *Kurswechsel* 01–2005. Online. Available HTTP: http://www.republicart.net/disc/aeas/folbre01_en.htm (accessed 30 April 2007).

Folbre, N. and Pujol, M. (1996) "Introduction," *Feminist Economics*, 2(3), 121.

Forget, E. (1997) "The Market for Virtue: Jean-Baptiste Say on Women in the Economy and Society," *Feminist Economics*, 3(1): 95–111.

—— (2001) "Saint-Simonean Feminism," *Feminist Economics*, 7(1): 79–96.

Fourier, C. (1808) *Degradation of Women in Civilization*. Online. Available HTTP: http://www.binghamton.edu/womhist/awrm/doc2b.htm (accessed 30 April 2007).

Friedl, B. and Kreimer, M. (2007) "Segregation und gläserne Decke als Stolpersteine weiblicher Erwerbskarrieren," paper presented at the 4th Austrian Workshop of Feminist Economists, Vienna, University of Vienna.

Friedman, M. (1963) *Capitalism and Freedom*, Chicago: University of Chicago Press.

Fromm, E. (1965, 1994) *On Being Human*, ed. by Rainer Funk, New York: Continuum.

Furtmayr, H. (2005) *Freiheit und Wettbewerb: Eine Kritik des (neo)liberalen Verständnisses zweier grundlegender Begriffe*, IKSF Discussion Paper No. 32, Bremen: IKSF.

Gagnier, R. and Dupré, J. (1995) "On Work and Idleness," *Feminist Economics*, 1(3), 96–109.

Gamble, S. (2001) *Feminism and Postfeminism*, London: Routledge.

Geoghegan, V. (1987) *Utopianism and Marxism*, London: Methuen.

George, S. (1999) "A Short History of Neo-liberalism. Twenty Years of Elite Economics and Emerging Opportunities for Structural Change," speech at the Conference on Economic Sovereignty in a Globalizing World, Bangkok.

Gerschlager, C. (2002) "Adam Smith and Feminist Perspectives on Exchange," in Gerschlager, C. and Mokre, M. *Exchange and Deception: A Feminist Perspective*, Dordrecht: Kluwer Academic Publishers.

Gerschlager, C. and Mokre, M. (2002) *Exchange and Deception: A Feminist Perspective*, Dordrecht: Kluwer Academic Publishers.

Gilroy, P. (1992) *The Black Atlantic: Modernity and Double Consciousness*, Cambridge, MA: Harvard University Press.

Goldman, E. (1896) *"Anarchism and the Sex question," The Alarm*, Sunday, 27 September, 3. Online. Available HTTP: http://dwardmac.pitzer.edu/anarchist_archives/goldman/sexquestion.html.

—— (1910) "Woman Suffrage," in *Anarchism and Other Essays*, 2nd rev. edn., New York and London: Mother Earth Publishing Association. Online. Available HTTP: http://dwardmac.pitzer.edu/anarchist_archives/goldman/aando/suffrage.html (accessed 12 January 2007).

—— (1917) "Woman Suffrage," in *Anarchism and Other Essays*, 3rd rev. edn., New York: A.C. Fifield; London: Mother Earth Publishing Association.

—— (1925) *My Disillusionment in Russia*. Online. Available HTTP: http://sunsite3.berkeley.edu/Goldman/Writings/Russia/index.html (accessed 12 January 2007).

—— (n.d.) *Anarchism. What It Really Stands for*. Online. Available HTTP: http://dwardmac.pitzer.edu/Anarchist_archives/goldman/aando/anarchism.html.

Goutrié, C. and Schönpflug, K. (2004) *Dyke March 2004 Lesboliebe Kontra – Kommerzielle Utopien in Bewegung*. Online. Available HTTP: http://www.villa.at/v/index.php?artikelnr = 65&seitenkat = 1 (accessed 24 October 2007).

Grapard, U. (1995) "Robinson Crusoe: The Quintessential Economic Man?," *Feminist Economics*, 1(1), 33–52.

Gray, J. (2001) *Die falsche Verheißung. Der globale Kapitalismus und seine Folgen*, Frankfurt: Fischer.

Gregoriou, Z. (1998) *Learning Performances of Dislocation, Receptivity and Hybridity in Women's Utopian Writing*, thesis, Urbana, IL: University of Illinois at Urbana–Champaign.

Gudeman, R. and Gudeman, S. (1996) "Gender, Market and Community on Femecon in May and June 1994," *Feminist Economics*, 2(2), 1–39.

—— (1997) "Competition/Cooperation: Revisiting the May 1994 Femecon Debates," *Feminist Economics*, 3(1), 131–142.

Guérin, D. (1969) *Anarchismus. Begriff und Praxis*, Frankfurt: Suhrkamp.

Gupta, J. (1997) "Human Reproduction in Utopian Writings and Women's Emancipation," in Lenning, A., Bekker, M., and Vanwesenbeek, I. (eds.) *Feminist Utopias in a Postmodern Era*, Tilburg, Netherlands: Tilburg University Press.

Gutek, G. and Gutek, P. (1998) *Visiting Utopian Communities*, Columbia, S.C.: University of South Carolina Press.

Hacker, H. (2006) "Sind wir je homo/normativ gewesen? Elemente einer Bewegungsgeschichte oder queere Fiktionen des Vergangenen," talk at Heteronormativität und Homosexualitäten. Forschung in Anknüpfung an Michael Pollak, Linz, University of Linz, Austria.

Hammerton, J. (2003) *A Critique of Libertarianism*. Online Available HTTP: http://www.tardis.ed.ac.uk/~james/politics/libcrit.txt (accessed 9 June 2007).

Haraway, D. (1980) *Simians, Cyborgs, and Women*, London: Routledge. Online. Available HTTP: http://www.stanford.edu/dept/HPS/Haraway/CyborgManifesto.html (accessed 30 April 2007).

—— (1995) *Die Neuerfindung der Natur. Primaten, Cyborgs und Frauen*, Frankfurt am Main: Campus.

Harding, S. (1986) *The Feminist Science Question*, Ithaca, NY: Cornell University Press.

—— (1995) "Can Feminist Thought Make Economics More Objective?," *Feminist Economics*, 1(1): 95–111.

Harris, S. (1998) *The Invisible Hand Is a Gentle Hand*. Online. Available HTTP: http://www.theadvocates.org/library/gentle-hand.html (accessed 1 November 2007).

Hayek, F. (1945) *The Road To Serfdom* (condensed version, published in the Reader's Digest, April 1945 edition). Online. Available HTTP: http://www.btinternet.com/~jhpart/hayek45.htm (accessed 12 January 2007).

—— (1949, 1998) *The Intellectuals and Socialism (Rediscovered Riches 4)*, London: Institute of Economic Affairs.

—— (1976) *The Road to Serfdom*, Chicago: Chicago University Press.

Heine, H. (1997) *Deutschland. Ein Wintermärchen*, ed. Joseph Kiermeier-Debre, Munich: Deutscher Taschenbuch Verlag.

Hermsen, J. (1997) "No Man's Land Utopia, or: A place called Desire," in Lenning, A., Bekker, M., and Vanwesenbeek, I. (eds.) *Feminist Utopias in a Postmodern Era*, Tilburg, Netherlands: Tilburg University Press.

Hewitson, G. (1999) *Feminist Economics*, Cheltenham, UK: Edward Elgar.

Hodgson, G. (1999) *Economics and Utopia*, London: Routledge.

hooks, b. (1995) "Challenging Capitalism & Patriarchy," interview by Third World Viewpoint, *zmag*, December.

Hopkins, B. (1997) "Argument and Community in the Markets Debate," in *Feminist Economics*, 3(1), 113–120.

Hoppe, H. (2002) *Feministische Ökonomik*, Berlin: Sigma.

Hossain, R. (1925, 1988) "Padmarag," in *Sultana's Dream*, New York: The Feminist Press.

Hubbert, M. King (1975) *Exponential Growth as a Transient Phenomenon in Human History*. Online. Available HTTP: http://www.hubbertpeak.com/hubbert/wwf1976/print.htm (accessed 30 April 2007).

Hutchinson, F. (1995) "A Heretical View of Economic Growth and Income Distribution," in Kuiper, E. and Sap, J. (eds.) *Out of the Margin: Feminist Perspectives on Economics*, London: Routledge.

Huxley, A. (1931, 1998) *Brave New World*, New York: Harper Perennial.

Hyee, R. (2007) "Bargaining in the Family," paper presented at the 4th Austrian Workshop of Feminist Economists, Vienna, University of Vienna.

Hyman, P. (1996) *The New Zealand Experiment: Not the Major Success that Politicians Claim*, Wellington, New Zealand: Victoria University of Wellington.

—— (2000) "Globalization and Associated Economic/Social Change: What Are the Impacts on Lesbians, Lesbian Community(ies) and Lesbian Politics?," draft, Victoria university of Wellington, New Zealand. Online. Available HTTP: http://www.victoria.ac.nz/education/staff/education-studies/prues-publications.aspx (accessed 1 November 2007).

Ikle, F. (1994) *Our Perpetual Growth Utopia*. Online. Available HTTP: http://dieoff.org/page68.htm (accessed 30 April 2007).

Jefferson, T. and King, J. (2001) "Never Intended to be a Theory of Everything: Domestic Labor in Neoclassical and Marxian Economics," *Feminist Economics*, 7 (3), 71–101.

Kelley, J. (1997) *Bringing the Market Back In*, New York: New York University Press.

Kilcullen, J. (1996) *Robert Nozick, Anarchy State & Utopia*, Sydney: Macquire University.

Klamer, A. (1984) *The New Classical Macroeconomy. Conversations with New Classical Economists and Their Opponents*, Brighton, Sussex: Wheatsheaf Books.

—— (2001) "Making Sense of Economists: From Falsification to Rhetoric and Beyond," *Journal of Economic Methodology*, 8(1)1, 69–75.

Klapeer, C. (2007) *Queer Contexts*, Innsbruck: Studien Verlag.

Klarer, M. (1993) *Frau und Utopie. Feministische Literaturtheorie und utopischer Diskurs im anglo-amerikanischen Roman*, Darmstadt; Wissenschaftliche Buchgesellschaft.

Klatzer, E. and Mader, K. (2007) "Gender Budgeting als Beitrag zur Demokratisierung europäischer Wirtschaftspolitik," paper presented at the 4th Austrian Workshop of Feminist Economists, Vienna, University of Vienna.

Koeszegi, S. (2007) "Gender Salience in Electronic Negotiations," paper presented at the 4th Austrian Workshop of Feminist Economists, Vienna, University of Vienna.

Kreis, S. (1996) *The History Guide*, Lecture 21. Online. Available HTTP: http://www.historyguide.org/ (accessed 12 January 2007).

Kuiper, E. and Sap, J. (eds.) (1995) *Out of the Margin: Feminist Perspectives on Economics*, London: Routledge.

Le Guin, U. (1969) *The Left Hand of Darkness*, New York: Ace Books. Chapter 7 online. Available HTTP: http://cla.calpoly.edu/~bmori/syll/311syll/Darkness.html (accessed 17 October 2007).

—— (1971, 2003) *The Lathe of Heaven*, London: Harper Perennial Modern Classics.

—— (1974, 2001) *The Dispossessed*, London: Gollancz.

Lefanu, S. (1988) *In the Chinks of the World Machine. Feminism and Science Fiction*, London: The Women's Press.

Lenning, A. van (1995) "Rad van avontuur," *Krisis*, 15, 26–31, Amsterdam: De Balie.

Lenning, A., Bekker, M., and Vanwesenbeek, I. (eds.) (1997) *Feminist Utopias in a Postmodern Era*, Tilburg, Netherlands: Tilburg University Press.

Levin, L. (1995) *Toward a Feminist, Post-Keynesian Theory of Investment*, in Kuiper, E. and Sap, J. (eds.) *Out of the Margin: Feminist Perspectives on Economics*, New York and London: Routledge.

Levitas, R (1990) *The Concept of Utopia*, Syracuse, NY: Syracuse University Press.

Lippmann,W. (1997, 1921) *Public Opinion*, New York: The Free Press.

Loenen, T. (1997) "The Fundamental Right to Work: Grand Promise or Male Deceit?," in Lenning, A., Bekker, M., and Vanwesenbeek, I. (eds.) *Feminist Utopias in a Postmodern Era*, Tilburg, Netherlands: Tilburg University Press.

Lohschelder, S. (2000) *Anarchafeminsmus. Auf den Spuren einer Utopie*, Münster: Unrast.

Lorde, A. (1986) *Zami. Eine Mythobiographie*, Berlin: Orlanda Frauenverlag.

McCloskey, D. (1993) "Some Consequences of a Conjective Economics," in Ferber, M. and Nelson, J. (eds.) *Beyond Economic Man: Feminist Theory and Economics*, Chicago: University of Chicago Press.

McCord, W. (1989) *Voyages to Utopia*, New York: W.W. Norton & Company.

McIntyre, V. (1978) *Dreamsnake*, New York: Powell's Books.

Maier, F. (1993a) "Das Wirtschaftssubjekt hat (k)ein Geschlecht!," in Regenhard, U., Maier, F., and Carl, A. (eds.) (1994) *Ökonomische Theorien und Geschlechterverhältnis: Der männliche Blick der Wirtschaftswissenschaft*, *fhw-forschung 23/24*, Berlin: edition sigma.

—— (1993b) "Homo Oeconomicus – Zur geschlechtsspezifischen Konstruktion der Wirtschaftswissenschaften," *Prokla* 4, 551–571.

Martinez, E. and Garcia, A. (2000) *What Is "Neo-Liberalism"? A Brief Definition for Activists*, San Francisco: Global Exchange. Online. Available HTTP: http://www.corpwatch.org/article.php?id = 376 (accessed 2 November 2007).

Marx, K. (1844, 1932) "Comments on James Mill," in Marx, K. and Engels, F. *Gesamtausgabe*, 1/3, Berlin. Online. Available HTTP: http://www.marxists.org/archive/marx/works/1844/james-mill/index.htm (accessed 22 June 2007).

Marx, K. and Engels, F. (1972) "Das kommunistische Manifest," in *Karl Marx/Friedrich Engels – Werke*, Berlin: (Karl) Dietz Verlag.

Matthai, J. (1996) "Why Feminist, Marxist, and Anti Racist Economics Should Be Feminist-Marxist-Anti-Racist Economics," *Feminist Economics*, 2(2), 22–42.

Maurer, S. (1996) *Zwischen Zuschreibung und Selbstgestaltung: feministische Identitätspolitiken im Kräftefeld von Kritik, Norm und Utopie*, Tübingen: edition diskord.

Mautner, T. (1997) *The Penguin Dictionary of Philosophy*, London: Penguin.

Meaney, G. (1993) *Unlike Subjects. Women, Theory, Fiction*, New York: Routledge.

Mellor, M. (1999) "Ecofeminist Economics: Women, Work and the Environment," paper presented in Valencia, Spain, Northumbria University, May. Online. Available HTTP: http://www-rohan.sdsu.edu/faculty/dunnweb/rprnts.ecofemeconomics.html (accessed 12 January 2007).

Michalitsch, G. (2002) "Engendering Economics, Grundlagen feministischer Ökonomie," in *Kurswechsel. Zeitschrift für gesellschafts-, wirtschafts-und umweltpolitische Alternativen*, Vienna: Sonderzahl Verlag. Heft 1/2002: 10–21.

Michalitsch, G. and Schlager, C. (2007) "Back to the Roots: Österreichische Ökonominnen vor 1945," papre presented at the 4th Austrian Workshop of Feminist Economists, Vienna, University of Vienna.

Mies, M. (1978) "Methodologische Postulate zur Frauenforschung," in *Beiträge zur feministischen Theorie und Praxis*, 1(1), 43–61.

—— (1988) *Patriarchat und Kapital*, Fulda: Rotpunkt Verlag.

Mill, J.S. (1836) "On the Definition of Political Economy; and on the Method of Investigation Proper to It," in Comperz, T. (ed.) (1869) *John Stuart Mills gesammelte Werke*, Leipzig: Fues.

—— J.S. (1869) *The Subjection of Women*. Online. Available HTTP: http://www.constitution.org/jsm/women.htm (accessed 12 January 2007).

Mincer, J. (1962) "Labor Force Participation and Married Women," in *Universities National Bureau of Economic Research. Aspects of Labor Economics*, Princeton: Princeton University Press.

Mokre, M. (2002) "On Adam Smith and Gender Construction," in Gerschlager, C. and Mokre, M. *Exchange and Deception: A Feminist Perspective*, Dordrecht: Kluwer Academic Publishers.

More, T. (1516, 1992) *Utopia*, New York: W.W. Norton & Company.

Nelson, J. (1993) "The Study of Choice or the Study of Provisioning? Gender and the Definition of Economics," in Ferber, M. and Nelson, J. (eds.) *Beyond Economic Man: Feminist Theory and Economics*, Chicago: University of Chicago Press.

—— (1995) "Feminism and Economics," *Journal of Economic Perspectives*, 9(2), spring, 131–148.

—— (1996) *Feminism, Objectivity and Economics*, New York: Routledge.

—— (2001) "Economic Methodology and Feminist Critique," *Journal of Economic Methodology*, 8(1), 93–97.

North, R. (1976) *The World that Could Be*, New York: W.W. Norton & Company.

Norton, A. (1963, 1986) *Witch World (The Witch World Series)*, New York: Ace.

Nozick, R. (1974) *Anarchy, State, and Utopia*, New York: Basic Books.

Oetsch, W. (1993) *Die mechanistische Metapher in der Theoriengeschichte der Nationalökonomie*, Universität Linz Working Paper Nr. 313, Linz, Austria: University of Linz.

—— (2002) *Haider light: Handbuch für Demagogie*, Vienna: Czernin Verlag.

—— (2007a) *Bilder der Wirtschaft. Metaphern, Diskurse und Hayeks neoliberales Hegemonialprojekt*, Universität Linz Working Paper Nr. 0709, Linz, Austria: University of Linz.

—— (2007b) "Die kulturelle Evolution von 'Bildern' über die Wirtschaft und das Konzept der sozialen Verantwortung von Unternehmen," in Beschorner, T., Linnebach, P., Pfriem, R., and Ulrich, G. (eds.) *Unternehmensverantwortung aus kulturalistischer Sicht*, Marburg: Metropolis.

Okin, S. (1991) *Justice, Gender and the Family*, New York: Basic Books.

Olson, P. and Emami, Z. (2002) *Engendering Economics: Conversations with Women Economists in the United States*, London: Routledge.

Orr, D. (1997) "Not Only Gender: More on Debating Markets," *Feminist Economics*, 3(1), 121–126.

Orwell, G. (1948, 1993) *1984*, Charlotte, NC: Barker and Taylor.

Ott, N. (1992) *Intrafamily Bargaining and Household Decisions*, Berlin; Heidelberg.

Otto Peters, L. (1866, 1997) *Das Recht der Frauen auf Erwerb*, Leipzig: Leipziger Universitäts Verlag.

Ovid (1997) *Metamorphosen*, Ditzingen: Reclam.

Paul, T. (1980) *Karl Marx and the Anarchists*, London: Routledge.

Perkins Gilman, C. (1898, 1966) *Women and Economics*, New York: Harper Torchbooks.

—— (1911) *Moving the Mountain*, New York: Charlton Co.

—— (1915, 1997) *Herland*, New York: Pantheon Books.

—— (1916) "With Her in Ourland," *The Forerunner*, 7.

Perrons, D. (1995) "Measuring Equality in Opportunity," Kuiper, E. and Sap, J. with Feiner, S., Ott, N., and Tzannatos, Z. (eds.) *Out of the Margin: Feminist Perspectives on Economics*, London: Routledge, pp. 198-215.

—— (2000) "Care, Paid Work, and Leisure: Rounding the Triangle," *Feminist Economics*, 6(1), 105–14.

Peters, M. (1999) "Neoliberalism. Introduction: Hayek and the Austrian School," *Encyclopedia of Philosophy of Education*. Online. Available HTTP: http://www.vusst.hr/ENCYCLOPAEDIA/neoliberalism.htm (accessed 12 January 2007).

Peterson, S. (1992) *Gendered States. Feminist (Re)Visions of International Relations Theory*, Boulder and London: Lynne Rienner Publishers.

Pharr, S. (1988) *Homophobia – A Weapon of Sexism*, Little Rock, AR: Chardon Press.

Piercy, M. (1976, 1997) *Woman on the Edge of Time*, New York: Ballantine Books.

—— (1991) *He, She, and It*, Greenwich, CT: Fawcett.

—— (2005a) *Sex Wars*, New York: William Morrow.

—— (2005b) "Utopistische feministische Visionen," transcribed video by Ressler, O., Cape Cod, USA, 2003, in *Kurswechsel* 1/2005. Online. Available HTTP: http://www.republicart.net/disc/aeas/piercy01_en.htm (accessed 12 January 2007).

Pizan, C. de (1405, 1994) *Book of the City of Ladies*, New York: Persea Press.

Poldervaart, S. (1997) "Utopianism and Feminism: Some Conclusions," in Lenning, A., Bekker, M., and Vanwesenbeek, I. (eds.) *Feminist Utopias in a Postmodern Era*, Tilburg, Netherlands: Tilburg University Press.

Pujol, M. (1984) "Gender and Class in Marshall's Principles of Economics," *Cambridge Journal of Economics*, 8, 217–234.

—— (1995) "Out of the Margin!," in Kuiper, E. and Sap, J. (eds.) *Out of the Margin: Feminist Perspectives on Economics*, London: Routledge.

Raab, H. (1998) *Foucault und der feministische Poststrukturalismus*, Dortmund: Edition Ebersbach.

Ramazanoglu, C. (2002) *Feminist Methodology: Challenges and Choices*, London: Sage Publications Ltd.

Redmount, E. (1995) *Toward a Feminist Econometrics*, in Kuiper, E. and Sap, J. with Feiner, S., Ott, N., and Tzannatos, Z. (eds.) *Out of the Margin: Feminist Perspectives on Economics*, London: Routledge.

Regenhard, U., Maier, F., and Carl, A. (eds.) (1994) *Ökonomische Theorien und Geschlechterverhältnis – Der männliche Blick der Wirtschaftswissenschaft*, *fhw-forschung 23/24*, Berlin: edition sigma.

Robertson, L. (1996) "'Debating Markets': A Rhetorical Analysis of Economic Discourse," *Feminist Economics*, 2(1), 98–113.

Robeyns, I. (2000) "Is There a feminist Economic Methodology?" Online. Available HTTP: http://www.ingridrobeyns.nl/Downloads/method.pdf (accessed 1 November 2007).

Roesch, M. (1999) *What Does Neoliberalism Mean?*, Tübingen: Eberhard-Karls-University. Online. Available HTTP: http://tiss.zdv.uni-tuebingen.de/webroot/sp/barrios/themeA2a.html (accessed 12 January 2007).

Rohrlich, R. and Hoffman Baruch, E. (1984) *Women in Search of Utopia. Mavericks and Mythmakers*, New York: Schocken Books.

Rosinsky, N. (1984) *Feminist Futures. Contemporary Women's Speculative Fiction*, Ann Arbor, MI: UMI Research Press.

Ross, K. (1997) *Feminism*. Online. Available HTTP: http://www.friesian.com/feminism.htm (accessed 24 October 2007).

Rothbard, M. (1977) "Robert Nozick and the Immaculate Conception of the State," *Journal of Libertarian Studies*, 1, 45–57, Oxford: Pergamon Press.

Russ, J. (1975, 2000) *The Female Man*, Boston: Beacon Press.

—— (1998) *What Are We Fighting For?: Sex, Race, Class, and the Future of Feminism*, New York: St. Martin's Press.

Samuelson, P. (1958) "An Exact Consumption-Loan Model of Interest with or without the Social Contrivance of Money," *Journal of Political Economy*, 66(6): 467–482.

San Juan, E. Jr. (2003) "Marxism and the Race/Class Problematic: A Re-Articulation," *Cultural Logic*. Online. Available HTTP: http://clogic.eserver.org/2006/2006.html (accessed 12 January 2007).

Sargisson, L. (1996) *Contemporary Feminist Utopianism*, London and New York: Routledge.

—— (2001) "What's Wrong with Ecofeminism?," *Environmental Politics*, 10(1), 52–64.

Saunders, L. (1997) "If You Can't Stand the Heat," *Feminist Economics*, 3(1), 127–129.

Schratzenstaller, M. (2007) "Gender Budgeting in Theorie und Praxis: Das Beispiel Oberösterreich," paper presented at the 4th Austrian Workshop of Feminist Economists, Vienna, University of Vienna.

Schröter, S. (2002) *FeMale. Über Grenzverläufe zwischen den Geschlechtern*, Frankfurt: Fischer.

Scott, M. (1993) *Trouble and her Friends*, New York: Tor Books.

Sellers, S. (1994) *The Hélène Cixous Reader*, London: Routledge.

Shafi, M. (1990) *Utopische Entwürfe in der Literatur von Frauen*, Bern: Peter Lang.

Shelley, M. (1818, 2000) *Frankenstein*, Boston, MA: Bedford Books.

Shiach, M. (1997) "Hélène Cixous and the Possibilities of Resistance," Lenning, A., Bekker, M., and Vanwesenbeek, I. (eds.) *Feminist Utopias in a Postmodern Era*, Tilburg, Netherlands: Tilburg University Press.

Shor, J. (1997) "*Utopias of Women's Time*," in Lenning, A., Bekker, M., and Vanwesenbeek, I. (eds.) *Feminist Utopias in a Postmodern Era*, Tilburg, Netherlands: Tilburg University Press.

Siriani, C. and Negrey, C. (2000) "Working Time as Gendered Time," *Feminist Economics*, 6(1), 59–76.

Smith, A. (1759) *The Theory of the Moral Sentiments*, London: A. Millar. Online. Available HTTP: http://www.econlib.org/library/Smith/smWN1.html (accessed 30 April 2007).

—— (1776, 1904) *An Inquiry into the Nature and Causes of the Wealth of Nations*, ed. Edwin Cannan, 5th edn., London: Methuen and Co., Ltd.Online. Available HTTP: (accessed 13 October 2007).

Spenser, E. (1579) *The Shepherd's Calendar*, London: Hugh Singleton.

Starhawk (1993) *The Fifth Sacred Thing*, New York: Bantam.

Staveren, I. (2003) "Feminist Fiction and Feminist Economics: Charlotte Perkins Gilman on Efficiency," in Barker, D. and Kuiper, E. (eds.) *Toward a Feminist Philosophy of Economics*, London: Routledge.

Stiglitz, J. (2002) *Globalization and Its Discontents*, W.W. Norton & Company.

Strassmann, D. (1993) "Not a Free Market: The Rhetoric of Disciplinary Autority in Economics," in Ferber, M. and Nelson, J. (eds.) *Beyond Economic Man: Feminist Theory and Economics*, Chicago: University of Chicago Press.

—— (1995) "Creating a Forum for Feminist Economic Inquiry," *Feminist Economics*, 1(1).

Sidney, P. (1593) *The Countess of Pembroke's Arcadia*, 2nd edn., ed. H. Sanford.

Tod, I. and Wheeler, M. (1978) *Utopia*, New York: Harmony Books.

Thomas, P. (1980) *Karl Marx and the Anarchists*, London: Routledge.

Vaughan, G. (1997) *The Gift Economy*. Online. Available HTTP: http://www.gift-economy.com/theory.html (accessed 12 January 2007).

Ve, H. (n.d.) *Gracias a la Vida. On the Paradigm of a Gift Economy*. Online. Available HTTP: http://www.gifteconomyconference.com/pages/Articles/veathanor.html (accessed 12 January 2007).

Vollmer, A. (1986) *Kein Wunderland für Alice? Frauenutopien*, Hamburg: Konkret Literatur Verlag.

Walker, A. (1993) *Her Blue Body, Everything We Know: Earthling Poems 1965-1990 Complete*, Fort Washington, PA: Harvest Books.

Waring, M. (1988) *If Women Counted: A New Feminist Economics*, London: Harper.

—— (2002) "Looking Forward," speech at the 2002 Public Service Senior Management Conference, New Zealand.

Waugh, P. (1989) *Feminine Fictions Revisiting the Postmodern*, New York: Routledge.

Weizsaecker, E. and Armory, B. (1998) *Factor Four: Doubling Wealth, Halfing Ressouce Use*, London: Earthscan.

Whitford, M. (1991) *The Irigaray Reader*, Oxford: Blackwell.

Whitney, E. (2006) "Capitalizing on Camp: Greed and the Queer Marketplace," *Text and Performance Quarterly*, 26(1), January: 36–46.

Wilk, R. (1996) "Taking Gender to Market," *Feminist Economics*, 2(1), 90–93.

Willemsen, T. (1997) "Feminism and Utopias. An Introduction," in Lenning, A., Bekker, M., and Vanwesenbeek, I. (eds.) *Feminist Utopias in a Postmodern Era*, Tilburg, Netherlands: Tilburg University Press.

Wolff, J. (2002) *Robert Nozick, Libertarianism, and Utopia*, London: University College. Online. Available HTTP: http://www.quebecoislibre.org/020413-19.htm (accessed 12 January 2007).

Wollstonecraft, M. (1792) *A Vindication of the Rights of Woman*. Online. Available HTTP: http://www.bartleby.com/144/4.html (accessed 12 January 2007).

Wolmark, J. (1994) *Aliens and Others. Science Fiction, Feminism and Postmodernism*, Iowa City: University of Iowa Press.

Woolf, V. (1938) *Three Guineas*. Online. Available HTTP: http://gutenberg.net.au/ebooks02/0200931.txt (accessed 12 January 2007).

Woolley, F. (1996) "Getting the Better of Becker," *Feminist Economics*, 2(1), 114–20.

—— (2000) "Degrees of Connection: A Critique of Rawls's Theory of Mutual Disinterest," *Feminist Economics*, 6(2), 1–21.

Yurtoglu, B. and Zulehner, C. (2007) "The Gender Gap in Top Corporate Jobs Is Still There," paper presented at the 4th Austrian Workshop of Feminist Economists, Vienna, University of Vienna.

Zimmer Bradley, M. (1978) *Stormqueen!* (The Darkover Series), New York: DAW.

Zweimüller, M. (2007) "Competition and the Gender Wage Gap. A Cross-Country, Time-Series Analysis," paper presented at the 4th Austrian Workshop of Feminist Economists, Vienna, University of Vienna.

Index